AFRICAN AMERICAN ENVIRONMENTAL THOUGHT

AMERICAN POLITICAL THOUGHT

Wilson Carey McWilliams and Lance Banning,
Founding Editors

AFRICAN AMERICAN
ENVIRONMENTAL THOUGHT

FOUNDATIONS

KIMBERLY K. SMITH

UNIVERSITY PRESS OF KANSAS

Published by the University Press of Kansas (Lawrence, Kansas
66045), which was organized by the Kansas Board of Regents and is
operated and funded by Emporia State University, Fort Hays State
University, Kansas State University, Pittsburg State University, the
University of Kansas, and Wichita State University

Library of Congress Cataloging-in-Publication Data
Smith, Kimberly K., 1966–
African American environmental thought : foundations /
Kimberly K. Smith.
p. cm. — (American political thought)
Includes bibliographical references and index.
ISBN 978-0-7006-1516-2 (cloth : alk. paper)
1. African Americans—Intellectual life. 2. Environmentalism—
United States—History. 3. Human ecology—United States—History.
4. Douglass, Frederick, 1818–1895—Political and social views.
5. Washington, Booker T., 1856–1915—Political and social views.
6. Du Bois, W. E. B. (William Edward Burghardt), 1868–1963—
Political and social views. 7. Locke, Alain LeRoy, 1886–1954—
Political and social views. 8. African Americans—Politics and
government. 9. Agriculture—Social aspects—Southern States—
History. 10. Racism—United States—History. I. Title.
E185.6.S63 2007
305.896'073—dc22
2006034358

British Library Cataloguing in Publication Data is available.

Printed in the United States of America

10 9 8 7 6 5 4 3 2 1

The paper used in this publication meets the minimum
requirements of the American National Standard for Permanence of
Paper for Printed Library Materials Z39.48-1992.

Behold, the Lord thy God hath set the land before thee:
go up and possess it, as the Lord God of thy fathers hath
said unto thee; fear not, neither be discouraged.

—DEUTERONOMY 1:21, quoted in Edward Blyden,
"The Call of Providence to the Descendants
of Africa in America," 1862

Let us go on and possess the land.

—MARTIN DELANY, *The Condition, Elevation,
Emigration, and Destiny of the Colored People
of the United States*, 1852

CONTENTS

PREFACE

In the fall term of 2000, I was teaching a course called "American Environmental Thought." It's a standard course taught in many environmental studies programs, designed to introduce students to the canon of American environmentalism. My course featured Henry David Thoreau, John Muir, Aldo Leopold, Rachel Carson, and Wendell Berry, among others. On the first day, a student approached me after class, handed me the syllabus, and asked, "Why are there no black people in this course?"

I don't know whether the double entendre was intentional, but it captured nicely a problem that had frequently worried me. There were no black writers on the syllabus, and it probably wasn't coincidental that there were no black students (or many minority students at all) in the class. The environmental justice movement was already twenty years old, but most environmental studies programs remained dominated by white middle-class students and white middle-class perspectives. If a major goal of environmental studies was to prepare students to tackle the most pressing environmental issues, we were missing an important part of our audience and an important part of the conversation.

This book is a partial response to that problem. It represents my effort to listen to some of the voices that didn't make it into the standard histories of American environmental thought—in particular, the voices of nineteenth- and early-twentieth-century black Americans. They aren't always easy to hear. Black Americans had a lot to say about nature, but they didn't write about wilderness in the same way that Thoreau or John Muir did. They were deeply concerned with agriculture and urban landscapes, but not for the same reasons that Liberty Hyde Bailey and Lewis Mumford were. As we would expect, talk of freedom and equality and of the devastating effects of racial oppression permeate their works, almost drowning out what they were saying about our relationship to the natural world. *Almost*—but not quite. Indeed, much of what they say about racial oppression makes sense only against a background of claims about humans' proper relationship to the natural world. In order to recover that background, I had to abandon the received understanding of both "environmental thought" and "black political thought" and read the works of black writers from a different angle. The result, I hope, is a new perspective on American environmental thought, and a new appreciation for black Americans' contributions to our common conversation about the natural world.

This project benefited from advice, support, and encouragement from many sources. Carleton College generously supported my research. I learned a great deal from conversations with Carol Rutz, Larry Cooper, Barbara Allen, Melvin Rogers, Baird Jarman, Michael Kowalewski, William North, Dale Jamieson, Jen Everett, David Schlosberg, Joe Lane, Dianne Glave, and Sheri Breen, and I am grateful for their help. Finally, thanks to Jessica Rodriguez, the student who started this by asking me the right question.

AFRICAN AMERICAN
ENVIRONMENTAL THOUGHT

INTRODUCTION

Herein the longing of black men must have respect:

the rich and bitter depth of their experience, the unknown

treasures of their inner life, the strange rendings of nature

they have seen, may give the world new points of view.

—W. E. B. Du Bois, *The Souls of Black Folk*[1]

One might think that 250 years of slavery would have left black Americans permanently alienated from the American landscape. Forced for generations to work the earth without just reward, without the right to own land, without even the freedom to travel, what meaning could they find in America's pristine wilderness? Locked in a struggle for social justice, what interest could they have in the claims of nature?

And yet W. E. B. Du Bois took time in the midst of his campaign for racial equality to reflect on the beauty of Bar Harbor, Maine:

> There mountains hurl themselves against the stars and at their feet lie black and leaden seas. Above float clouds—white, gray, and inken, while the clear, impalpable air springs and sparkles like new wine. The land sinks to meadows, black pine forests, with here and there a blue and wistful mountain. Then there are islands—bold rocks above the sea, curled meadows; . . . all the colors of the sea lie about us—gray and yellowing greens and doubtful blues, blacks not quite black, tinted silvers and golds and dreaming whites.[2]

Published in Du Bois's 1920 collection *Darkwater*, this essay, "Of Beauty and Death," is contemporary with the first flourishing of environmentalism in the United States; in fact, it describes Acadia, one of the first national parks. It suggests that Du Bois's appreciation for the beauty of the American landscape equaled that of John Muir and Aldo Leopold.

Still, we won't find this passage in our standard chronicles of American nature writing. Indeed, we don't read this essay as an expression of progressive environmentalism at all; we read it as a discourse on social justice. Du Bois's description of Bar Harbor is, after all, merely preparing the ground for a different point: to explain why he doesn't spend more time in such inspiring places. "Why do not those who are scarred in the world's battle and hurt by its hardness travel to these places of beauty and drown themselves in the utter joy of life?" he asks. It is a question worthy of Thoreau, who similarly wondered why so many men live lives of quiet desperation. But Du Bois's answer dwells less on nature's glory than on grim social realities: "Did you ever see a 'Jim-Crow' waiting room? . . . Usually there is no heat in winter and no air in summer. . . . The agent browbeats and contradicts you, hurries and confuses the ignorant, . . . and sends you and me out on the platform, burning with indignation and hatred!"[3] Thoreau, of course, wasn't subject to such indignities. From Du Bois's very different perspective, the beauty of nature wasn't so easily disentangled from the ugliness of racial injustice.

Nor was the environmental movement itself. Early twentieth-century environmentalism had significant ideological and political connections to white supremacy; it is not purely coincidental that early preservationists included proponents of scientific racism such as Madison Grant and Henry Fairfield Osborn.[4] That legacy has been hard to shake. Contemporary debates about population and immigration control among preservationists still rehearse Madison Grant's fears about the nation's landscape being submerged in a rising tide of color. In addition, the environmental movement has drawn criticism for distracting attention from antipoverty and other social justice causes, as well as for its failure to put people of color in leadership positions.[5] Environmentalists, for their part, have complained that black Americans aren't interested in environmental politics, a claim resting on early studies of environmental attitudes suggesting that blacks have less concern for the environment than do whites.[6]

These tensions help to explain why we haven't included Du Bois, or any other black writer, in the conventional canon of American environmentalists and nature writers: Du Bois belongs to a political tradition we understand as not just distinct from but in conflict with environmentalism. This picture, however, overstates the political and ideological divide between environmentalism and black politics. Recent public opinion research, for example, shows that while white environmental activism may exceed that of blacks, the two groups have roughly equal interest in and concern about the environment.[7] In fact, studies in the emerging field of African American environmental history suggest that environmental activism in black communities dates back at least as far as the Progressive era.[8] To be sure, that activism looks different from the conservation and wilderness preservation campaigns of that era: it was generally local in focus and aimed at such issues as access to urban parks and other green spaces, combating urban pollution, and protecting public health. Moreover, black activists usually framed their concerns as civil rights issues. But they are civil rights issues based on the assumption that environmental amenities and freedom from environmental harms are critical to the good life and should be available to all—an assumption that informs the contemporary environmental justice movement as well. Indeed, its sudden emergence and rapid growth in the 1980s suggests that the environmental justice movement has deep roots in black politics and black political thought, reflecting long-standing concerns of civil rights activists.[9]

The goal of this study is to explore those ideological roots as they evolved from the abolition movement through the Harlem Renaissance period. I argue that contrary to conventional wisdom, black Americans have not been indifferent to environmental values; there is, in fact, a rich tradition of black environmental thought. Du Bois and many other black writers—including Henry Bibb, Martin Delany, Frederick Douglass, Booker T. Washington, George Washington Carver, Alain Locke, Jean Toomer, and Langston Hughes—had a great deal to say about how slavery and racial oppression affected black Americans' relationship to the land, and their arguments offer valuable insights into humans' relationship to nature in general. Their works belong in the canon of American environmentalism.

That claim requires some clarification, however. We usually think of "environmental thought" as a set of ideas and arguments aimed at preserving the wilderness and maintaining a viable ecosystem, and defined by or tending toward ecocentric values.[10] Under that definition, there is little in the black political tradition that qualifies. But that definition is too narrow, I believe; it excludes too many voices and perspectives on humans' relationship to nature, and it tends to obscure the environmental dimension of black political activism. Accordingly, I define "environmental thought" more broadly, as a set of ideas concerning the relationship between humans and the natural environment, including the norms that ought to govern that relationship. Under this broader definition, there is a great deal in the black political tradition to explore (more, indeed, than I can hope to cover in one book). We may not discover a black Thoreau—nor should we expect to. But we may discover new points of view on the relationship between humans and the natural world.

I begin with some assumptions: black literary, political, and philosophical traditions are not independent of white intellectual traditions. Rather, we should approach black thought as a conversation, with white Americans and with each other, about problems common to black Americans or about more general problems from the perspective of black Americans. Black writers drew on whatever intellectual resources were available to make sense of their world and to communicate with their various audiences. But they had choices about which concepts they relied on and how they interpreted those concepts. Those choices express their aspirations and their perspectives, thus giving a distinctive inflection to the traditions they were drawing on.[11]

This is true, as well, of their engagement with the intellectual traditions that inform the environmental movement. This movement began as part of a multifaceted reaction to problematic features of modernity in late nineteenth-century America, including the decline of religious authority and resulting void of spiritual meaning; the effects of industrial exploitation of nature on agricultural fertility and human health; the increasing social diversity that drew into question national identity; and the spread of powerful technologies that tended to control and not just facilitate human action. White middle-class Americans dominated the early environmental movement, and the language that grew out of it has traditionally been interpreted as reflecting their experiences of fin de siècle alienation and malaise. However, black theorists also used this language and these concepts for their own purposes. They were engaged with white Americans in a common conversation about humans and nature—but they entered that conversation from a different standpoint.

Black Americans experienced modernity differently. Broadly speaking, nineteenth-century and early twentieth-century black Americans inhabited the same ecological space and intellectual universe as white Americans. But they viewed industrialization from the standpoint of a group still seeking access to the industrial economy. Debates about national identity and between evolutionary biology and religion were for them filtered through the rhetoric of scientific racism. Industrial exploitation of nature, for many black Americans, involved exploitation of their labor (a problem as well for many white farmers, but carrying a different social meaning). Black Americans living in cities were, on the whole, more vulnerable to disease and pollution than were white Americans, but the roots of their greater vulnerability lay in a distinctive history of racial oppression.

Accordingly, when black theorists talked about the natural environment, they often used the same language that white writers used, but they put this language to different uses, with a different set of problems and experiences in mind. First, they used arguments drawn from the mainstream environmental tradition in order to engage white audiences, bringing the problems of the black community within the ambit of white consciousness. Additionally, they used this language to speak to black audiences—to suggest ways to affirm their value and sense of self against the onslaught of racial oppression.[12] Thus black theorists were engaged in a kind of double translation. On one hand, they were translating the problems of black Americans into terms familiar to white audiences—terms that, quite often, spoke of humans' relationship to the natural world. On the other hand, they were translating to black Americans what this environmental discourse might mean *to them*— what concepts like stewardship and harmony with nature could mean to a people in their condition.

The result was a tradition of black environmental thought—a tradition deeply related to dominant traditions of environmental thought but characterized by a particular concern with how these traditions could be applied to problems generated by racial oppression. Recovering this tradition is an important step toward documenting the full range of American environmental thought, and that is my primary motivation for pursuing this project. But those less interested in such a recovery project should still find this tradition worth exploring. First, it helps to explain where the environmental justice movement came from. The rhetoric of that movement was not invented, suddenly, in the 1980s; rather, it evolved over many decades of political activism aimed at rectifying blacks' relationship to the land. Understanding this history of black environmental thought helps us to recognize and make sense of the environmental dimension of black politics. Second, black environmental thought offers a valuable perspective on the relationship between racial justice and environmental stewardship—a subject that has received comparatively less attention from white environmentalists. The mainstream tradition of American environmental thought has had a great deal to say about humans' duties to future generations and to nature itself, as well as the value of individual experience with the natural world. But (as some social ecologists and ecofeminists have pointed out) equality and social justice have not received much attention from the mainstream environmental movement. Even those canonical figures who connected their environmental concerns to social justice, such as Gifford Pinchot and Robert Marshall, gave little attention to how *racial* oppression interferes with fulfilling our duties to nature or affects the quality of our experience of the natural world.[13] Black theorists, in contrast, have addressed precisely that question: how humans' relationship to the environment is affected—and often distorted—by racially oppressive political, social, and legal institutions and practices.

Finally, the black tradition directly addresses the organic and essentialist theories of race and nation with which environmentalism was closely associated in the early twentieth century. The mainstream tradition of environmental thought remains troubled by notions it inherited from those essentialist theories—most prominently, the idea that human culture should be determined in some way by the natural environment. Progressive black theorists explicitly rejected racial essentialism, along with the strong environmental determinism on which it rested. In its place, they developed a more pragmatic framework for thinking about the proper relationship between culture and nature. Exploring this framework should help environmental theorists think more productively about the interrelationships among natural environment, identity, and culture. The black tradition is not, of course, the only American intellectual tradition that offers valuable insights into these questions. But it is one such tradition, and it deserves careful attention in its own right.

Before we begin, however, we need to define our subject. Black environmental thought has multiple roots, including elite intellectual traditions, folk traditions of white and Native American communities, and the folk traditions and experiences of black Americans themselves. There are a number of ways to approach this complex body of thought. I've chosen to concentrate on elite discourse: the ideas and arguments developed by the political and intellectual leaders in the black community, and specifically the canonical black writers. These include the abolitionists, the nineteenth-century black nationalists, and the early twentieth-century progressives. Martin Delany, Henry Bibb, and Booker T. Washington figure prominently, but not as prominently as W. E. B. Du Bois and Alain Locke, who dominate the final chapters. I concentrate on these figures because their works are particularly rich in environmental themes, because they provide an insightful counterpoint to the mainstream tradition of environmental thought, and because they have had a good deal of influence on twentieth-century black politics.

Unfortunately, this choice means that my study (like many works on early black political thought) is dominated by male voices—not simply because there were fewer published female writers during this period but also because focusing on the best-known writers allows me to build on a substantial body of scholarship. In addition, addressing the specific concerns and perspectives of black women writers—and generally integrating gender issues more fully into this study—would have expanded its scope beyond manageable proportions. There is clearly a great deal more to be done in this area; I intend only to provide a starting point for further investigations.

In addition to the works of the canonical black writers, I have given a great deal of attention to the white Euro-American intellectual traditions they were engaging, such as democratic agrarianism, scientific racism, and pragmatism. In this I have followed the approach of George Hutchinson, whose study of Harlem Renaissance writers similarly develops the broader cross-racial conversations in which they were immersed.[14] There is of course some value to considering black writers in isolation from these Euro-American traditions, but Hutchinson's approach is more conducive to my goal: identifying what black writers contribute to the dominant modes of environmental discourse. To be sure, the traditions I highlight—such as scientific racism and pragmatism—are not the ones we usually consider central to American environmental thought. But I would suggest that our conventional understanding of American environmental thought has been too narrow; these other discourses were important parts of the wide-ranging conversations about nature taking place at the turn of the nineteenth century.

Finally, I have also given attention (in admittedly broad strokes) to the environmental and political context in which this elite black tradition developed. But I have not attempted to explore mass attitudes and folk culture in any depth. These would require other methods—those of the social and environmental historian—to investigate. However, the questions and theories posed by black writers suggest many promising avenues of empirical research for social and environmental historians. As I will discuss in the conclusion, I believe this study can contribute to that project.

I argue in the following pages that the black environmental tradition developed primarily in response to two problems. First, black theorists reasoned that race slavery and post-Emancipation racial oppression put black Americans into a conflicted relationship to the land—by coercing their labor, restricting their ability to own land, and impairing their ability to interpret the landscape. Second, the ideology of scientific racism that developed to legitimate this oppression promoted an environmental determinism that insisted blacks, as a race, had virtually no capacity for free creative action. In response to these problems, black theorists have focused on the importance of freedom, understood particularly as creative agency, in humans' relationship to nature. A central theme in this tradition is the claim that denial of freedom to black Americans has distorted their relationship to the natural environment; indeed, it has scarred the land itself. To black writers working in this tradition, America—not just the political community but the physical terrain—is a land cursed by injustice and in need of redemption.

Contrast this perspective with that taken by such nature writers as Henry David Thoreau, George Perkins Marsh, John Muir, Rachel Carson, and Aldo Leopold: for them, pristine nature or wilderness—the natural world as it exists independent of human manipulation—is the central value, and humans' duty lies in preserving untouched nature as far as possible. This is the perspective that has informed the environmental movement for decades. Indeed, according to William Cronon, "wilderness" with all its romantic associations "serves as the foundation for a long list of [environmental] concerns that on their face seem quite remote from it." The influence of this wilderness concept is, in his view, "pervasive."[15] It underlies the central message of American environmentalism: that humans should be relatively constrained in their interactions with the natural world so as to avoid disrupting it too much. Thus the mainstream environmental tradition advocates humility, restraint, and respect for the integrity of natural systems.

The black tradition, in contrast, highlights an older, less romantic theme in Western thought, conceptualizing the American landscape not as pristine and innocent wilderness but as a corrupted land in need of redemption.[16] Humans, in turn, are to be active, creative, co-equal partners in giving meaning to and redeeming the natural world. Their central question is not how to protect the natural world from human interference but how to facilitate responsible and morally beneficial interaction with nature. I don't mean to overstate this contrast, of course; both traditions are complex, and each is influenced by the other. But I do want to underscore how the specific concerns and perspectives of black writers deepen certain dimensions of American environmental discourse.

Black writers show us how this conception of the fallen world can serve as the starting point for analyzing how social justice affects an individual's and a community's relationship to the land—or, more specifically, the question of how an oppressed, disenfranchised group comes into possession of the land. "Possession" is a rich concept here; we find in this tradition at least three understandings of what the land is and how one might rightfully possess it. First, land may be simply a commodity, something to be owned or traded. This conception seems to reduce the meaning of one's relationship to the land to mere economics, but for black Americans the debate about who can rightfully possess the land extended beyond economics into questions of citizenship, of membership in the political community. Black theorists had to address who had the right to buy and sell the land, and what social and economic conditions are necessary for a group to effectively exercise that right. Thus from the perspective of black Americans, owning land means more than acquiring wealth; it means civic membership, political autonomy and personality, and community integrity. One's relationship to the land is integrally connected to one's relationship to the political community.

Second, for black theorists influenced by nineteenth-century Romanticism, the land could be a source of creative energy, the particular manifestation of a universal life-force. Possessing the land means coming into contact with the creative energy animating nature, and letting that vital force guide cultural production. This conception is tied to nineteenth-century notions of the folk, race, and nation. Under this view, possessing the land has to do with creating a folk culture "in harmony" with the natural landscape: a culture conducive to a group's survival and flourishing. Drawing on this romantic discourse, black theorists debated whether blacks as a race (or folk) could thrive on the American continent—or, alternatively, whether white Americans were already too far from the creative force of nature to maintain a vital folk culture.

These questions about the relationship between race, culture, and nature would continue to engage black political thought, but most early twentieth-century black progressives eventually rejected the romantic concept of nature, along with racial essentialism. For them, the land is best conceived in its social aspect as common ground, the thing a social group holds in common. Under this view, the land is an important source of the collective experiences that create a common consciousness; it is the foundation of community. Possessing the land, in turn, requires overcoming the segregation, poverty, and injustice that destroy the bonds of community and alienate the oppressed from their physical environment.

The following chapters will explore these ideas—or, more properly, these conversations about black Americans' relationship to nature generally and to the American landscape specifically. Chapter 1 sets the stage, reviewing what we know and don't know about how slave culture related blacks to the land. The central argument of that chapter is briefly stated: the slave system forced slaves into an intimacy with the natural environment but also tended to alienate them from it. This ambivalent legacy permeates black environmental thought; a central question in this tradition is how black Americans could overcome the negative effects of slavery and create a home for themselves in a land cursed by injustice.

Chapters 2 and 3 explore how black writers during the nineteenth century made sense of slavery's effect on slaves' relationship to nature. This section traces the evolution of a particularly influential environmental discourse—black agrarianism—from its abolitionist origins to the post-Emancipation period. Black agrarians argued that agriculture was man's natural calling, and when conducted by free, responsible proprietor-farmers, it confers the moral, economic, and spiritual benefits claimed by the Jeffersonian yeoman farmer. But slavery and peonage corrupt agriculture, turning what should be a creative interaction with nature by co-equal stewards into a struggle for power between master and slave. Oppressing agricultural labor, they concluded, impairs the physical integrity of the land, as well as its spiritual and moral value.

These chapters leave us with a fairly bleak image of black Americans as strangers in a strange land, striving to come into rightful possession of a land of their own. Chapters 4 and 5, addressing the late nineteenth and early twentieth centuries, turn to a more positive but still problematic image of black Americans as the true American peasantry—America's folk—and a key source of cultural vitality. That image was bound up with late nineteenth-century race theory, so Chapter 4 examines the rise of scientific racism and black theorists' response to white supremacy. That debate led black progressives to reject racial essentialism and the notion that culture is determined by a race's natural environment; they argued instead that history and individual creativity chiefly shape human races and cultures. But that argument in turn raised questions about what it means for a culture or group to be "close to nature," and in what sense black Americans could claim to be America's folk.

Chapter 5 takes up those questions, exploring the influence of artistic primitivism and pragmatism on black progressive thought. These influences resulted in a new way of thinking about the relationship between nature and culture, privileging *experience* rather than racial essence as the key connection between humans and their physical environment. Under this view, history—including the history of racial oppression—becomes a key factor in determining the meaning of the natural landscape; tradition and collective memory play a central role in how a group relates to nature. This understanding of the relationship between culture and nature offered a powerful alternative to the romantic, essentialist ideas that were dominating American environmental thought in the early twentieth century—and a new way to explain black Americans' distinctive contribution to American culture. Moreover, this progressive discourse offered a new perspective on urban environments, a major theme in black environmental thought in the late 1920 and 1930s. This conversation is the subject of Chapter 6, which explores how the tradition of black environmental thought informed depictions of the city during the Harlem Renaissance period and beyond. The perspectives on urbanization discussed in this chapter laid the groundwork for the environmental justice movement and continue to influence our thinking about urban environmental reform.

I don't want to oversimplify this complex tradition, but I do want to highlight some of the more prominent themes we will encounter. A central claim implicit or explicit in most of the texts we'll consider is that humans' relationship to the natural world is affected by the justice or injustice of their social arrangements. Ideally, we would come to the natural world as co-equal members of a community—as carriers of traditions, rights, duties, and capacities that allow us to fulfill our role as (under one understanding) co-partners with God in "finishing creation." This role does require us to exercise dominion over the land, but that dominion is best understood as a collective duty of stewardship, of homemaking. As I interpret this perspective, our proper stance toward the natural world is one of *creative response:* the world we encounter as individuals has been funded with value (social, aesthetic, spiritual, economic) by ongoing cultural practices; our duty is to modify it to make it an appropriate home for humans—mindful, always, of its meanings and of our position as members of a community of co-equal stewards.

But when oppression destroys the foundations of community, our ability to interact creatively and responsibly with the natural world is similarly put at risk. The oppression of labor—particularly agricultural labor—can make creative, sensitive response to the land difficult, if not impossible. Exclusion from membership in the political community, suppression of a group's collective memory, denial of economic and artistic opportunity—all of these things similarly impair one's capacity to interact appropriately with the natural world. The environmental history of black Americans is a history of struggle against these forces of alienation and dispossession. As such, it lays bare the social conditions of environmental virtue and the failure of Americans to realize those conditions. Racial oppression, as Du Bois put it, has worked a strange rending of nature. This study explores what that rending means for humans' relationship to the natural environment.

CHAPTER ONE
STRANGE RENDINGS OF NATURE

White immigrants to New England in the seventeenth century described the landscape they encountered as a "hideous and desolate wilderness, full of wild beasts and wild men." Separated by an ocean from "all civil parts of the world," "the whole country, full of woods & thickets, represented a wild & savage hue." But it was teeming with "Fowles in abundance, Fish in multitude," and "goodly groves of trees," and colonists believed that the desolate wilderness was destined to be transformed, by faith and labor, into a new Canaan.[1]

The story is familiar to students of American environmental thought. The English colonists drew on the intellectual legacy of the Old World to give meaning to the American landscape. "Wilderness" meant the part of the landscape that was not under agricultural cultivation or human settlement of the European pattern. It was the abode of savages and beasts, a place of danger. But it was also a place governed by a natural order, in opposition to the human order reflected in rural and urban landscapes. It could therefore be a place of spiritual or political refuge, or a place to start over and create a paradise.[2]

This conventional story, however, doesn't include the Africans enslaved and forcibly transported to the American colonies in the seventeenth and eighteenth centuries. How did they view the American landscape? We know less about these involuntary immigrants, but apparently the New World could be frightening to them as well. Olaudah Equiano's *Narrative*, published in 1789, recounts in vivid detail just how strange this world could look: he described his "astonishment" at the unfamiliar animals—flying fishes, sharks, grampuses—and the mysterious devices used by his captors during his voyage. The world was full of spiritual as well as social menace; when the ship to England encountered bad weather, he thought "the Ruler of the sea was angry" and expected his captors to sacrifice him to the fish in order to calm the waters. Men on horseback, portraits hanging in his master's room—"everything about me," he declared, "was magic. These people were full of nothing but magical arts."[3]

Like the white colonists, enslaved Africans came to the New World with concepts and categories that would help them make sense of this strange land. Although West African peoples were religiously diverse, most shared Equiano's faith in magic and some form of animism: a belief system teaching that the natural world is infused with spirits that can be propitiated and to some extent controlled through ritual and sacrifice.[4] They also encountered new ideas—Christianity, folk beliefs, western literary traditions, and scientific theories—that would replace, modify, or meld with African intellectual traditions. Drawing on these resources, slaves would attempt to give their own meaning to the American landscape.

Of course, the experience of slavery itself, with its wide-ranging implications for blacks' social, political, and economic status, had a profound influence on their experience with and interpretation of the environment. The South (where most slaves would end up) was more densely forested, hotter, and less healthy than the northern colonies. Southern agriculture organized the landscape differently, as did the racial and class hierarchy that structured southern society. The laws and practices of slavery also shaped slaves' relationship to the natural world directly—by affecting their ability to own land and livestock, cultivate a garden, and hunt and gather in the forest—as well as influencing the meaning of these activities. As we will see, slavery created a complex relationship between slaves and the landscape, forcing most of its victims into an intimacy with the immediate natural world but also, in some respects, alienating them from it.

But the slave system was not the only source of meaning in nature. Slave culture was a mosaic of beliefs, offering multiple perspectives on the natural world. In addition to western scientific and folk beliefs, for example, slaves could turn to African and Christian religious traditions to find their own sacred meaning in the landscape. Rather than describing a single coherent view of the natural world, then, this chapter explores the variety of intellectual resources that slaves could use to give the landscape political, moral, and spiritual meaning, focusing in particular on those resources that would contribute to the development of the black intellectual tradition.

SLAVERY AND THE AMERICAN SOUTH

If the New England colonists encountered a desolate wasteland, southern colonists encountered a warm and fetid one. Much of the American South was a hot, humid, dense pine forest relieved mostly by swamps. The southeast, where the first English colonies were established, rises from the coastal plain—a region of swamps and marshes—to the Piedmont, the remnants of an old mountain range worn down to a smooth, rolling landscape. West of the Piedmont, settlers found a diverse region of higher elevation including the Blue Ridge Mountains, the Great Valley of Virginia, and the Cumberland Plateau; even farther west they encountered the bluegrass region and the Ozarks and Ouachita mountains. But the Lower South, the states that would be dominated by plantation agriculture and slavery, consisted mostly of the marshy river deltas and pine forest of the Gulf Coastal Plain, along with the "Black Belt"—a stretch of fertile soil along the Coastal Plain uplands—and the alluvial valley of the Mississippi.[5]

Two features of this environment were particularly salient to southern slaveholders: its hospitability to certain diseases, and its climate. The warm, wet South hosted malaria and yellow fever, along with other diseases that devastated colonial populations in the seventeenth century and continued to make the South an unhealthy region throughout the nineteenth century. Africans (particularly those imported from the West Indies) had acquired immunities to many of these diseases, and they also usually arrived already acclimated to the heat. Both factors led to the lower mortality rate among blacks than whites in the seventeenth century.[6] It was only a slight advantage, since blacks were vulnerable to other diseases, and whites acclimated quickly. But colonists found in this small advantage a useful justification for race slavery, and blacks' physical robustness was a persistent theme in discourses on race, nature, and slavery well into the nineteenth century.[7]

Also contributing to the South's regional identity were the forest and the soils. Despite the warmth, humidity, and long growing season, the South was not quite the fertile paradise that early settlers envisioned.[8] Until the 1880s, the American South was blanketed by a longleaf pine belt, stretching from Virginia to eastern Texas, with shortleaf pines and hardwoods covering the higher elevations. The colonists' best efforts to clear this forest had little impact until after the Civil War. Thomas Clark estimates that in 1880, 10 billion board feet of lumber still stood in the forests of North and South Carolina, and the pine forests of Florida, Georgia, Alabama, Mississippi, Louisiana, Arkansas, and eastern Texas remained virtually untouched.[9] Throughout the eighteenth and nineteenth centuries, the South was a frontier society, besieging and besieged by wilderness. And when the forest was cleared, the would-be farmers discovered poor, thin soil highly vulnerable to erosion. Colonists in South Carolina and Georgia (and later, Louisiana) learned to improve soils with marsh mud and flooding. But the Piedmont area, a sloping region running from Virginia to eastern Alabama, was exceptionally vulnerable to erosion, and cotton culture in the early nineteenth century would aggravate the problem.[10] Much of the southwest was also plagued with sandy, inferior soils (with the important exceptions of the Black Belt and Mississippi Valley).[11] Both the poor, eroding soil and the persistence of forest created the impression, to northern (and some southern) critics, that southerners were lazy and careless farmers.

Southern agricultural practices—perhaps unfairly—reinforced this reputation. In the Chesapeake region, for example, the fragile soil and abundant land encouraged many farmers to clear land, use it for a few years, and abandon it, leaving the landscape dotted with fallow and ragged fields ranged by unpenned cattle and pigs. Others dealt with the low natural fertility of the soil by rotating crops, which left patches of weedy openings and regrowth forest interspersed among the fields. These practices were efficient from the farmer's point of view, but they created a "transient landscape" of "shifting fields, abundant old fields, and ragged vegetation in various stages of succession" that looked disorderly and ugly to observers accustomed to the look of the northern colonies.[12] Images of abandoned, exhausted fields surrounded by wild pine forests supported southerners' reputation as inefficient and indolent farmers; both the image and reputation would become commonplace in black writers' descriptions of the South in the nineteenth century.

The South was, however, economically and ecologically diverse. Moravian settlers in North Carolina, for example, practiced careful mixed agriculture, producing farms that looked neat and attractive. South Carolina pursued large-scale indigo and rice cultivation and developed Charles Town (now Charleston) into a large city.[13] (Charles Town, a major center for the slave trade, did little for southerners' reputation; to northern critics, this city, along with the great plantations, represented luxury and other vices that afflicted southern society.) Georgia resisted the introduction of slavery longer but by 1750 had turned to plantation agriculture, relying mostly on rice, cotton, and sugar.[14] Transappalachia was a more diverse region: farms in the Great Valley resembled those in Pennsylvania; the mountains and Cumberland Plateau would long remain home to small, isolated subsistence farmers; grazing and hemp production dominated the Bluegrass region; and cotton plantations dominated southern Tennessee.[15] In the early decades of the nineteenth century, southerners migrated toward the fertile plains of the

Black Belt and the great alluvial valley of the Mississippi in large numbers. There they established cotton and, in Louisiana, sugarcane plantations.[16] This broad region south and east of the Appalachians became known as the Deep South, the heart of the cotton kingdom and home of the most brutal forms of plantation agriculture.

Throughout the South, corn was the most common staple and the small subsistence farm the most common unit of production.[17] Nevertheless, by the nineteenth century, the southern economy relied heavily on plantation agriculture and slave labor, and slaves imported to the American South typically ended up on plantations. Initially most slaves worked on small plantations; in 1725, the median slave plantation in the Chesapeake had only about 10 slaves. But the southeast colonies turned to tobacco, rice, and indigo cultivation in the eighteenth century, leading to the development of larger plantations and more heavy reliance on slave labor. By the 1760s, over half of the labor performed by slaves went to cultivating tobacco, rice, and indigo. That proportion increased dramatically when cotton emerged as a major southern staple crop in the early nineteenth century.[18] Nevertheless, most slaves still lived on small or medium-sized plantations. By the nineteenth century about one-quarter of slaves lived on holdings with 1 to 9 slaves; half lived on holdings with 10–49 slaves, and the rest on holdings with more than 50 slaves.[19] The relatively small size of American plantations, along with the high proportion of American slaves born in the New World, interfered with the emergence of a distinctive African-based slave culture comparable to those of other New World slave societies.[20] However, African influences on American slave culture are well documented, and some regions, such as the low country of South Carolina and Georgia, had concentrations of slaves so large that an independent Africanized slave culture could emerge, with an orientation and worldview different from that of most white Americans.[21]

This southeast region has often appeared in the scholarly literature as representative of slave culture in general. In fact, however, slave culture varied widely from region to region, and not all slaves shared in it to the same extent. Moreover, it varied over time—and not necessarily in a uniform direction. For example, historian Ira Berlin suggests that the first generation of slaves in the American colonies, coming from creole enclaves on the western coast of Africa, may have been more broadly traveled and enjoyed more language skills than later arrivals from interior West Africa, and therefore may have had a decidedly different worldview than did later generations. Moreover, those later arrivals sometimes came in large numbers, overwhelming the second- or third-generation slaves already present. Thus neither the Americanization nor the Africanization of slave culture was a steady, uniform process.[22] Exploration of all these variations is beyond the scope of this project, however; my focus is the most familiar and well-studied slave culture, the southeastern plantation culture—the Old South—as it had developed by the late eighteenth and early nineteenth centuries. I do not claim that the experiences of slaves on these southeast tobacco, rice, and cotton plantations are representative, but they are a useful starting point for considering how slavery affected slaves' relationship to nature. Moreover, because this culture is what most black theorists would have in mind when they wrote about slavery, it is also a useful starting point for exploring those aspects of slave culture that influenced the development of black intellectual traditions.

Central to the plantation slave's relationship to the natural world was the way plantation agriculture imposed control on nature and human labor. Mart Stewart's excellent study of Georgia slave agriculture in the early nineteenth century describes plantations as complex agroecological and social systems designed to control nature and labor simultaneously, and requiring careful management.[23] Controlling nature was critical not only to the plantation owner's economic success but to his social and political standing. In colonial America and the early republic—especially in the agrarian South—economic, social, and political status depended heavily on ownership of and effective control of productive land. Indeed, a long tradition in Anglo-American thought linked land ownership with economic and political independence; as J. Hector St. John de Crèvecoeur famously put it, the land "has established all our rights; on it is founded our rank, our freedom, our power as citizens, our importance as inhabitants of such a district."[24]

But controlling nature meant controlling the labor force needed to impose a human order on nature—and vice versa. Here was one significant source of slaves' complex and conflicted relationship to the land: plantation slaves were intimately engaged with their natural environment, but they had to be coerced under threat of violence into performing what was often difficult labor—just as the natural world had to be disciplined to make it a fit environment for this sort of coerced, regimented labor. Stewart uses rice plantations as an example: a rice plantation is a "hydraulic machine" that calls for a skilled and disciplined workforce. Slaves had to move massive amounts of earth to create the irrigation system, prepare the soil, and plant seeds before the first full tide of spring. Once the crop was in, they had to regulate the flow of water through the culverts, adjusting to compensate for rain and prevent stagnation, and make sure the rice squares were flooded and drained uniformly. Tobacco and cotton cultivation, although less mechanized, also called for a trained labor force that could be fully mobilized during crucial production periods. But controlling the workforce was difficult when hurricanes or disease threatened the plantations, or when the surrounding forests and swamps provided opportunities for escape. So in order to maintain a disciplined, involuntary workforce that could consistently produce a crop, the master had to give attention to maintaining a healthy environment, to building defenses against severe weather, and to regulating the borders of the plantation.[25]

Perfect control, however, was neither possible nor desirable. For example, planters often allowed slaves time and land to grow their own food, thus giving slaves some opportunity to exercise their own control over nature. This practice in turn tended to undermine planters' authority by providing slaves sources of independence and self-control. In fact, the very skill and knowledge that slaves needed to be effective agricultural workers gave them the means to resist planters' control; as Stewart points out, knowledge was power on a plantation.[26] Thus plantation agriculture could be a source of suffering and degradation for slaves, but it could also be a means to autonomy. To be sure, masters had to produce crops reliably in order to maintain their status as independent land-owners, but they depended on slaves to do so—and therefore had to give slaves some autonomy by allowing them some independent control over the natural world.

This connection between individual autonomy and control of nature was an important theme in most American subcultures, but slave agriculture made it particularly salient and problematic for black Americans. The plantation slave system linked self-possession to possession of the land. As subsequent chapters will show, for slaves, achieving freedom would mean, prominently, achieving the right to the land on which they labored so that they could produce food for themselves and their families. And achieving that right, in turn, depended in part on demonstrating that they *could* make the land productive—that they had the intelligence and self-discipline to master nature. In short, plantation slaves experienced the American environment in the context of a struggle against the slave system to achieve self-mastery through mastery of a disordered and often hostile natural world. That struggle made the connection between nature and freedom—between possessing the land and possessing oneself—a central theme in black political thought.

SLAVE CULTURE

Slaves brought to this struggle a rich set of conceptual resources—ideas and practices that inscribed the landscape with social, political, and spiritual meanings that would inform the black literary and political tradition well into the twentieth century. Before we investigate those ideas and practices, though, a few caveats are in order concerning the problems of interpreting slave culture. First, southern culture in general was a tapestry of folk cultures, and slave culture—in addition to changing over time—was also syncretic, melding African and European elements.[27] Therefore, we must avoid simplistic contrasts between slaves and whites concerning their respective views of nature. Much of what we know about white American culture on this point—their scientific or Christian views of the natural world, their orientation toward dominating and exploiting it—is derived from the study of white elites. But if we want to understand how slaves' cultural background and experience affected their understanding of nature, surely the relevant comparison is between black folk beliefs and white folk beliefs.[28] Those comparisons are hard to draw. A variety of ethnic groups settled the South, and these groups often shared in and even borrowed from blacks' and Native Americans' beliefs in the supernatural, as well as Christian religious traditions.[29] The research necessary for a useful comparison has yet to be done, and I don't intend this chapter to contribute to that project. What follows is a survey of those aspects of slave culture that seem relevant to slaves' understandings of the natural world, without any sustained attempt at comparing them to white folk beliefs.

Even this limited project, however, raises problems of interpretation. Broadly speaking, we can say that American slave communities developed symbolic cultures that reflected a distinctive orientation toward nature. We can approach those cultures as texts—from religious practices to folk songs and stories to patterns of food production and medical practices—conveying concepts, categories, and theories that participants in the culture could draw on to make sense of the natural world. But members of a cultural group may disagree over whether a text is in fact part of their culture. The status of African folk beliefs, for example, was contested among blacks during the nineteenth century, rejected by some as primitive superstition and embraced by others as an important tie to the fatherland. And even if they agree over the status of a text, they may disagree over its meaning. Elements of symbolic culture are often open to multiple interpretations. Indeed, that is part of their value; they can hold many meanings and be used in many ways.

Take, for example, the most familiar aspect of slave culture, the animal tale. Slave culture was rich in folk tales, including the Br'er Rabbit stories collected and popularized by Joel Chandler Harris. These stories would seem an obvious place to look for insight into slaves' view of nature, and a number of scholars have done so. Indeed, animal tales have had a significant impact on scholarly interpretations of slave culture. But it's not clear what, if anything, the stories tell us about humans' relationship to the natural world.

Consider this story about Mr. Wolf. Br'er Wolf, a dangerous bully in the animal world, was being chased by dogs. He ran to Br'er Rabbit for help. Br'er Rabbit was happy to oblige and offered to hide Mr. Wolf in a big chest. After sitting by the chest and thinking awhile, he came up with a plan to get rid of the troublesome Wolf. First he heated a kettle of water, telling Mr. Wolf he'd make some tea. Then he started boring holes in the chest, telling Wolf they were air holes. When the water was hot, he poured it into the holes in the chest, telling Wolf the pain was just flea bites. By this clever strategy he killed Br'er Wolf with boiling water. The story ends with Br'er Rabbit celebrating the victory with his neighbors in a big jubilee.[30]

Rabbit and Wolf hardly enjoy the harmonious relations one might expect from their use of the friendly title "Brother" (Br'er). Does the story then teach us that despite superficial appearances, nature is a conflict-ridden state, red in tooth and claw? Probably not. Lawrence Levine's influential interpretation of the animal tales argues that the animals represent *human* characters and behavior patterns:

> The world they lived in, the rules they lived by, the emotions that governed them, the status they craved, the taboos they feared, the prizes they struggled to attain were those of the men and women who lived in this world. The beings that came to life in these stories were created to be human enough to be identified with but at the same time exotic enough to allow both storytellers and listeners a latitude and freedom that came only with much more difficulty and daring in tales explicitly concerning human beings.[31]

Under this view, the animal tales teach us nothing about how slaves viewed the natural world; rather, they are about the social world and social relationships. The story of Mr. Wolf, for example, is a cautionary lesson for bullies, teaching us how the weak can triumph over the strong through deception.

But Levine isn't consistent on this point. He goes on to insist that the tales encouraged slaves to identify with animals, and thus to "see themselves as part of a unified world in which Man, beasts, spirits, even inanimate objects, were a natural part of the order of things."[32] Leaving aside the question of what is orderly or unified about a natural world where one boils one's enemies alive, we might well ask what it means to identify with an anthropomorphic animal: are we identifying with its animal nature, or its human characteristics? Nevertheless, Levine's reading has had considerable influence on scholarly interpretation of the animal tales, and thus on interpretations of slaves' relationship to nature. For example, Charles Joyner contends on one hand that the stories highlight the *unnaturalness* and contingency of social relationships. The Wolf story, under this reading, involves inverting the usual social order and allowing the weak to defeat the strong. But he also suggests that "through the symbolic identification of nature with society, the animal trickster tales define the trickster and his actions as both necessary and good."[33] Under this view, the social relationships described in the story are both natural and unnatural.

Can the animal tales bear these competing interpretations? Certainly the stories are, and should be, open to multiple interpretations, and they may mean different things in different contexts. But Levine's first argument underscores a key point: references to natural phenomena do not always reveal attitudes about nature. In the animal tales, using natural phenomena as metaphors for social phenomena reinforces the *difference* rather than the similarity between nature and human society. Although they do make use of the fact that some human behaviors are similar to animal behaviors (bullies do in some respects resemble wolves), the displacement strategy Levine refers to—using animals to disguise the fact that the stories actually depict human behaviors—assumes that the audience recognizes animals are not humans. The stories work because we understand that real rabbits don't make tea and boil their enemies alive; the animal characters are meant to transport us to a different, fabulous world where such things can happen. Nor do the stories suggest (*pace* Joyner) that such behaviors are good or even necessary merely because they're performed by animals. Br'er Rabbit is a classic trickster, and the defining characteristic of the trickster—a figure common to African, Native American, and slave culture—is that he is *amoral*. He is a chaotic force that disrupts the conventional moral universe.[34] Nothing a trickster does is necessary, and little is unqualifiedly good.

The animal tales are notoriously ambiguous, however, and their meaning must rest in large part on the context in which they are related—a point that applies to much of slaves' symbolic culture. Indeed, rather than treating slave culture as a coherent, unified body of beliefs that outfitted its members with a single perspective on nature, I would argue that slaves' cultural context made available different belief systems (magical, Christian, scientific, etc.), allowing the individual to take up whichever one seemed appropriate in a specific context. A slave explaining to his master why a rice crop failed might use scientific terms, looking at the natural world as a mechanism subject to rational comprehension and manipulation. Returning to slave quarters, he might consult a witch doctor for protection against a curse that might have caused the crop failure, or reflect on the inscrutability of God's providence in afflicting the plantation. Slaves were no less capable than their masters of moving among fundamentally different worldviews.

Making complete sense of slaves' view(s) of nature would require exploring debates and conflicts over interpretations of folk beliefs, as well as how beliefs are mobilized in various social settings. In others words, we would have to investigate the variety of belief systems available in any given place and time, and when and how they matter. I won't do that here; my purpose is more modest. I intend only to identify some of the important sources of meaning available to slaves as they attempted to make sense of their natural environment.

STRANGERS IN A STRANGE LAND

Unlike most of the white colonists, the first generation of slaves did not come to North America by choice. They came as exiles, not to take possession of the land or make a home for themselves on it. Indeed, there is evidence that many of these first-generation slaves remained psychologically in exile and never looked on America as their home. According to historian Mechal Sobel, their exile may have been spiritual as much as physical. Many slaves believed that the spirits of their ancestors could not cross large bodies of water, so that in leaving Africa, they were also leaving their spiritual guides and protectors. Some slaves, Sobel notes, were even buried with small canoes, apparently in the hopes that their spirits would be able to return to Africa.[35]

By the second and third generation, this expectation of returning to Africa diminished and slaves' connection to Africa became more tenuous and conflicted. On one hand, there is evidence that a sense of African identity persisted among American slaves into the nineteenth century. Even as late as the 1870s, reports Lawrence Levine, descendants of slaves remembered stories told by African-born parents and grandparents. Slaves would talk about Africa among themselves, share stories of the fatherland, and express pride in their heritage.[36] On the other hand, some slaves and free blacks objected to being called African, arguing that claiming their African heritage would make it more difficult to win acceptance into American society.[37]

This conflict over how "American" slaves were undoubtedly complicated their relationship to the American landscape. To the extent that law and social practices (along with slave culture itself) reinforced the idea that slaves were aliens to the American community, they created conditions unfavorable to developing a sense of connection to the land over which that community claimed authority. Thus for slaves, the process of forming an emotional bond to the land and developing a sense of identity that was connected to the immediate landscape must have been quite different than it was for free persons (especially free white persons). But that doesn't mean such connections didn't develop. How they developed and what they looked like—all the complexities and ambiguities of the slaves' relationship to the American and African landscapes—would become a major theoretical issue in black political thought, as subsequent chapters will discuss. Empirical research on this question is still quite limited, however; scholars have focused primarily on the extent to which blacks identified as Africans rather than on their ideas and feelings about the land on which they lived, and the extent to which their relationship to the natural world could serve as a basis for their sense of self. The following lines of investigation nevertheless offer some insight into the various conflicting meanings the slave system and slave culture imposed on the American landscape.

LANDSCAPE AND POWER

David Hackett Fischer, in his magisterial *Albion's Seed,* notes an oddity of Virginian folk culture in the eighteenth and nineteenth centuries: house slaves often slept in the same room with their masters, but field slaves generally were not allowed to enter the house.[38] Many nineteenth-century abolitionists commented on this apparent inconsistency as well. But there is no inconsistency; indeed, to Virginians, black and white, there was nothing odd about it at all. Field hands were of lower status than house slaves, and status, in southern society, determined where one could go: which doors one could use, which rooms one could enter, where one could stand, sit, travel, live.

Southern society was fundamentally, insistently hierarchical, and social practices in the Old South inscribed these hierarchical relations on the landscape, giving the natural world important social meanings. According to Dell Upton, planters designed plantations and arranged their buildings to reinforce status. Tidewater, Chesapeake, and Piedmont plantations were modeled on the estates of the English aristocracy; planters sought to create an ordered, processional landscape in which every barrier—rows of trees, terraces, porticoes, doorways, halls, chambers—helped to define status. They typically organized the estate around the main house, which was often raised higher than the other buildings and surrounded by gardens and terraces. Slave quarters were part of the "working landscape," located around or behind the main house with the other outbuildings. Architecture and the use of space marked the difference between slave and white quarters; slaves' yards, for example, were extensions of their cabins, a productive area where vegetables were grown and livestock raised. The grounds surrounding the master's house, in contrast, usually had formal, ornamental landscaping that proclaimed the master's wealth and taste.[39]

Slaves, according to Upton, were not part of the audience these landscapes were intended for, and they could often cross barriers that white persons could not—hence the freedom of house slaves to sleep in their masters' rooms.[40] Thus the processional landscape held meaning for white southerners that it did not hold for black slaves. But slaves faced their own set of barriers and meanings; power relations also inscribed their landscape. Slave society like white society was hierarchical; proximity to the great house conferred higher status, and the higher the status, the more barriers one could cross. House slaves could go where field slaves could not. No slave, however, could leave the plantation without permission. To do so was to risk capture by patrollers, to suffer punishment and imprisonment.[41] Moreover, because white southerners typically assumed that blacks were slaves unless they could prove otherwise, the restrictions on slaves often served to restrict the movement of all blacks. The conventions put in place to control the movement of slaves therefore created a landscape of racial barriers.

The social and legal conventions that barred slaves from moving freely through the landscape served to associate the status of freedom with the freedom of movement enjoyed by whites. Exclusion from and attachment to particular places were marks of slavery. To be sure, racial segregation was not as prominent a feature of southern society as it would become after Emancipation. Nevertheless, the accounts of fugitive slaves suggest that the southern landscape was inscribed with racial meaning long before Jim Crow. Henry Bibb, for example, described what the world looked like to him as he attempted to escape from slave catchers in Louisville, Kentucky. The forest was not a safe refuge for Bibb: "I dared not go into the forest, knowing that I might be tracked by bloodhounds, and overtaken." Instead, he found a hiding place under a pile of boards between two workshops. After dark, he emerged into a city filled with slaveholders and slave hunters. "To me," he declared, "it was like a person entering a wilderness among wolves and vipers." He found his way blocked everywhere, not by walls but by "the gaze of patrols, or slave catchers." He finally escaped the city through a tunnel used by livestock. Fortunately an old black man was able to tell him where he could find something to eat. He then set off for the North, avoiding the public highways that would be patrolled by slave catchers and hiding in the forest or about the plantations, where he could enlist the help of other slaves.[42]

Of course, Bibb's account was written for a white audience for specifically political purposes, and it cannot be taken as a simple reflection even of his own worldview, much less that of other slaves. Nevertheless, it is significant that Bibb—no doubt by virtue of his position as a slave—was able to see and describe a very different landscape than the one inhabited by white men. Where they saw streets and highways along which they could move freely, Bibb saw blockades patrolled by a white gaze; where they saw two workshops side by side, a domain controlled by white power, Bibb saw the neglected space between the buildings. The roads, buildings, and taverns that represented civilization to whites were a "wilderness" to Bibb; the most civilized landscape he encountered was the border between plantation and forest, where he could escape the gaze of white patrols and receive help from other slaves.

Bibb and other black southerners, it seems, negotiated a landscape infused with white social power—a landscape in which they must have often felt like an alien and unwelcome presence. But as Bibb's narrative suggests, white control was far from perfect. By the end of the eighteenth century, slaves on many plantations in the Old South had gardens and were allowed to hunt and fish for food, as well as travel to other plantations and to town. In the years following the American Revolution, plantation maps from the southeastern low country started to give greater prominence to slave cemeteries and to the paths used by slaves to visit other estates, suggesting that slaves were successfully imposing their own meanings on the landscape. Philip Morgan reports that in this region, slaves often had enough leisure and freedom of movement to raise livestock, trade produce, and acquire significant wealth.[43] Such independent food production—the opportunity to exert some independent control over nature—in turn gave rise to ideas of family, property, status, and connection to place independent of one's relationship to one's master.[44] Slaves often referred to their customary "rights" to free time and property, and such claims were widely respected by masters. Not all slaves enjoyed these privileges, of course; Frances Kemble's journal of her residence on a Georgian plantation reports that slaves weren't allowed to hunt or keep livestock and seldom tended their gardens.[45] Nor were such customary rights secure. They were not legal rights; masters saw them as privileges and might revoke them at any time. Morgan describes the conflict over customary rights in South Carolina, where slaves were at various times prohibited from selling produce and even from growing corn, peas, and rice.[46] Those laws were too difficult to enforce and eventually abandoned, but they serve as a reminder that slaves enjoyed only an insecure control over property, compared to the rights held by even the poorest whites.

Still, customary rights to a garden or to hunting privileges could become the basis for an attachment to place—an attachment based on one's positive relationship to the land rather than on the legal barriers to movement. Slaves clearly valued the ability to exert some control over nature and their own labor, and to make a home for their families. In interviews of former slaves conducted by the Federal Writers' Project, among the most common memories were those of gardening and hunting, and interviewees could describe in loving detail the flowers, trees, birdsongs, and landscape where they grew up. A former slave called Aunt Clussey, for example, recalled with surprising eloquence "de way de shadows of de moon fell across our house; de call of do whip-poor-will over de ridge at night an' de song of de thrush early in de morning."[47] Admittedly, these interviews, distorted by nostalgia and suspicion of the white interviewers, undoubtedly produced an overly positive picture of plantation society. But most observers of slave society agreed that slaves valued their gardens and customary rights to raise and sell produce, and many developed a strong attachment to their homes.[48] In fact, this desire to establish a secure home and engage in independent production seems to be a common feature of virtually all slave cultures in the United States by the nineteenth century and would become an important element of slaves' and freedmen's conception of freedom.

In sum, the social and legal conventions designed to support racial hierarchy, at least in the Old South, invested the landscape with racially charged
meaning. Slave status, and hence blackness, determined which boundaries
one could cross and what it meant to cross them. How such conventions operated elsewhere in the South—how they persisted or were transformed in
frontier areas, in regions where plantation agriculture did not predominate,
and in towns and cities—requires further exploration, of course. But all
slaves probably faced some set of barriers to movement. And for virtually all
slaves, slave status determined the security (or insecurity) of one's right to
use the land for independent food production. These practices treated slaves
as aliens, as strangers in a strange land. But slaves apparently did not acqui-
esce in this status, and through their homemaking and food production established their own sense of right and belonging to the American landscape.
That sense of right would be central to the meaning of freedom in the black
political tradition, which included prominently both the ability to control a
particular piece of land and the ability to move freely through the landscape—in other words, the right to make a home and the right to leave it.

HERB LORE

White social power was not the only source of meaning in the slaves' landscape. The slaves' natural world was also a "pharmocosm," a storehouse of
plants and animals filled with healing and harming spiritual power.[49] During the eighteenth and nineteenth centuries, plant medicine formed the
core of rural health care for both blacks and whites, and plantation slaves'
herb lore was, by all accounts, extensive. They typically enjoyed an intimate
knowledge of their local environment and added to their inheritance of
African beliefs a wealth of information from whites and Native Americans
about the uses of local herbs. Slave doctors explored the local terrain, gathering flag root, jimson weed, garlic, calamus root, arrowroot, dogwood,
snakeroot, pokeweed, peach leaves, sassafras, privet root, mayflower root,
cotton root, and a vast variety of other herbs and roots to treat afflictions
ranging from headaches to rheumatism to malaria. Female slaves in particular were in a position to develop botanical knowledge, since they were often
responsible for gathering roots and herbs. Thus enslaved women often became the chief herbalists for their communities.[50] This detailed knowledge
of the local environment probably reinforced their attachment to it; like
gardening, it offered them some measure of control over nature and over

themselves. But herb lore had a deeper significance than did mere garden-ing expertise. Knowledge of roots and herbs conferred spiritual as well as social power.

Plantation slave communities in the Old South combined African ani-mistic beliefs with folk beliefs learned from whites and Native Americans to create a distinctive health culture, a culture that viewed the natural world as infused with spiritual power affecting human health for good or ill. Those blessed with the healing gift and educated in the proper traditions could draw on this spiritual power to heal (or harm). Illness, under this view, might be the result of spiritual forces unleashed against one because of some conflict or disturbance in one's relationships with neighbors, family mem-bers, or ancestors. Such afflictions required treatment from a conjuror or healer who understood the spiritual power of roots and herbs. Using herbs was therefore not just pharmacology but ritual, a way to harness the spiritual power residing in the natural world.[51] For slave healers in such health cul-tures, the natural landscape held meaning that was independent of the meanings imposed by white society; mastery of the natural landscape through knowledge of the local plant life was a source of spiritual power in-dependent of the master.

Masters recognized this challenge to their authority. Like independent food production, mastery of herb lore and folk healing practices posed a threat to masters' control over slaves, which rested in part on masters' con-trol of access to medical care. Thus some masters tried to discourage slaves from seeking help from conjure doctors and relied instead on standard western scientific medicine.[52] Mart Stewart explains this struggle over con-trol of slaves' bodies as a conflict between black slaves' and white elites' health cultures; he argues that white elites made a clear distinction between the spiritual and the material worlds, attributing disease to purely physical or psychological causes. Black slaves, in contrast, occupied a "sacred land-scape" that included both material and spiritual beings. Humans were "in-extricably entwined into this tightly woven fabric of spirits and matter"; illness could have physical, social, and spiritual causes at the same time.[53] Under this view, slave and white cultures offered fundamentally different and opposed attitudes toward nature.

There is considerable evidence, however, that white Americans—even white elites—often shared their slaves' beliefs in magic and herb medicine. Frances Kemble tells us that her doctor treated her husband's rheumatism by tying tulip leaves around his knees, a cure he learned from the Negroes.

Sharla Fett reports similar examples of white masters on nineteenth-century slave plantations resorting to "Negro cures" and even seeking help from black conjurors.[54] Masters were not above using slaves' belief in magic to bolster their control. Moreover, slaves didn't always embrace these folk beliefs (or at least said they didn't).[55] And some slaves learned quite a lot from their masters about western science. Agriculture reformer Edmund Ruffin, for example, was surprised at how much his slave Sykes understood about his agricultural experiments.[56] Admittedly, such complex health cultures— in which competing views of nature existed side by side—were probably more typical of the late eighteenth and early nineteenth centuries than of earlier periods. Colonial culture may not have been penetrated as deeply by scientific worldviews, and slaves probably enjoyed differing levels of access to white culture depending on their language skills and length of residence in America. Nevertheless, we should be cautious of assertions that slaves believed one thing and masters another. In many communities, it would be more accurate to say that different belief systems coexisted among slaves and masters and could be mobilized by either when appropriate.

But how different are these belief systems? After all, both the scientific and magical use of herbs required extensive and particular study of the natural world; in fact, white botanists often relied on black healers for information about local plants. Conjurors studied the effects of roots and herbs to determine their uses and developed theories to explain the underlying principles of their practices—not unlike the theories developed by eighteenth-century scientists.[57] Nevertheless, there is a tradition in western social theory of distinguishing scientific from magical ways of relating to nature, describing science as a more analytic, rational, and less participatory approach to the natural world. It is a controversial tradition, though. It teaches that magic and animism start from the assumption that humans share an intimate spiritual connection to nature that must be felt or intuited rather than grasped analytically. Under this view, the natural world for practitioners of magic is not differentiated from the spiritual or social world; nature and humans are united by mystic connections that are felt rather than comprehended analytically.[58] This tradition thus supports the claim that peoples with animistic beliefs relate to the natural world intuitively rather than analytically and are therefore "closer" to nature than western industrialized peoples (who presumably share a common scientific, rationalized understanding of nature).

This tradition, as we will see in Chapter 5, will have some influence on early twentieth-century black thought. However, modern scholars are rightly wary of it. Although it has given us valuable insight into animistic belief systems, it also reinforces problematic racial stereotypes and fails to capture the complexity of both western and nonwestern cultures. Magical belief systems, understood on their own terms, may be analytic and rational, and scientific belief systems may incorporate intuitive and emotional elements. Moreover, the prevalence of magical and religious beliefs among western industrialized peoples undermines the claim that their worldview is fundamentally scientific.[59]

In any case, there is the abundant evidence that neither slaves nor their masters consistently viewed nature from a single perspective. The slaves' world could be magical, religious, or scientific, and which view they adopted depended critically on their relationships to other human beings. For example, slaves could use their herb lore to enhance their status in the slave community and with their masters. Their knowledge had practical uses to planters, and many planters seemed to respect and fear slave conjurors as much as other slaves did. Herb lore was thus a source of social power. However, that kind of knowledge (in contrast to scientific knowledge) also marked one's status as a slave. White elites often denigrated herb lore as "Negro cures" and "Negro superstition" (even while admitting it had some value) and cultivated scientific knowledge as a marker of their superior social status.[60] Thus slaves' herb lore, like their attachment to place, had a complex relationship to their social status; it could both support and undermine their bids for autonomy and social recognition.

Such a social environment made it possible, and indeed often necessary, for slaves to deploy different understandings of nature strategically. Consider, for example, how Frederick Douglass's 1845 *Narrative* exploits the ambiguous status of root medicine in slave and white society: First Douglass suggests that a magical root given to him by his friend may have endowed him with the strength to stand up to his brutal overseer. But he quickly qualifies that suggestion; he *might* have thought there was some power in the root "had [the conflict] been on any other day than Sunday."[61] His white audience is left to speculate on whether Douglass's strength came from his Christian faith or from a different form of spiritual power. The message, though, is clear: either way, they should be wary of crossing him. Slave culture offered more than one source of power and more than one way to master the spiritual and material landscape.

SLAVE COSMOLOGY

As the discussion of herb lore suggests, the power relations and production practices established (or allowed) by the slave system could give meaning to the landscape, but so could the cosmological beliefs shared, to a greater or lesser extent, by slaves who participated in the plantation culture of the Old South. Slaves' religion made available a distinctive understanding of the relationship between humans and nature and between physical and spiritual reality. Like other aspects of slave culture, however, slaves' religious discourse poses interpretive challenges.

Scholars once endorsed the view of Franklin Frazier that slavery destroyed all vestiges of African religious ideas, leaving slaves with only the fatalistic and quietist version of Christianity offered by slaveholders.[62] That view has been largely discredited; although Christian churches certainly played a major role in the black community from the nineteenth century on, we now have considerable evidence of African survivals and the persistence in the slave community of belief in nature spirits, ghosts, and other supernatural phenomena that do not fit into a conventional Christian cosmology. John Blassingame, for example, points to a striking passage from Henry Ravenal's 1936 *Recollections of Plantation Life:* "Another very general belief among the negroes, was that every spring or fountain of water had a presiding Genius, or guardian spirit, which lived there. They called this thing 'Cymbee.' . . . If anyone disturbed the spring, the Cymbee would be angry. If it was destroyed or much injured from any cause, the Cymbee would leave it, and the waters would dry up."[63] This passage suggests that despite immersion in a predominately Christian culture, animistic beliefs and practices persisted among slaves into the nineteenth century and influenced slaves' conception of nature.

How did such animistic beliefs relate to the slave Christianity that developed in the nineteenth century? Were they part of an integrated worldview, or merely remnants of a largely abandoned tradition? Melville Herskovits's influential discussion of slave religion argues that animistic beliefs persisted because they could be merged with compatible Christian ideas. For example, he suggests that Baptists were popular among the slaves because the baptism ritual echoed the water rituals of West African river cults.[64] Under this view, slave religion may have been largely African in content although Christian in form. Margaret Creel's equally influential study of the Gullah community supports that interpretation. Creel shows that efforts at

Christianization in the Old South were intermittent and largely ineffective until the 1830s, allowing for the persistence of African rituals and beliefs. She points in particular to "seekin" rituals—a religious conversion process practiced among the Gullahs, in which the seeker goes into the wilderness to pray and experience visions. "Seekin," she argues, is similar to common West African religious initiation rituals, which involve going into "the bush" to encounter the nature spirits that dwell there. Like Herskovits, Creel concludes that the Gullahs' religious experience was based on a worldview more African than Christian.[65] (She attributes the appeal of the Baptists, however, to their more intense recruitment efforts and willingness to give slaves more institutional autonomy than other denominations.[66])

Lawrence Levine offers the most developed version of this thesis. Levine contends that slave religion reflects a fundamentally African consciousness. He points to evidence that slaves retained many of their animistic beliefs, syncretizing them with the folk beliefs of white Americans.[67] The persistence of African beliefs made slaves' version of Christianity distinctive. Slave religion, according to Levine, does not differentiate material and spiritual reality as sharply as does the Christianity of white Americans. Rather, like West African animistic beliefs, slave religion conceptualizes the spiritual and material world as intertwined. Spirits inhabit *this* world alongside men and animals, rather than transcending it. Eugene Genovese, elaborating on this point, argues that "African ideas place man himself and therefore his Soul within nature," and that Christian slaves similarly rejected "otherworldly" understandings of the soul and Heaven. For example, he contends that references to Heaven in slave spirituals should be interpreted as referring to both a spiritual condition *and* a physical place (such as the North) where slaves would enjoy freedom.[68]

Whether slave religion reflects a fundamentally African consciousness (or whether there is in fact such a thing as an undifferentiated "African consciousness") would require a more nuanced exploration that takes into account regional and temporal differences among slave communities. But Levine's claim that slave spirituals and other religious discourse infuse the material landscape with spiritual—and specifically biblical—meaning is compelling, at least with respect to nineteenth-century slave culture in the Old South. The Bible permeated the symbolic culture of these slave communities. Black spirituals used vivid biblical nature imagery and referred frequently to biblical landscapes: Slaves sang "O Canaan, sweet Canaan, / I am abound for the land of Canaan"; they called on the river to "roll, Jordan, roll" and asked "Did yo' ever / Stan' on mountain / Wash yo' han's / In a cloud?" Black troops marched into war singing "Go in de wilderness, / Jesus call you. Go in de wilderness / To wait upon de Lord."[69] They were particularly drawn to the story of the Israelites' captivity and deliverance and to Old Testament figures such as Daniel, Joshua, and Moses—historical figures who were delivered from slavery in *this* world rather than in a future end-time. They even acted out the story of the Israelites' deliverance in ring dances; according to Albert Raboteau, in such dances "time and distance collapsed, and the slaves became the children of Israel. With the Hebrews, they traveled dry-shod through the Red Sea; they, too, saw Pharaoh's army 'get drownded'; they stood beside Moses on Mount Pisgah and gazed out over the Promised Land."[70]

Under Levine's interpretation, these religious practices gave spiritual meaning to the slaves' contemporary reality: "The sacred world of the slaves was able to fuse the precedents of the past, the conditions of the present, and the promise of the future into one connected reality."[71] Christian theology encourages this fusion by treating Old Testament figures as *types*—persons, objects, or events of Old Testament history that prefigure persons or things revealed in the new dispensation. Slaves' religious and political discourse went even further, treating Moses and Jesus as types of contemporary liberators such as Abraham Lincoln. In this way, Moses, Jesus, and Abraham Lincoln could fuse into a single figure, giving contemporary political events spiritual meaning by linking the biblical past, the present, and a millennial future. Genovese in fact reports that after the Civil War, black preachers told freedmen in South Carolina that the Republican gubernatorial candidate, Franklin Moses, was actually the biblical Moses, come to lead them to the Promised Land.[72] A striking but not unusual example; according to Colonel Thomas Wentworth Higginson, who observed black Union soldiers during the Civil War, "their memories are a vast bewildered chaos of Jewish history and biography; and most of the great events of the past, down to the period of the American Revolution, they instinctively attribute to Moses."[73]

For our purposes, the critical point is that use of Old Testament types could invest geographic places with spiritual significance. To take a familiar example, Frederick Douglass informed his audience that when slaves referred to "Canaan" they meant both Heaven and the North: "the north was our Canaan."[74] The South, conversely, was often referred to as "Egypt," the land of captivity. Similarly, the Mississippi could be the river Jordan or the

Red Sea, and wild spaces could become the desert in which the children of Israel wandered. Melvin Dixon points out further that slave spirituals used features of the vernacular landscape as metaphors for slaves' religious feelings: valleys represented depression and despair; mountains were figures for personal triumph and witness; the wilderness represented a state of spiritual seeking.[75] Such rhetorical practices resulted in a typological map—a sacred geography investing the American landscape with spiritual meaning.

This tendency to interpret the landscape in biblical terms was pervasive in nineteenth-century black culture, among both elites and masses. Although white Americans also drew heavily on biblical imagery to give meaning to the landscape, this use of biblical types to fuse the spiritual with the material world seems to be more pronounced and persistent in black American culture. We find a striking example in Martin Delany's serial novel, *Blake*. Henry, the hero, has escaped from a plantation with the intent of leading a slave revolt. As he enters the wilderness and reaches the Red River, he is overwhelmed by the task in front of him:

> Standing upon a high bank of the stream, contemplating his mission, a feeling of humbleness and a sensibility of unworthiness impressed him. . . . Henry raised in solemn tones amidst the lonely wilderness:
>
> > Could I but climb where Moses stood,
> > And view the landscape o'er;
> > Not Jordan's streams, nor death's cold flood,
> > Could drive me from the shore!

The modern reader might be struck by the sudden emergence of an Old Testament landscape in the American wilderness, but Henry is thoroughly at home in this biblical world. He climbs his mountain and crosses the alligator-infested Jordan, his faith "now fully established."[76]

Nor was this rhetorical practice confined to literary discourse or to the antebellum period. Nell Painter quotes a participant in the 1879 Kansas Fever Exodus: complaining about being stranded in St Louis east of the Mississippi, he exhorts his followers,

> We've been fooled about that railroad and land and mule biz. And then this here gentleman asks us whether we'd not go back to Egypt (the South). Children, I've been giving him the 'wing of old Mississippi. I knows what you thinks, and I told him you'd rather join hands and walk into Jordan's tide.

Painter's Exodusters also referred to the Mississippi as the Red Sea:

> We's like the children of Israel when they was led from out o' bondage by Moses. . . . Now child, just listen to me. This is our Red Sea, right here in St. Louis, between home and Kansas, and if we sticks together an' keeps up our faith we'll get to Kansas and be out o' bondage for sure.[77]

The imposition of biblical geographies onto the American landscape persists in African American literature and political discourse, constituting an important legacy of slave culture to the development of the black intellectual tradition. But how much it tells us about slaves' view of nature is harder to say. As argued earlier, religious texts—like folk tales—are subject to multiple interpretations, and slaves had access to more than one worldview. Although slave testimony reveals an abundance of religious imagery and sentiments, it just as commonly reveals a purely practical orientation toward the natural world, attributing phenomena to natural causes without putting them into a spiritual context at all. Thus the religious worldview Levine describes may have operated less as an all-encompassing orientation toward the natural world than as a set of beliefs that could be put on and off as the situation warranted.

Consider, for example, the story told by the former slave Tommie Bryant to a Federal Writers' Project interviewer:

> When I was a youngster I always liked to go muddin for fish, 'twas easier than hook 'n' bait, so I always used this way when I got chance. Then was days when a boy could 'preciate a few hours to loaf.
>
> Once I went a muddin and just as the fish begins to jump about all around and just as I was a fixing to get my catch I heard a peculiar sound. I looked towards where I heard the sound to a old hollow stump a sitting there in the water near the bank and what do you reckon? Lo an' behold, Fletis McGetis (good gracious) there a staring me in the face was a big old brown slick snake or old moccasin snake, just seeming to dare me to get airy one of them fish. He licked out his tongue at me. Then I thinks about the snake which messed Adam and Eves' business, I thinks about that beautiful garden, with all them fruit trees, then I thinks about 'twas no such thing as work, then I thinks about how tired I gets and so I ups and gets blasted mad. I tolls him 'you low cussed deceiving liar, you fooled Eve but you won't bluff me.' So I gets to land to get me a stick to bust him open but when I returns he done hid from me. I stood there, calling him all kinds of deceivers but he didn't appear. I told him I wasn't scared of him. I did feel sort of funny and somehow my mind never led me to go mudding there again.[78]

In this story, Tommie Bryant moves effortlessly into a biblical interpretation of nature. As soon as he is reminded of the snake in the Garden, the snake actually *becomes* Satan, and Tommie becomes a spiritual warrior. This is all consistent with the argument that southern blacks inhabited a sacred world in which biblical types fused with present reality, infusing the material world with spiritual meaning. It suggests that Bryant saw spiritual meaning derived from the Old Testament in the natural world.

On the other hand, the story is clearly meant to be humorous, and the humor works because we (and the storyteller) recognize the silliness of seeing a stray moccasin as the devil incarnate. Tommie Bryant is *making fun* of this rhetorical practice, distancing himself from it by inviting us to laugh at it—or perhaps he is making fun of his white audience, offering to them what he thinks they expect from a poor southern black man. He may even be playing a more serious game, giving the interviewer the kind of folk tale he expects in order to avoid answering questions that might reveal a more sophisticated and subversive belief system. He could in fact be doing all of these things, making use of the richness of the text, the rhetorical situation, and his own skills as a raconteur.

We must be cautious, then, in generalizing about slaves' beliefs about nature without paying close attention to the rhetorical context in which those beliefs are deployed. Nevertheless, we can draw some conclusions about the legacy of slave culture to the black intellectual tradition. The way the slave system controlled space, along with the Afro-European symbolic culture developed on plantations, invested the American landscape with political, spiritual, and moral significance and created a racialized landscape that would receive further elaboration after Emancipation under segregation laws. Slave agriculture and the systems of control it depended on put slaves in a conflicted relationship to the land, and they also created a strong association between the concept of freedom and certain ways of interacting with and controlling nature. In particular, slavery deprived slaves of property rights and the right to travel, and it restricted their ability to engage in independent food production. This feature seems to be characteristic of American slavery generally, and as we will see, these rights would become critical components of the freedom sought by black Americans, linking self-possession with possession of the land.

If the slave system prohibited slaves from some sorts of economic activities, though, it required or at least allowed other sorts. Many slaves engaged in gardening, hunting, and gathering roots and herbs. These production practices and the knowledge they reflected undoubtedly served as the basis of an attachment to place for plantation slaves, as well as a potential source of selfhood and social power. That attachment and knowledge, however, could also be a marker of slave status; their meaning was therefore ambiguous and would be contested in the black political tradition. Finally, we find in slaves' religious culture a strong tendency to imbue the landscape with moral and spiritual significance—a tendency that spills over frequently into political and literary discourse. Biblical typological discourse infused the physical landscape with spiritual meaning, reinforcing the fusion of spiritual and material reality found in African religious traditions. This trend, too, persisted in elite political and artistic discourse well into the twentieth century.

Nevertheless, slave culture did not inform elite black discourse in a simple and straightforward way. Elites often tried to distance themselves from slave culture in order to secure their authority with white audiences. When they did draw on slave culture, they did so selectively and strategically. For example, black elites drew on typological discourse in part because they were trying to communicate with the black masses but also because it was an effective rhetorical strategy for white audiences, who were also well versed in the Old Testament. Moreover, European and Anglo-American intellectual traditions accorded value to folk traditions—even black folk traditions. As subsequent chapters will discuss, white elites during the late nineteenth and early twentieth centuries increasingly valued folk culture as a source of cultural authenticity and vitality. Black intellectuals and activists could therefore use elements of slave culture to assert to white audiences their authority to speak for the black community and to demonstrate their mastery of the primitive sources of high culture. At the same time, their validation of slave culture could suggest to black audiences that pride in this culture could be a foundation for their sense of self.

Still, there is an important sense in which black elites were speaking from a common black culture and experience: they were, by and large, subject to and talking about the system of racial oppression rooted in race slavery, particularly plantation slavery. That system, and slaves' response to it, therefore shaped in vital respects what they had to say about nature. Most significantly, it led them to focus on how slavery and freedom affect humans' relationship to the natural world. These theoretical links between freedom and humans' relationship to nature would be elaborated in the nineteenth-century tradition of black agrarianism.

CHAPTER TWO

A LAND CURSED BY INJUSTICE

In 1833 the Third Annual Convention for the Improvement of the Free People of Color considered the American Colonization Society's plan to send free blacks to Liberia. The participants did not wish to emigrate to a foreign country, they decided, but to "those who may be obliged to exchange a cultivated region for a howling wilderness, we would recommend, to retire back into the western wilds, and fell the *native forests of America*, where the *ploughshare* of prejudice has as yet been unable to penetrate the soil—and where they can dwell in peaceful retirement, under their own vine and under their own fig tree."[1] Many free blacks and fugitive slaves did just that, establishing several planned agrarian communities in the United States and Canada.[2]

These experimental communities represent a deep-rooted aspiration of black Americans to the property ownership, independence, and equality enjoyed by other American farmers. Such agrarian aspirations also inform the first major body of black political theory, the writings of black abolitionists. The antislavery movement was, after all, an agricultural reform movement: it aimed at disassembling the plantation system of controlling nature and labor and promoting a different system of agriculture—the system celebrated by Thomas Jefferson and other American democratic agrarians. Under this alternative system, workers are not under a master's control but establish their own control over the natural world from a position of individual independence and political and social equality. That position allows them to develop an interest in and affection for the land that should lead to good stewardship. In short, antislavery advocates argued that only when the land was worked by free and equal citizens would agriculture thrive.

Black abolitionists in particular developed this agrarian critique of slavery. Drawing on Jeffersonian democratic agrarianism, along with arguments by eighteenth-century economists and agriculturalists, they explored how slave agriculture affected both the meaning of nature and the incentives to stewardship. The result was a tradition of black agrarianism that emphasized the role of free labor and social and political equality in establishing a sustainable and morally beneficial relationship to the natural world.

SLAVERY AND ANTISLAVERY IN ANTEBELLUM AMERICA

Slavery was not, of course, confined to agriculture. Slaves were craftsmen, traders, foresters, shipbuilders—virtually any economic activity could make use of slave labor. But the South throughout the nineteenth century remained a predominately agricultural society, and most of its slaves (like most of its white citizens) were agricultural workers. A number of factors contributed to the slow pace of industrial development in the South, including the harsh disease environment, a political climate favoring laissez-faire policies and weak government, limited investments in the transportation infrastructure, resistance among southerners to federal spending on internal improvements, and possibly the slave system itself.[3] This industrial lag allowed southerners to develop a regional identity as a traditional agrarian society. Indeed, by exploiting Thomas Jefferson's ambiguous stance on slavery and inequality, southerners could claim to be the true inheritors of Jefferson's agrarian vision for the United States.

But the South was in fact a highly mobile and changing society. For example, after the Revolutionary War, the tobacco monoculture of the Chesapeake region gave way to a more intensive mixed farming regime based on wheat, which required different skills and work patterns from the slave labor force. This regime demanded less unskilled field work and more specialized work from plowmen, herdsmen, and dairy maids, as well as a mobile workforce that could process and transport grain. The resulting economic diversity stemming from this transition diminished the slaves' isolation, giving them more freedom of movement and more control over their labor. More generally, these economic changes weakened the slave system and led to the growth of a free black community. As historian Ira Berlin puts it, the Upper South moved from a slave society to a society with slaves.[4]

In the Lower South, however, plantation slavery expanded. In fact, between 1810 and 1861, southerners and slavery spread west in a migration so vast that it has been called the "Second Middle Passage." The migration was in part a response to declines in soil fertility in the Old South, and soil stewardship, accordingly, became a major theme in Southern public discourse during this period. Those hoping to stem the westward migration looked to the successful wheat farmers in the Upper South, with their mixed farming regime allowing for crop rotation and heavier use of fertilizer, as a model for reforming southern agriculture generally. But arguments for mixed farming made little headway in the tidewater region, which remained dominated by cotton and rice monoculture. Maintaining soil fertility under such a regime posed serious challenges; agricultural science was still in its infancy, and even if the reformers knew how to improve soil fertility, farmers generally couldn't afford their remedies—especially when land was so cheap. Instead, they left behind the exhausted fields and rigid social hierarchy of the Old South, moving in large numbers to the more fertile Gulf region.[5]

This migration to the Gulf region resulted in the creation of the large, highly regimented cotton and sugar plantations that came to represent the worst form of chattel slavery. The resulting demand for field hands led to the expansion of the internal slave trade; in the 1830s, slave traders uprooted an estimated 300,000 black men, women, and children.[6] But recreating slave society wasn't easy. The settlers faced harsh frontier conditions, cotton production was labor-intensive and hard to master, and it was difficult to establish planter authority in the absence of the complex social structures that supported slavery in the east.[7] In fact, even in the Old South, planter authority could seem fragile; Nat Turner's 1831 revolt in Virginia fueled slave owners' fears of slave rebellion as well as increasing anxiety about runaway slaves. And to make matters worse (from the slaveholders' point of view), northerners were starting to interfere with the "peculiar institution."

The spread of slavery into what was then the southwest discouraged those northerners who had hoped the institution would die a natural death, thus helping to radicalize the antislavery movement. In the 1830s a small contingent of antislavery advocates, led by William Lloyd Garrison, abandoned colonization as a solution and began calling for an immediate end to slavery. The publication of Nat Turner's *Confession* provided this radical abolition movement with an important new weapon: the *Confession*'s popularity encouraged Garrison to promote abolition through the publication of testimony by fugitive slaves—a strategy that proved to be remarkably successful in bringing attention to the cause, as well as creating a rich body of black abolitionist literature.[8] Also helpful to the abolitionist cause was growing concern in the North about southerners' influence in federal government and anxiety among northern workers about competition with slave labor. By the 1840s, these concerns made antislavery (if not Garrison's radical abolitionism) a respectable position in northern politics, embraced first by the Free Soil Party and then by the Republicans.[9]

The abolition movement was the first flowering of black political thought in the United States. White abolitionists promoted black political activism by giving a platform to black speakers, including former slaves such as Frederick Douglass, William Wells Brown, Sojourner Truth, James Pennington, Lewis Clarke, and Henry Bibb. But radical abolitionism also had roots in the free black community. As early as 1817, three thousand blacks met in Philadelphia to denounce the American Colonization Society and declare their solidarity with their enslaved brethren, reflecting a deep commitment to emancipation in the northern black community. One of the first militant calls for immediate emancipation was *David Walker's Appeal* (published shortly before Turner's rebellion), whose author was a member of the Massachusetts General Colored Association, one of many black organizations promoting abolition.[10] Blacks also participated in the American Anti-Slavery Association and many of its satellite and auxiliary organizations, and it was apparently the influence of free black abolitionists that turned Garrison against colonization.[11]

Abolitionism was thus an interracial movement, despite persistent conflicts between black and white abolitionists. Not only did abolitionists seek support from both races, they actively encouraged blacks to speak to white audiences.[12] Therefore, black abolitionists drew primarily on intellectual traditions and rhetorical conventions familiar to such audiences (although they often used those traditions and conventions in unexpected and creative ways). As a result, slave narratives and other political writings by black abolitionists (which were often written in collaboration with white abolitionists) are not simple reflections of slaves' or free blacks' worldview. Rather, they are complex rhetorical acts growing out of and reflecting both blacks' unique experiences and the broader northern political culture. They are, as Henry Louis Gates writes, "two-toned," participating in both the dominant American culture and a distinct black tradition.[13]

Two elements of northern political culture in particular influenced American abolitionism. Radical abolitionists relied most heavily on humanitarian arguments against slavery, linking the antislavery movement to other nineteenth-century humanitarian and moral reform efforts. But abolitionists and other antislavery advocates (such as radical Republicans) also drew on the political tradition of democratic agrarianism and liberal economic theories developed by eighteenth-century agricultural reformers. This agrarian strain of antislavery thought focuses on the virtues of independent yeoman farmers and the deleterious effects of unfree labor, large-scale agricultural operations, and absentee owners on agricultural productivity and soil fertility. Such arguments pervaded American environmental thought during the nineteenth century; antebellum antislavery advocates used them to explain the effects of slavery on stewardship and on humans' relationship to nature. The result was a distinctive variety of agrarianism, consistent with the dominant democratic agrarian tradition but centered on issues growing out of the experience of slavery.

DEMOCRATIC AGRARIANISM AND SLAVERY

Black agrarianism was only one version of an environmental philosophy that has shaped western thought for centuries. Like any robust intellectual tradition, agrarianism has been more of a conversation than a static, internally consistent body of principles. But central to this tradition in its many permutations is the idea that man's natural calling is to cultivate the earth. Christian agrarians have dignified this calling with the claim (based on Genesis 1:28) that God gave humans stewardship over the lower orders of nature, including the authority and duty to domesticate animals and cultivate plants. Indeed, a long-standing theme in this tradition characterizes humans as "co-creators" whose function is to "finish" Creation, transforming the wilderness into a garden suitable for human flourishing.[14] As we will see, this "co-creator" concept has been particularly salient in the black tradition, which consistently emphasizes the creative agency—and the equality among humans—implied by this understanding of stewardship.

Stewardship is a central theme in white American culture as well, of course. In fact, by the eighteenth century, agrarianism was integral to American intellectual life, permeating religious, moral, literary, and—especially—political discourse. Agrarian ideology had a number of political uses. For example, colonists could justify conquering and displacing the natives on the grounds that the earth rightfully belongs to those who use it as God intends—that is, creating out of the wilderness a civilization based on European-style agriculture.[15] Thomas Jefferson, in contrast, used democratic agrarianism to support policies favoring agriculture over commerce and manufacturing (policies that he believed would benefit the South). Such a rich and versatile tradition was not easily confined, however; Federalists and their successors also drew on democratic agrarianism to criticize southern slavery.

Democratic agrarians' central claim was that owning a farm and cultivating it through one's own labor creates a character ideally suited to republican government.[16] Echoing seventeenth-century English republicans, agrarians contended that owning productive land provides economic and therefore political independence.[17] Ideally, therefore, a majority of citizens in a republican polity should own their own farms. But agrarians also wanted citizens to *work* their own farms. They typically endorsed John Locke's view that the right to property derives originally from one's labor in cultivating the earth—an argument that small farmers could deploy against owners of large slave plantations (as well as Native American hunters and gatherers, when necessary).[18] In addition, agrarians argued that agricultural labor cultivates virtues conducive to good citizenship, including self-sufficiency, industriousness, humility, spirituality (through contemplation of God's creation and the cycle of birth and death), and prudence. "Corruption of morals in the mass of cultivators is a phenomenon of which no age nor nation has furnished an example," Jefferson famously declared in *Notes on Virginia*. Therefore "let us never wish to see our citizens occupied at a workbench, or twirling a distaff."[19]

This focus on the moral value of labor is the primary difference between democratic agrarianism and its aristocratic cousin, a minority tradition that developed in the South in order to justify slavery. Aristocratic agrarians agreed that the South's agrarian society was more virtuous than the busy, money-mad commercial society to the north, and that ownership of productive land should be a requirement for citizenship. But they claimed that their civic virtue was the result of *leisure* activities such as studying history, natural history, and philosophy—leisure made possible by large-scale slave agriculture. Slavery, they argued, was essential to creating a virtuous citizenry capable of republican government because it relieved the political class from the degrading effects of manual labor.[20]

Democratic agrarians disagreed. Not all were opposed to slavery on a small scale, but they strongly criticized the economic, social, and political inequality that characterized southern slave society, as well as the luxury and moral corruption that such inequality led to. Hector St. John de Crèvecouer's classic work, *Letters from an American Farmer*, contains a particularly cogent example of this agrarian critique of slavery—a critique that would become common among Federalists and appear later in abolitionist literature. An important element of that critique, of course, was the humanitarian objection to slavery.[21] But I wish to focus here on the other two elements: a theory of social evolution that characterized slavery as a sign of a civilization's moral decline, and the economic argument for free agricultural labor.

Crèvecoeur's narrator condemns the South through invidious contrasts with the northern colonies. The slave-trading city of Charles Town (Charleston, South Carolina), he explains, is "what Lima is in the south; both are capitals of the richest provinces of their respective hemispheres," both filled with "inhabitants who enjoy all those gradations of pleasure, refinement, and luxury which proceed from wealth." But while the inhabitants of Charles Town enjoy their wealth, "scenes of misery overspread in the country" where the slave "grubs the ground, raises indigo, or husks the rice, exposed to a sun full as scorching as their native one, without the support of good food, without the cordials of any cheering liquor." In contrast, the middle colonies are characterized by independent freemen: industrious, prudent, jealous of their rights but tolerant of religious difference. The northern colonies are not agrarian utopias, however; as one approaches the western frontier, men become even more independent and indifferent, as well as idle and ruder in their manners. They live not by farming but by hunting—a "licentious idle life" that degrades their character.[22] The natives, in contrast, are less degraded, exhibiting a primitive nobility and rude virtue.

This description of American regional variation follows a theory of social evolution that took shape by the middle of the eighteenth century and remained orthodoxy until the twentieth.[23] According to this theory, human society begins with the primitive savage inhabiting a wilderness and living by hunting. The savage, a largely solitary creature, is innocent of both social virtues and social vices; he lives a leisurely life of independence and freedom. But eventually primitive society evolves, first into nomadic pastoralism and then into an agricultural community of independent farmers enjoying a rough economic and political equality. Each stage witnesses an improvement in manners and morals; individuals in agrarian society reach the apex of moral development and are eminently suited for republican government—that is, a government of free and equal citizens seeking the public good. Unfortunately, as agricultural society becomes more prosperous, it begins to engage in commerce. Commerce produces riches; cities and empires arise, and the citizenry suffer moral degeneration as a result of idleness and luxury. The citizens, thus degraded, trade independence for the opportunity to indulge their thirst for domination, leading to social inequality, slavery, and tyranny.

Crèvecoeur uses this theory of social evolution to create a moral geography, distributing the historical stages of civilization over the landscape from east to west: Europe under this view is an overdeveloped commercial civilization whereas the American continent is a younger, more virtuous republic of small farmers.[24] Still moving east to west, American society becomes more virtuous as it becomes more primitive—until it reaches the frontier and living conditions become too primitive to sustain agrarian virtues. This was all quite conventional in American political discourse by the late eighteenth century, of course. But Crèvecoeur also distributed the historical stages from north to south: The northern frontier is still a primitive society, while the New England and mid-Atlantic colonies represent virtuous agrarian communities. The South, in contrast, is an overdeveloped, corrupt society characterized by inequality and slavery—as bad as and perhaps even worse than aristocratic, tyrannical Europe.

Under this view, the northern colonies (particularly the farming communities of New York and Pennsylvania) are well suited for republican government. Moreover, they should remain so, as long as they are protected from moral degeneration by the frontier. According to Crèvecoeur's narrator, the frontier is an important political and moral resource: the work of subduing the wilderness "regenerates" political character, turning a degraded and dispirited victim of tyranny into an independent, resourceful, rugged individual. On the frontier, he explains, the idle become employed, the useless become useful, and the poor may become rich (in lands, cattle, and good houses, rather than pernicious luxuries).[25] As we will see, this belief that Americans' interaction with the wilderness—specifically, transforming the wilderness into farms—forms a character uniquely suited for republican government would eventually prove helpful to blacks seeking citizenship.

But the South had a frontier as well. Why did this political regeneration fail to occur among slaves and their masters? This question brings us to the second element of Crèvecoeur's case against slavery: Under his reasoning, the moral benefit of agriculture is available only under a *free* labor system. Crèvecoeur explains that it is both the laws and industry that regenerate European immigrants to America: because of the "indulgent" laws, "they receive ample rewards for their labours; these accumulated rewards procure them lands; those lands confer on them the title of freemen, and to that title every benefit is affixed which men can possibly require."[26] Clearly this regenerative process only works for those who can accumulate wealth from their own labor—which excludes both slaves and those who live off slave labor. The South started down the path to moral degeneration because, from the beginning, it relied too heavily on slaves.

Crèvecoeur's narrator favors free labor, then, for its moral and political benefits. He contrasts the favorable situation of American freeholders with that of the "Russian boor and Hungarian peasant," "condemned to a slavery worse than that of our Negroes," and attributes Americans' happiness to the "freedom of action, freedom of thoughts," and rule "by a government which requires but little from us." But he also favors it for its economic benefits: free workers, he believes, are more productive. "We are all animated with the spirit of an industry which is unfettered and unrestrained," he explains, "because each person works for himself." His own slaves, he assures us, enjoy a great deal of liberty, which makes them happy and good workers. He even lets his bees work in freedom: "Were I to confine them, they would dwindle away and quit their labour."[27]

Crèvecoeur doesn't explicitly use this argument in his critique of southern slavery—he describes the South as quite wealthy, despite its reliance on unfree labor. But others would. Indeed, the claim that free workers are more productive than slave labor would become a central element of the economic case against slavery, appearing in Federalist critiques of southern society, antebellum antislavery ideology, and black abolitionism. It did not begin with abolitionists, however; it derives from eighteenth-century debates about agriculture reform among progressive European agriculturalists and economists, including Arthur Young, Lord Kames, Adam Smith, and the French Physiocrats, as well as American intellectuals such as Thomas Jefferson and John Taylor of Caroline.[28] In general, these reformers were more concerned with improving the productivity of agriculture through application of scientific and technological advances than with combating slavery. (Southern reformers were in fact usually slaveholders.) Nevertheless, they promoted an ideal conception of farming that tended to support small farms and free labor over large slave plantations.

This ideal is rooted in ancient traditions that link good husbandry to improved soil fertility. Classical and Christian traditions both taught that the more labor one applies to the soil, the more fertile the soil will become; the price of indolence is infertile fields, lower productivity, and poverty.[29] Eighteenth-century agricultural reformers agreed with this tenet and could cite in support the success of "convertible husbandry" or "improving agriculture," a labor-intensive regimen derived from English farming practices. Farmers under this system plow deeply and use small fields intensively rather than cultivating large amounts of land using less labor-intensive methods. This intensive use of small plots prevents soil erosion. Farmers also enhance fertility by rotating crops and using manure as fertilizer, which therefore must be carefully husbanded and spread on the fields (also an extremely labor-intensive enterprise, and another reason to keep fields small). Reliance on manure, of course, means that the farmer must raise manure-producing livestock (ideally, cattle) along with crops. And he must be a scientist as well, as it requires a good deal of expertise to determine how much manure to use. Since soil analysis was not available until the mid-nineteenth century (and even then it often produced unreliable results), the farmer had to learn the quality of his soils through careful observation.[30]

English experience had shown that such intensive mixed farming methods could be both productive and sustainable—but they required considerable labor, expertise, and attention to the soil. Hence the reformers' preference for both small farms and free labor: they reasoned that small holdings could be more attentively cultivated than large ones and that slaves lacked the skill and intelligence for such careful and complex farming. (Indeed, the complexity of the farming regimen became one commonly cited explanation for the decline of slavery in the northern states.[31]) They also recognized that relying on slaves rather than hired labor often required planters to cultivate more acres than they could reasonably manage under this regime, in order to keep their slaves fully employed.[32] Thus reformers generally favored free labor over slave labor, and small landholdings carefully and intelligently farmed.

Economists such as Adam Smith further developed the reformers' case for free labor and small farms by arguing what would become a common theme in nineteenth-century antislavery discourse: that slave labor is more expensive and less efficient than free labor. Slaves, Smith argued, are usually unskilled and uneducated, poorly cared for, and lack the incentives to work hard. Moreover, Smith noted that slaves are seldom inventive—probably because masters are not inclined to take advice from slaves, suspecting them of simply trying to avoid work. These factors make slave labor less efficient and therefore more costly—thus reducing the farmer's income and therefore the amount he can invest in the long-term productivity of the farm. Tobacco and sugar planters, Smith suggested, could afford the luxury of slave labor (which they desired because it fed their thirst for domination). But English grain farmers, with a smaller profit margin, could not.[33]

Of course, the American experience suggests that Smith's assumptions about the quality of slave labor did not always hold true. Americans used slave labor for complicated tasks like rice farming, and slaves probably did account for some innovations in American agriculture, particularly in rice cultivation and raising cattle.[34] And, as will be discussed, slaves themselves often claimed to be diligent and efficient farmers. Even so, the reformers' link between free labor and sustainable farming may have some foundation in the American experience. There is reason to believe that it was more difficult to use slave labor for mixed farming than for conventional plantation agriculture. For example, in those regions (such as Virginia and Maryland) where farmers moved from tobacco monoculture to a mixed farming regime, slaves had to develop more skills and enjoyed more freedom of movement. They were therefore better able to assert their autonomy—even while the intensive farming methods demanded more labor from them.[35] Planters still made use of slave labor, but it appears that they had to either invest more in supervision to maintain their authority or move toward economic incentives (that is, treat the slave more like a free worker.) This dynamic suggests that slave labor can inhibit good stewardship—not because slaves don't work hard but because sustainable farming methods typically require a workforce with more various skills, flexibility, judgment, and initiative. Developing those characteristics in a degraded, uneducated slave labor force can be quite difficult and can threaten the master's control. Under this reasoning, reliance on slave labor encourages routinized, factory-like farming methods that are easy to learn and monitor, instead of flexible, sophisticated approaches that would be more responsive to environmental conditions.

Even if this argument is not persuasive, however, Smith offered other reasons large-scale plantation agriculture might lead to poor stewardship. First, he pointed to Europe's great proprietors, arguing that they were reluctant to pursue their economic interest in stewardship and other capital improvements because their aristocratic ethos leads them to value "ornament" over profit. That charge could just as easily be leveled against southern planters, as the abolitionists would demonstrate. Moreover, Smith argued that large landholdings are problematic in themselves. Some economists favored larger landholdings because they produced greater profits, which could be put into improving cultivation.[36] But Smith highlighted the principal-agent problem raised by large estates: if the landowner rents his land, he will find that tenants (particularly with short or insecure leases) have no incentive to make improvements. If he tries to cultivate the whole estate himself, he will end up relying on "idle and profligate bailiffs, whose abusive management would soon degrade the cultivation . . . of the land."[37] Again, the same argument could be leveled against large-scale slave agriculture.

These economic arguments favoring small landholdings worked by free proprietors would inform European land reform movements during the nineteenth century and eventually find their way into twentieth-century environmentalism.[38] But they were also prominent in antislavery thought. Historian Linda Kerber notes that Federalists critical of southern political leadership frequently condemned slavery for its tendency to degrade agriculture. Connecticut congressman Robert Griswold, for example, noted in 1800 that the poverty of the South was thinly masked by the planters' custom of starving and overworking their slaves. Southern slave owners, he suggested, "having never been taught to take hold of the plough themselves, or to perform any manuel [sic] labour . . . cannot enter with sufficient spirit into the business to acquire any real knowledge of the best mode of managing lands." Comparing Maryland's poverty to Pennsylvania's prosperity, he concluded that slavery harms agricultural productivity because it fails "to give the cultivators of the soil an interest in the improvement which they make."[39] Thirty years later Henry Clay would use similar reasoning in his speech to the American Colonization Society, predicting the demise of slavery: "That labour is best . . . in which the labourer knows that he will derive the profits of his industry; that his employment depends upon his diligence, and his reward upon his assiduity." Therefore, "wherever the option exists to employ, at an equal hire, free or slave labour, the former will be decidedly preferred." He concluded that "farming agriculture"—meaning the mixed farming regime described earlier—could not support slave labor; it was only the high price of cotton that was maintaining such an inefficient institution.[40]

So well accepted was this belief that even as vocal a defender of slavery as Edmund Ruffin—the leading agriculturalist in the South during the antebellum period—admitted that the most productive and careful agricultural laborers were free proprietor-farmers. They were, he conceded, "the most diligent, hard-working, careful and frugal of laborers" because they had the incentives—self-interest, family affection, and pride of ownership—to exertion and care.[41] By the 1850s these economic arguments for free labor, land, and agriculture reform would be combined with the political arguments for favoring small family farms to form the core of the antislavery ideology adopted by the Republican Party.[42] Radical abolitionists, in contrast, were somewhat wary of the economic arguments against slavery; in their view, slavery would be wrong even if it were profitable. Nevertheless, abolitionists could and did highlight the moral dimension of the economic and political arguments. For example, Adam Smith had condemned slavery and large

landholdings in part because of the aristocratic ethos such a system cultivated—an argument consistent with abolitionists' claim that slavery led to
moral corruption. And black abolitionists were drawn to the economic and
political arguments for additional reasons: free labor, land reform, and
agrarian ideals not only supported their critique of slave agriculture but
served to guide their vision of what freedom ought to look like.

BLACK AGRARIANISM

Judging from the narratives of fugitive slaves, what slaves wanted most from
freedom was the opportunity to pursue the agrarian ideal. Fugitive slave
William Wells Brown wanted nothing more from freedom than to purchase
"a little farm" and his "own FREE HOME" in Canada.[43] Solomon Northrup
aimed at "the possession of some humble habitation, with a few surrounding
acres."[44] Josiah Henson advised his fellow free blacks to invest in land, to
"undertake the task . . . of settling upon wild lands which we could call our
own; and where every tree which we felled, and every bushel of corn we
raised, would be for ourselves; in other words, where we could secure all the
profits of our own labor."[45] This course, he argued, would create in blacks
the same "indestructible character for energy, enterprise, and self-re-
liance" enjoyed by the Yankees.[46]

Free blacks in the north were also encouraged to pursue agriculture, although they were apparently less than receptive to the suggestion.[47] Lewis
Woodson, who helped to found a black farming community in Ohio, supported agriculture as a "means of changing our present dependent and pre-
carious position, into one of comfort and independence."

> The possession of houses and lands, and flock and herds, inspires the possessor
> with a nobleness and independence of feeling, unknown to those in any other
> business. Every thing by which he is surrounded tends to the preservation of his
> morals, and the integrity and elevation of his soul. The lofty hill, the deep valley,
> the golden fields of waving grain, the green carpeted meadows of luxuriant grass,
> the bleating flocks and herds of cattle, the beautiful landscape, the painted flow-
> ers, the rich odours of the balmy breeze, are scenes and associations amongst
> which to dwell without the most exalted emotions, we must be either more or less
> than human.

Despite this eloquent endorsement, Woodson warned that farming takes
skill and diligence and is not appropriate for everyone. But for those who are

not thriving in the cities, he advised that removing to the country would take their children "from the degrading drudgery and domineering of others; and from their exposure to the pollutions of idleness, vice, and crime."[48] Frederick Douglass for similar reasons counseled free blacks to turn their attention to agriculture rather than working as servants in the city. "Go to farming. Be tillers of the soil. . . . Our cities are overrun with menial laborers, while the country is eloquently pleading for the hand of industry to till her soil, and reap the reward of honest labor." By this means they would become "equally independent with other members of the community." It is impossible, he explained, "that we should ever be respected as a people, while we are so universally and completely dependent upon white men for the necessaries of life." Woodson and Douglass thus echoed Thomas Jefferson, who also favored agriculture for its promise of economic self-sufficiency—which, under republican principles, was a crucial basis for citizenship.[49]

Considerable evidence suggests that this agrarian rhetoric accurately captured widely shared aspirations among slaves for homes and farms of their own.[50] As was discussed in Chapter 1, the slave system made the right to property and independent food production markers of free status; slaves felt keenly the deprivation of these rights. Democratic agrarianism, in identifying freedom with property ownership and control over one's own agricultural labor, thus resonated with their experience. But black abolitionists had another reason for drawing on agrarian rhetoric: it was an effective strategy for criticizing the southern plantation system and establishing their right to citizenship.

This agrarian critique of slavery is particularly prominent in the narratives of fugitive slaves. Aimed at painting a vivid and detailed picture of slave society, the narratives are a rich source for ideas about the effect of slavery on humans' relationship to the land. For example, the narrative of Charles Ball (written in collaboration with the white attorney Isaac Fisher) closely follows the Federalist critique of slavery, giving sustained attention to its impact on agriculture and developing themes that will become commonplaces in later slave narratives. Ball begins with the claim that slavery gets more cruel and oppressive as one travels farther south, and then describes the degeneration of agriculture he encounters as he travels south in a slave gang. "Under the bad culture which is practiced in the south," he tells us, "the land is constantly becoming poorer, and the means of getting food, more and more difficult." Immediately upon leaving Maryland, they pass "the house of a poor gentleman." "The land was the very picture of sterility,

and there was neither a barn nor stable on the place. . . . It was with difficulty that we obtained a bushel of corn." He encounters more impoverished
and abandoned farms in Virginia. In some places, civilization disappeared
altogether: "cedar thickets . . . continued for three or four miles together,
without a house to enliven the scene." What turned this "former rich and
populous country, into the solitude of a deserted wilderness?" Virginia has
become poor, he explains, "by the folly and wickedness of slavery, and dearly
has she paid for the anguish and sufferings she has inflicted upon our injured, degraded and fallen race." Although the land was fertile, the original
settlers "valued their land less than their slaves" and "exhausted the kindly
soil by unremitting crops of tobacco." Thus "they declined in their circumstances, and finally grew poor."[51]

As Chapter 1 discussed, there were ecological and economic reasons that
southern agriculture created such transient, disorderly landscapes; southern planters were not necessarily poor farmers or economically irrational.
Ball's description also fails to capture the regional variations in slavery, a
fault endemic in this abolitionist tradition (although slave narratives in general were more attentive to such variations than other forms of abolitionist
literature). His point, however, had less to do with ecology than with southern moral and political culture: He attributed environmental degeneration
to the South's aristocratic ethos and reliance on slave labor—characteristics
of an overcivilized, corrupt society. The sons and daughters of the wealthy
planters "are gentlemen and ladies by birthright" and therefore disdain to
work. Ignorant of and uninterested in agriculture, they instead turn to un-
wholesome pursuits like "riding about the country" or "reading silly books."
Their "vicious idleness" leads to ruin, after the usual fashion of Gothic romances—they get into debt, make poor choices, and lose economic and social status. As the family degenerates, the slaves are treated even worse,
since "somebody must suffer" the consequences of their bad habits. Interestingly, the narrator also suggests that planters keep more slaves than they
actually need (perhaps feeding their thirst for domination?). If the planters
were skillful cultivators and kept only as many slaves as necessary to work
the soil properly, plantations would be more profitable and the slaves would
suffer less. As it is, however,

They are attempting to perform impossibilities—to draw the means of supporting
a life of idleness, luxury, and splendour, from a once generous, but long since
worn out and exhausted soil—a soil, which, carefully used, would at this day have

richly repaid the toils of the husbandman, by a noble abundance of all the comforts of life; but which, tortured into barrenness by the double curse of slavery and tobacco, stands, as . . . *a monument to the poverty and punishment which Providence has decreed as the reward of idleness and tyranny.*[52]

In short, the cause of the South's environmental degeneration is the ignorance, idleness, and moral corruption that results from southerners' aristocratic ethos—an ethos resulting from reliance on slave labor.

Other narrators agreed that slavery and moral corruption had devastated the land. Frederick Douglass famously contrasted the poverty of Maryland with the wealth of New Bedford, Massachusetts, where everything looked "clean, new and beautiful." Similarly, James Pennington attributed the exhaustion of the soil in Maryland to the "bad cultivation peculiar to slave states." Like Ball, he told stories about the rapid moral degeneration caused by slavery; the children of planters, he argued, are poorly educated and frequently fall into gambling and other vices, causing the once-prosperous estates to decay. Lewis Clarke, noting the comparative wealth of the north, concluded that slavery "curses the soil, the houses, the churches . . . it curses man and beast." And John Thompson, commenting on a region populated by wealthy and humane planters, reasoned that "the land being less cursed by cruelty, was rich and fertile"[53]—thus making a direct connection between humane treatment of slaves and the productivity of the land. Treating slaves badly makes them less efficient and diligent, and the fertility of the soil will suffer under their care.

Henry Bibb, in contrast, offered a less ecological view of how slavery curses the land, focusing instead on how it affected one's moral and aesthetic relationship to the American landscape. As he was being taken south by slave catchers, he paused a moment to "gaze on the beauties of nature," writing, "on free soil, as I passed down the river, things looked to me uncommonly pleasant: The green trees and wild flowers of the forest; the ripening harvest fields waving with the gentle breezes of Heaven; and the honest farmers tilling their soil and living by their own toil. These things seem to light upon my vision with a peculiar charm."

But his pleasure dimmed when he reflected on his fate: "to be sold like an ox, into hopeless bondage, and to be worked under the flesh devouring lash during life, without wages."[54] Returning north to freedom, he again contrasted nature's beauty with the horrors of slavery. As he gazed on "the green hill-tops and valleys of old Kentucky," he reported, his "soul was pained to look upon the slaves in the fields . . . still toiling under their task-masters without pay."[55] Such contrasts between pastoral beauty and human misery echo Jean-Jacques Rousseau's striking image in *A Discourse on Inequality* of "vast forests . . . transformed into pleasant fields which had to be watered with the sweat of men, and where slavery and misery were soon seen to germinate and flourish with the crops."[56] The image indicts the social order by contrasting its ugliness with the beauty inherent in the divine order of nature. Presumably, a more natural social order would not pain the soul.

But one could also read this recurring spectacle of poverty and suffering in the midst of natural beauty as undermining the value of that natural beauty. Under this reading, injustice does not only physically degrade the land but can also degrade the *meaning* of the landscape, and therefore the observer's moral relationship to it. Indeed, Crèvecoeur had made precisely this claim sixty years earlier, complaining that the miserable scenes produced by human injustice blinded him to the beauty and glory of God's creation. After spending time in slave society, he could no longer see in the natural world evidence of God's justice and benevolence. Instead, the world became to him "rather a place of punishment than delight": "View the frigid sterility of the north," he lamented, and "the arctic and antarctic regions, those huge voids where nothing lives," "the parched lands of the torrid zone," "those countries of Asia subject to pestilential infections," and all the other "poisonous" and desolate landscapes.[57] Fugitive slave Harriet Jacobs would echo him in her narrative, reflecting on how the beauty of the "dancing sunlight" and the "bright, calm light" of the stars seemed to mock her sadness.[58] Bibb's message, I think, is similar: the meaning and value of nature's beauty is affected by its juxtaposition with human oppression. Instead of teaching one to have faith in the God of nature, such scenes highlight the impotence of natural law to restrain and govern human society—a message of pessimism and despair that robs one of any pleasure in natural beauty.

Such rhetorical tropes infused the landscape with a distinctive moral and political meaning, just as the use of Biblical typological discourse in slave culture infused it with spiritual meaning. Characterizing the North as an agrarian paradise and the South as a corrupt tyranny resonates with the practice in slave culture of referring to the North as "Canaan" and the South as "Egypt." Slave narrators sometimes drew on this typological discourse. For example, Henry Bibb explains that the first time he tried to run away, he was halted by the Ohio River: "To me it was an impassable gulf. I had no rod wherewith to smite the stream, and thereby divide the waters. I had no

Moses to go before me and lead the way from bondage to the promised land. Yet I was in a far worse state than Egyptian bondage; for they had houses and land; I had none."[59]

Interestingly, this use of Biblical imagery emphasizes how *different* is Bibb's situation from that of the Israelites. Unlike Martin Delany's hero in *Blake*, Bibb is unable to imagine himself as Moses or to find hope in the story of the Israelites. Nevertheless, the Biblical story provides a powerful analogy for the slaves' political condition. This is not to say that Bibb confused his quest for political freedom with his quest for spiritual salvation, however. Although the slave narratives did borrow from the conventions of spiritual autobiography, slave narrators were typically careful to distinguish spiritual conversion from political liberty.[60] Still, to the extent that they fused the abolitionists' north-south moral geography with the sacred landscape of the slave spirituals, they created a moral landscape with both political and spiritual meaning.[61]

For abolitionists, though, the chief point of this moral geography was to illustrate the theoretical connection between slavery and the physical degeneration of the land established by eighteenth-century agriculturalists. Defenders of slavery would dispute that theory, arguing that if the landowner has an economic interest in good stewardship, the slave's dependence on the master should give him a comparable interest. But black abolitionists pointed out that the brutality used to support an unfree labor system tends to make the slave disinclined to serve the master's interests, and also makes it possible for the master to keep for himself most of the economic benefits of their labor. Therefore, slaves lack the incentives to work hard or carefully. As narrator John Brown explained, slaves "will work well enough for themselves, but they do not care to work for the benefit of another, unless they are forced to do it. . . . In order to compel them to labour for the sole advantage of another, the whip and all sorts of coercive means are employed."[62] Charles Ball noted that slaves simply do not care whether the master's cotton is harvested—especially if they can work for wages in another field.[63]

This argument suggests at the very least that slave plantations will not be cultivated with as much care and diligence as farms worked by free labor. The poor quality of an unmotivated, overworked slave labor force might account for soil erosion and other kinds of waste and inefficiencies that allegedly plagued southern agriculture. But the argument also suggests that reliance on slave labor could constrain the master's ability to adopt sustainable farming methods, such as the convertible husbandry described earlier.

The bitter, dispirited slaves depicted by the black abolitionists won't coop-erate in such a regime; they will instead resist, impede, or refuse to learn new methods—or they will take advantage of their increased responsibility under the new system to defy the master's control. In general, the abolition-ists' description of the psychology and incentive structure of slavery sup-ports the view that relying on slave labor will encourage farming methods that enhance the master's control of the workers—and that in the struggle for control, neither the master nor the slave is likely to be focusing on the long-term productivity of the land.

Importantly, this reasoning supports a free labor system but not neces-sarily widespread ownership of land by agricultural laborers. If agricultural labor were performed by workers whose best efforts were secured purely by economic incentives, then the worker's economic dependence on the owner would create no disincentives to innovation or good stewardship. Neverthe-less, under the black agrarians' reasoning, a free labor system alone might not be enough to ensure good stewardship; it is also important to afford po-litical and civil equality to agricultural workers, which might in turn involve ownership of land by laborers. One of the abolitionists' chief criticisms of slavery is that it led to poor farming because it *degraded* labor by associating it with slave status—with social subordination and political inequality. The slave system, according to white and black critics alike, created throughout the South a contempt for agricultural labor that did not bode well for careful stewardship of the soil. According to Lewis Clarke, southern whites some-times complained that slavery made it a disgrace for a white man to work.[64] As Charles Ball's narrative explained, in the South "exemption from labour is [the] badge of gentility," so the wealthy will not work or permit their chil-dren to work.[65] Thus the masters are frequently described as living on the slaves' earnings "in idleness and luxury."[66] That contempt for labor offers a further explanation for the South's soil erosion and declines in fertility: if neither blacks nor whites were diligent farmers, it would hardly be surpris-ing to find the region dotted with impoverished, failing plantations.

The solution to this contempt for agricultural labor is to grant those who work the land the status of free citizens. Widespread land ownership could accomplish that goal: owning land would give agricultural workers the inde-pendence that (under classical republican principles) is the chief basis for citizenship, thus raising their status and giving dignity to their labor. Of course, the United States was not a classical republic, and land ownership was not a requirement of citizenship in the mid-nineteenth century. In fact, owning land would be less important to civil equality as the nation became more industrial—for white workers, at least. As we will see in the next chapter, for blacks, land ownership would remain important to achieving equality and securing the conditions for free labor. But in an ideal industrial polity, where workers already enjoy social and political equality with landowners, the workers are not exploited, and owners do in fact have a long-term interest in the productivity of the land, good stewardship should be possible even if most agricultural workers don't own their own land. As Adam Smith warned, though, if the owner has only a short-term interest in the land, or owns so much land that he must rely on managers or tenants with insecure leases, stewardship will suffer—all good reasons to favor small family farms over plantations.

The land tenure issue would persist in black political thought long after Emancipation, and it would continue to rest on black agrarians' central point: that slavery degraded the land by degrading those who work the land. It's a powerful argument—but it depends on the claim that slaves were not diligent and careful farmers. This was a tricky theme for the slave narrators. Slaves' alleged lack of skill and contempt for labor could serve as an indictment of slavery, but it could also undermine the agrarian premise of that indictment. Some of the slave narratives in fact read as picaresques, romanticizing the rootless, cosmopolitan life of the adventurer even while paying lip service to agrarian ideals.[67] That picaresque motif reflects the importance of the right to travel—a right denied by the slave system—to slaves' conceptions of freedom. Although the right to own land and the right to travel shouldn't be mutually exclusive, it was hard (given the available rhetorical conventions) to insist on the value of one without devaluing the other. Similarly, some narrators, such as Solomon Northrup and James Pennington, the "fugitive blacksmith," clearly valued craftsmanship more than agricultural labor. This judgment reflects the high status accorded skilled craftsmen in slave and free black communities.[68] These desires to escape, to seek broader opportunities and higher status than mere husbandmen, provide a persistent counterpoint to agrarianism in black thought.

Nor is this antiagrarianism the only tension in abolitionists' indictment of slavery. Not all black abolitionists endorsed the claim that slaves were poor farmers or that southern agriculture was failing. On the contrary, that position conflicted with the other important theme in black abolitionism—the use of democratic agrarianism to establish blacks' right to the land and citizenship. Black activists' arguments for citizenship drew on the right of civilization, the civic republican tradition, and agrarianism, emphasizing again the connection between freedom and possessing the land. If, as democratic agrarianism teaches, it was agricultural labor that earned one the right to the land, then surely the slaves who did the bulk of agricultural labor in the South had the best claim to it. And if agricultural labor produced the virtues one desired in republican citizens, slaves should have a good claim to that as well. Thus there was some value in insisting to white audiences that slaves were productive farmers and that southern agriculture was thriving under their care. And the same argument could suggest to black audiences that their agricultural labor, instead of being a mark of ignominy, should be viewed as a source of pride, a strong basis on which to build their sense of self.

Thus slave narrators often made a point of their skill and diligence, taking obvious pride in their superior abilities. John Brown reported "without unduly boasting, that at farming, at carpentering, and at any and all kinds of labour, [he] was a match for any two hands." John Thompson put his master's estate in such good order that he was made foreman of the plantation.[69] Josiah Henson noted the difficulty of the work he performed on the plantation but asserted that he "grew to be a robust and vigorous lad, and at fifteen years of age, there were few who could compete with [him] in work. . . . [He] was competent to all the work that was done upon the farm." Challenging the stereotype of the lazy, dispirited slave, he claimed he was motivated by "pride and ambition," which slavery did not always extinguish. He eventually became superintendent of the farm, reporting that it prospered under his care.[70]

Martin Delany's major work, "The Condition, Elevation, Emigration, and Destiny of the Colored People of the United States" (1852), dwells at length on the superiority of black labor in order to combat the charge of racial inferiority and establish blacks' right to citizenship. That right, Delany claimed, "in all democratic countries" is accorded to those who "have made contributions and investments in the country"—soldiers, farmers, and mechanics, for example.[71] According to Delany, blacks contributed substantially to the country through their agricultural labor. He argued that Africans were enslaved not because they were unfit for freedom but because they were better workers than Native Americans—and, importantly, more resistant to the diseases decimating colonial populations. He thus turned a common justification for slavery into an argument for citizenship: Spaniards and Portuguese tried to enslave the natives, but that race "sunk by scores under the heavy weight of oppression." European laborers also failed to adjust to the tropical climate of South America. Africans, however, were well suited to the task. They "had been known as an industrious people, cultivators of the soil. The grain fields of Ethiopia and Egypt were the themes of the poet."[72] Delany went on at great length to describe West Africa as an agricultural paradise. Travelers, he pointed out, described the country as "beautiful and pictur-esque . . . the fields as in a high state of cultivation, clothed in the verdure of husbandry, waving before the gentle breezes, with the rich products of in-dustry—maize, oats, rye, millet, and wheat, being among the fruits of cultiva-tion. . . . Their cattle were fine and in good order. . . . The fruit groves were delightful to the eye of the beholder."[73]

These Africans brought their skills to North America just in time to save the European settlers from starvation. "It is evident, that [neither] the whites nor the Indians were equal to the hard and almost insurmountable difficulties [of settling North America]. An endless forest, the impenetrable earth; the one to be removed, and the other to be excavated. Towns and cities to be built, and farms to be cultivated—all these presented difficulties too ar-duous for the European then here, and unknown to the Indian." Africans were not only up to the challenge, they were superior farmers: "From their knowledge of cultivation, the farming interests in the North, and planting in the South, were commenced with a prospect never dreamed of before."[74] In fact, "it is notorious, that in the planting States, the blacks themselves are the only skillful cultivators—the proprietor knowing little or nothing about the art, save that which he learns from the African husbandman." Delany gave blacks credit for the success of southern agriculture, asking, "Are not these legitimate investments in the common stock of the nation, which should command a proportional interest?"[75] Under his view, it was not white Americans but the slaves who cleared the southern wilderness, and this agricultural labor gave them a compelling claim to the land, citizenship, and self-respect.

Many of the slave narrators agreed with Delany that southern agriculture flourished under the care of black labor. Although there are plenty of claims like Ball's that slavery impoverished the South, there are also frequent images of an abundant agriculture. Solomon Northrup described his master's plan-tation in Louisiana as a "little paradise in the Great Pine Woods," an "oasis in the desert" bursting with "crimson and golden fruit" and garlanded with "blossoms of the peach, the orange, the plum, and the pomegranate."[76] Fred-erick Douglass claimed that his master's plantation produced crops in "great abundance" and his garden was "abound[ing] in fruits of almost every description." Douglass used the device to contrast the master's wealth and plenty to the slave's poverty and need.[77] But it also helped to support the claim that blacks were good farmers and therefore deserved citizenship. After all, it was slaves who tended that plantation and "finely cultivated garden."

Thus we find two competing views of southern agriculture in the slave narratives: a failing enterprise prosecuted by a dispirited and degraded workforce and a thriving enterprise prosecuted by a skillful and industrious (but exploited) workforce. There are a number of ways to resolve this tension. In some cases, the conflict may simply result from the narrator's imperfect control of his argument, or from the fact that some slaves (like Pennington and Douglass) held up under slavery better than others (perhaps *they* were skillful and disciplined but their less rugged peers languished). Or one might argue that the slaves themselves were competent farmers but were forced into bad habits by ignorant masters—or that masters forced an undisciplined workforce into reasonably good habits. Charles Ball's narrative suggests that the abundance of southern agriculture was due entirely to the native fertility of the soil and disappeared as soon as the soil was exhausted, which may have been true in some areas or for some plantations. Ultimately, however, this tension reflects the black agrarians' struggle with a fundamental question about the nature of slavery—a question that would become a central problem in black environmental thought: does slavery create disincentives to stewardship and irredeemably alienate workers from the natural world—or do slaves adapt, finding their own reasons for and meaning in tending the land? From a different angle, the question is whether an oppressed people can find in their own forced labor a foundation for their sense of self: a way to express themselves and serve their own ends by means of their interaction with the physical world. Black agrarians did not offer a single, uniform answer to that question. But in exploring it they developed the concepts and hypotheses that would continue to guide black theorists' understanding of the effect of injustice on humans' relationship to nature.

A BLACK ENVIRONMENTAL THEORY

Black agrarianism persists as a major axis of black thought long after Emancipation. The environmental critique of slavery in fact finds its fullest expression in 1873, in a speech by Frederick Douglass to the Tennessee Colored Agricultural and Mechanical Association. Douglass praised the black farmers for setting a "noble example" of industriousness and progress toward "civilization, culture and refinement."[78] He approved their choice of occupation. Echoing Delany, he declared that "it is pleasant to know that in color, form, and features, we are related to the first successful tillers of the soil; to the people who taught the world agriculture. . . . While the Briton and Gallic faces wandered like beasts of prey in the forests, the people of Egypt and Ethiopia rejoiced in well cultivated fields and abundance of corn."[79] Sadly, prejudice and hostility to blacks have "driven the Negroes in great numbers from the country into the large cities, and into menial positions, where they easily learn to imitate the vices and follies of the least exemplary whites."[80] Douglass encouraged blacks to resist this trend and to view agriculture as their best means of advancement.

He then asserted that "emancipation . . . was not only a triumph of justice, but a triumph of agricultural industry." After all, "what possible motive had the slave for a careful, successful cultivation of the soil? What concern could he have for increasing the wealth of the master, or for improving and beautifying the land?" On the contrary, he claimed that wealthy masters were less likely to work in the fields with the slave, so wealth served to increase the distance and break down the sympathy between master and slave. Therefore, "it was in the interest of the slave to make the rich man poor and the poor man poorer."[81]

Even worse, under slavery the soil itself "was cursed with a burning sense of injustice." Slavery fostered anger and hatred in the slave, and "your fields could not be lovingly planted nor faithfully cultivated in its presence." Farm animals were mistreated as well: "The ox and the mule shared the general feeling of indifference to rights naturally engendered by a state of slavery. The master blamed the overseer; the overseer the slave, and the slave the horses, oxen and mules, and violence and brutality fell upon the animals as a consequence." Fortunately, with liberty came "respectability of labor" and a concern for the "general welfare" that promised to lead to a prosperous agriculture.[82] Douglass counseled the farmers to treat their farm animals with respect and kindness and to be careful of soil fertility (but to "make war" upon the destructive insects that threaten crops). His chief piece of advice to them, however, was to "accumulate property." "Property . . . will purchase for us the only condition upon which any people can rise to the dignity of genuine manhood; for, without property, there can be no leisure." Without leisure, there is no thought, no invention, no progress.[83]

Douglass's speech expands on many of the themes we find in abolitionist literature, offering a thoughtful analysis of the relationship between social justice and environmental stewardship. In the absence of secure property rights, he argues, farmers have no economic incentive to be careful of soil fertility—a familiar tenet in agrarian thought. But Douglass develops the point further: exploited agricultural workers feel no common interest with owners in the continuing productivity of the soil. Nor are they psychologically disposed to be careful, responsible stewards or to respect the rights of animals. Under this view, secure property rights create economic and emotional incentives for good stewardship, and an equitable labor system creates a respect for labor that encourages good, careful farming.

It's a compelling argument, but there are other compelling explanations for the state of southern agriculture. Given the soil conditions in much of the South, the cheapness of land compared to labor, and the limited knowledge of soil chemistry, it is likely that reliance on free labor would have produced the same environmental results as slave agriculture. Central to this theory is the assumption that the landowner has an economic interest in the long-term productivity of the land—but if land is cheap and labor is not, or if the landowner has no idea how to ensure the land's long-term productivity, he may choose to mine the soil's fertility and move his capital to another plantation or to other enterprises. This lack of economic incentives may be the major difficulty facing environmental regimes relying on private stewardship. Nevertheless, black agrarians have a good argument that this difficulty is compounded by an unfree labor system. They identified both economic and psychological reasons for believing that black farmers would have been more efficient and creative if they had been free—or at least that a free labor system would have allowed landowners greater opportunities to experiment with more complex, innovative sustainable farming methods.

Even in the absence of a careful regime of soil stewardship, however, slave agriculture may have been more successful than Douglass contends. Although Douglass's view of the productivity of slave agriculture was once orthodoxy, most historians now accept Robert Fogel's judgment that the South was more prosperous than the abolitionists claimed, and that slave labor is not necessarily more expensive than free labor. Nevertheless, many still contend that the slave system retarded agricultural productivity and economic development to some extent. William Mathews, for example, argues that the plantation system as a whole interfered with the development of a more entrepreneurial culture and a transport system that would have facilitated the adoption of progressive agricultural reforms.[84] And slavery's impact on the masters' attitudes toward labor is also hard to evaluate. David

Hackett Fischer claims that southerners' aristocratic disdain for labor was part of the folk culture imported by English settlers from south and west England.[85] Under this view, slaves learned their work ethic from their masters. Eugene Genovese, however, attributes the southern work ethic to African influences. He argues that the planters took people accustomed to the rhythms of labor in the traditional agrarian communities of West Africa and attempted to subject them to a more rigid discipline—a discipline inappropriate to many forms of agricultural production. Slaves did work hard, they just didn't like to work *regular*; they would work in short, intense bursts of activity but then adopt a more leisurely approach to less pressing tasks. Moreover, Genovese suggests that white planters adapted to the slaves' rhythms; they, too, worked hard but not regular.[86] So according to Genovese, both masters and slaves might have seemed lazy to northern sensibilities, but both groups contributed substantially to the productivity of southern agriculture.

In general, it appears that the master's economic incentives (and perhaps his emotional attachment to the land), combined with the discipline of the lash, forced slaves to work with sufficient care to ensure a productive agriculture in the short term, if not in the long term. Their resentment may have made it difficult for slaves to recognize or acknowledge that they shared an interest with the master in how the land was treated. But against that claim stood the testimony of the many slave narrators who insisted that they did serve their masters' interests faithfully. Slavery could put the interests of the workers and owners into direct conflict and fill the slave with anger and resentment, but that wasn't the only possible response. In many cases the slave showed resilience, pride, generosity, compassion, or an enlightened sense of his or her own interest. Indeed, the slave narrators suggested that agricultural labor could serve as a source of self-respect, not merely a source of degradation. The slave narratives thus qualify Douglass's argument: the experience of slavery suggests that exploitation of agricultural labor is one of several factors that can create barriers to good stewardship, but those barriers can be overcome, at least in the short term, either by greater reliance on violence on the part of the master or by extraordinary resources of character on the part of the slave.

Douglass's claim that mistreatment of slaves led to mistreatment of animals also needs qualification. It's undoubtedly true that animals suffered cruel treatment on slave plantations; Douglass's concern for the welfare of farm animals is in fact a new theme in nineteenth-century black thought, possibly reflecting the influence of the postwar animal welfare movement.[87]

Slave narrators, in contrast, frequently complained that they were treated like animals but seldom commented on how badly animals were treated. But David Hackett Fischer argues that cruelty toward animals, like the southern work ethic, was a cultural norm brought over from England rather than the result of the slave system. According to Fischer, the southern aristocratic ethos permitted the use of violence against persons of lower status and animals. Southern children were encouraged to play blood sports involving the torture of animals to prove their bravery, and black children were apparently exposed to these norms as well.[88] One former slave, for example, recounts that when he was a boy, his master tried to make him brave by making him hold stray cats while someone else cut their heads off.[89] Even so, some slaves did justify the cruel treatment of animals by referring to their own treatment. Leon Litwack reports that a freedman, when asked why he was skinning catfish alive, responded, "Why, this is the way they used to do me, and I'se going to get even with somebody."[90]

Thus slavery may have reinforced a norm of cruelty toward animals, even if it didn't create it. It is not clear, however, that respecting the rights of blacks would lead to greater respect for the rights of animals. A central element of abolitionists' case against slavery was that it erased the important moral distinction between men and animals. Douglass himself had condemned slavery for treating men like animals. "The slave," he insisted, "is a man . . . possessing a soul, eternal and indestructible." The first work of slavery is to "mar and deface those characteristics of its victims which distinguish *men* from *things,* and *persons* from *property.*" His point—and it is a point repeated endlessly by abolitionists—is that men should be treated better than animals, which are things that can be worked, flogged, hired, sold, and killed "with perfect impunity."[91] Thus a greater respect for freedmen's rights could rest not on a deeper commitment to humane treatment of all living things but on a more faithful adherence to the moral hierarchy that made humans superior to animals.

In sum, Douglass's intriguing argument is that good stewardship requires those who work the land to develop an attitude of affection and generosity toward the world, which grows out of a confidence that good care will be valued and repaid. That attitude, he contends, is hard to maintain in a land cursed by injustice. But other black abolitionists offered the equally intriguing suggestion that good stewardship can arise out of many different motivations and psychological dispositions, and that small, individual acts of redemption may be possible, even in a land cursed by injustice.

CONCLUSION

In criticizing slave agriculture and making their case for citizenship and land ownership, black agrarians developed a powerful theoretical framework for investigating how lack of freedom can distort humans' relationship to nature. Their central claim is that good stewardship is facilitated by a free labor system in which workers enjoy civil and political equality; ideally, workers should own their own farms, in order to ensure their economic interest in the land's productivity and their political independence and equality (which safeguards the dignity of agricultural labor). The basic problem with slavery, under this view, is that it uses violence instead of economic incentives to motivate workers, thus allowing the owners to exploit the workers and associating agricultural labor with coercion and social subordination. As a result, the people who own the land have little incentive to engage in farm labor themselves (since labor is a mark of low social status) and the people working the land have little incentive, beyond fear of punishment, for the careful workmanship that good stewardship requires (since they believe they will receive no benefit from it). Indeed, the violence used to coerce their labor creates a powerful disincentive to stewardship. Moreover, masters are unlikely to make use of slaves' knowledge, since doing so might undermine the master's authority. Slavery thus makes both masters and slaves less industrious and innovative by diverting or suppressing their creative energy; agriculture becomes a struggle for power instead of the fulfillment of humans' common calling to "finish Creation."

Slavery distorts slaves' moral and spiritual relationship to the land in other ways as well. The coercion necessary to hold workers in slavery makes it psychologically difficult to appreciate the beauty and order of nature, or to see in it evidence of God's benevolence. To the oppressed, the land may seem ugly and disordered—a hostile and desolate wilderness scarred by an unjust social order. (It may seem so to free citizens as well, unless they are completely desensitized to the suffering of slaves; it is not only the slave whose relationship to the land is harmed by slavery.) According to the abolitionists, whether America was a fertile paradise or a desolate wasteland depended critically on the justice of the American social order. Indeed, a striking feature of both slaves' religious discourse and black agrarian ideology is the close connection they posit between physical nature and human morality. Nature is not independent of human society; both its physical integrity and its moral meaning are deeply intertwined with and dependent on humans' moral decisions.

In sum, black agrarians argue that instead of cultivating agrarian virtues, slavery tends to create in the workers contempt for agricultural labor, hatred for the land, and a disposition to cruelty. Only freedom—granting political and social equality to slaves and allowing them to work for themselves— would rectify these perverse effects and redeem the land. The testimony of the fugitive slave narrators, however, reveals that the effects of slavery could be more complicated than this theory suggests. If forced labor made some slaves hate the land, it could also create in slaves a strong tie to the land and become a source of pride and self-respect. Moreover, some slaves may have learned to see in the landscape a natural order and beauty with which to contrast the unnaturalness and ugliness of the social order. These themes suggest that slaves were able to find ways to resist the degradation of slavery—to affirm their sense of self through their interactions with the natural world. Nevertheless, black agrarians offered a persuasive argument that under a free labor system both blacks and whites would have enjoyed a less conflicted relationship to the land. Emancipation brought a fleeting glimpse of what that relationship might have been. But instead of redemption, the end of slavery brought a long struggle for equality and independence—a struggle that led black writers to deeper explorations of how racial injustice affects the relationship between black Americans and the natural world.

CHAPTER THREE

POSSESSING THE LAND

As General William Sherman marched to the sea over the remains of southern resistance in 1864, George Perkins Marsh published the first American work on scientific forestry, *Man and Nature.* Marsh's work traditionally marks the beginning of American conservationism, warning Americans of the dire consequences of their unrestrained exploitation of natural resources. But it also reflects the continuing alliance of agrarianism and free labor ideology in American environmental thought. Marsh opens the book by explaining the decline of agriculture in ancient Rome as the result of "civil and ecclesiastical tyranny and misrule." Rome "imposed on the products of agricultural labor . . . taxes which the sale of the entire harvest would scarcely discharge. . . . She impoverished the peasantry by forced and unpaid labor." As a result, land was left uncultivated and exposed to the "destructive forces" of nature.[1]

Marsh apparently believed that Americans in the 1860s still needed to be reminded of the link between oppression of farm labor and the physical decay of the land. But as the pace of industrial development quickened, conservationists would increasingly take the free labor system for granted and focus instead on arguments for government control of natural resources. Conservationism and the other progressive environmental movements thus diverged from the black political tradition. For black Americans seeking to create a successful agriculture after Emancipation, the persistence of "forced and unpaid labor" would remain the central problem. Freedom, they believed, should have given freedmen the opportunity to take possession of the land and thereby achieve the autonomy denied by the slave system. But they discovered that to possess the land and secure the conditions for free labor, they first had to secure civil rights and the political status of citizens. Their efforts to establish a productive and sustainable relationship to the natural world thus remained intimately connected to their struggle for equality and rights.

Black agrarianism, with its emphasis on the relationship between stewardship and the status of labor, furnished black theorists a framework for understanding the situation of black farmers. Indeed, they developed this tradition further by drawing on the arguments of the radical agrarians of the late nineteenth century, examining the economic and political conditions that impeded the emergence of a free agricultural labor system. But the status of agricultural labor was only part of the broader question of how black Americans could create a home for themselves and a meaningful relationship with the natural world in a land cursed by injustice. Achieving that goal, according to many black theorists, required more than just abolishing slavery. It meant creating the conditions for independent, responsible agency—in other words, ensuring that black Americans had the authority, the means, and the incentives to exercise creative stewardship of the land. Their analyses of the environmental pathologies created by slavery and postwar peonage illuminate how oppressive labor relations and insecure civil rights can undermine such agency, thus distorting the community's economic, moral, aesthetic, and spiritual relationship to nature.

FREEDOM AND FARMING

The state of southern agriculture was, for most of the late nineteenth century, grim. The high price of cotton after the war encouraged the antebellum trend toward cotton monoculture in much of the South. Unfortunately, the price of cotton and other agricultural commodities declined steadily during the late nineteenth century, and the agricultural economy was disrupted by depressions in the 1870s and 1890s.[2] Other persistent problems in the South included declining soil fertility and soil erosion, high transportation costs, lack of credit and high interest charges, heavy debts, disease, and bad weather—all of which kept production costs high and farm incomes low.[3] Other parts of the country were also facing disruptions in the agricultural economy as the result of postwar industrial development, but none experienced a transformation as dramatic as the South's: the replacement of the slave plantation system with an industrial order based on the principles of free labor and rational resource development. Unfortunately for black farmers, that transformation was neither rapid nor complete.

For the freedmen, freedom meant, first and foremost, possessing the land. Owning land, they believed, would give them control over their own and their family's labor.[4] But their hopes were disappointed. The defeat of the Confederacy did create the opportunity to abolish the plantation system and redistribute confiscated estates to the freed slaves. General Sherman's Field Order No. 15, issued in January of 1865, declared as abandoned some 485,000 acres of land in the Sea Islands; General Rufus Saxton subsequently settled 40,000 freedmen on forty-acre plots on these lands. That March, Congress authorized the Freedmen's Bureau to distribute confiscated estates to freed slaves, and Thaddeus Stevens proposed seizing the land of the wealthiest Southerners and granting forty acres to each adult freedman. Those ambitious plans, however, went too far for President Andrew Johnson, who ordered the confiscated lands restored to their owners, and for many congressional Republicans, who rejected Stevens's proposal. Republicans did pass the 1866 Southern Homestead Act, which gave freedmen and loyal whites preferential access to public lands.[5] But most freedmen lacked the capital to take advantage of that opportunity, and the Homestead Act was revised in 1876 to favor what would become the true beneficiaries of postwar land redistribution: the railroad and timber interests.[6] The dominant trend after the war was in fact concentration of land ownership: tenancy rates in the South rose to nearly 50 percent by 1900, reaching 80 percent in some heavily black, cotton-growing counties.[7]

Plantation owners, for their part, were determined to maintain the plantation labor system in some form. In 1865 and 1866, several states enacted Black Codes, imposing severe political and civil disabilities on blacks in order to maintain white control of black labor. Most of the provisions of the Black Codes would become unconstitutional after the passage of the Fourteenth Amendment, but blacks continued to suffer legal and political disabilities as a result of laws passed after congressional Reconstruction ended, including restrictions on voting and marriage. Southern states also enacted laws against enticing workers away from plantations, made it a crime to break a contract, and required persons arrested as vagrants to sign a labor contract in lieu of imprisonment—all aimed at restricting freedom of contract.[8] Moreover, planters attempted to restore their authority over the workforce by offering contracts that prevented workers from leaving the plantation, holding meetings, or showing disrespect to their employers.[9] This emerging legal regime was backed by the extra-legal violence of the Ku Klux Klan and other vigilante groups, which made freedmen's rights even less secure than the formal laws would suggest.

Freedmen did not accede willingly to this regime. Refusing to work in gangs, most were eventually able to negotiate a sharecrop arrangement:

plantations were divided into small farms, and farmers would rent or buy the land and pay the landlord with a portion of the crop.[10] Sharecropping allowed black farmers to borrow against the anticipated crop, and in theory to build wealth and eventually acquire land. In practice, however, the system gave the landowner or merchant who supplied credit considerable control over what the farmer could grow (usually cotton or some other cash crop), and typically led the farmer into debt. Nevertheless, under this system freedmen were able to secure more control over their time and labor than they had enjoyed under slavery. Historian Albert Cowdry summarizes the situation:

> Widespread tenancy tended to disintegrate the unity of the workforce; to the extent that they were able, freedmen preferred to regulate their own time and efforts . . . [but] while plantation discipline waned, lack of capital compelled the creation of a jerry built credit system under which farmers borrowed against the expectation of making a crop. . . . Obliged to grow cotton to get credit . . . the farmer planted less food, which the merchant then obligingly sold him at a goodly markup.[11]

Reliance on cash crops like cotton did little to improve the environmental conditions facing southern agriculture. Both economic and social forces frustrated efforts to diversify and implement soil conservation measures. Cash crops were generally the only collateral accepted by creditors, so farmers had little choice but to devote as much land as possible to cotton, tobacco, or rice. Moreover, landowners were often reluctant to adopt complex farming practices that would require more supervision or allow sharecroppers more independent control. Advances in agricultural science and the availability of new fertilizers, such as guano, offered solutions to the persistent soil fertility problem—but only for those prosperous enough to take advantage of them. The majority of farmers in the South (black and white) worked farms too small to produce a significant profit, and they lacked both the capital and the knowledge to engage in more intensive, careful cultivation.[12]

Many freedmen, discouraged by these conditions in the countryside, left farming for the cities—between 1865 and 1870 the black population in the ten largest cities in the South doubled.[13] There were also periodic surges of interest in emigration throughout the late nineteenth century. The African emigration movements in the 1870s and 1890s never attracted mass support, but in 1879, about 6,000 blacks traveled west in the "Kansas Exodus," and another mass emigration to the southwest took place in 1888–90.[14]

However, most freedmen focused on acquiring land in the South. By 1910, southern blacks had acquired about 15 million acres of land, and nearly 17 percent of southern farm owners were black.[15] This number, as small as it is, represents an impressive achievement, given the barriers facing black farmers. Freedmen typically had little capital to begin with and limited access to legal services or credit. White landowners were often reluctant to sell to blacks. Faced with legal disabilities and a social climate infused with racism, buying and holding property was a constant challenge.

Not surprisingly, then, the problem of land ownership and its relationship to political and social equality was a major topic of black thought during this period. Black agrarianism, accordingly, remained a prominent theme in black political discourse. However, the intellectual landscape grew considerably more complex in the late 1890s, and those complexities had important influences on the evolution of black agrarian thought.

PROGRESSIVES, POPULISTS, AND AGRICULTURE

Late nineteenth-century America witnessed the rise of Darwinian biology, scientific racism, and progressive conservationism and preservationism, all of which influenced black Americans' ideas about nature. I will leave the discussion of race theory and related ideas to subsequent chapters, however, and focus here on the intellectual currents that were particularly relevant to agricultural thought. Those currents carried the agrarian tradition in different directions, fragmenting what had been a fairly unified view of the ideal agriculture as careful stewardship by a free proprietor-farmer. Conversations about agriculture became increasingly specialized during the late nineteenth century: the radical agrarians (the Populists and their fellow travelers) took the lead in analyzing the economic and political problems of farmers and the status of agricultural labor. Various progressive groups, in contrast, pursued agricultural science, conservation, and rural reform.[16] Black theorists—themselves speaking from increasingly diverse intellectual perspectives—would draw from all of these conversations in analyzing blacks' evolving relationship to the natural world.

Stewardship—or more properly, environmental science and management—was the central concern of the progressive environmental movements: conservationism, preservationism, urban reform, and scientific agriculture reform.[17] Responding to changes in the American landscape created by industrialization, urbanization, and western expansion, these movements were mostly the province of intellectual elites and the white middle class. There were differences among them: conservationists sought economic rationality in the exploitation of natural resources; preservationists were more concerned with the aesthetic, spiritual, and recreational value of pristine wilderness; and urban reformers were interested in beautifying the urban landscape and reducing pollution to improve public health. However, they shared the goal of putting America's natural resources under the care of professionals—experts educated in natural science and dedicated to the public interest in healthy, beautiful, and sustainable communities.[18]

Black Americans didn't participate in these progressive environmental movements in large numbers. That lack of interest calls for some explanation; after all, the South did have serious conservation and urban health problems. The end of Reconstruction ushered in what historian Thomas Clark calls a period of "frantic harvest" of the South's forests. During the 1880s, northern lumber companies (facilitated by the opening of the Southern Pacific Railroad in 1880) acquired millions of acres of public lands. Relying heavily on black labor, they began clear-cutting the vast acres of the southern pine belt. By 1914 the South's virgin forest was close to disappearing, replaced by millions of acres of land studded with stumps and roots, unsuitable for wildlife habitat, recreation, or agricultural production.[19] The notoriously unhealthy southern cities, too, were an obvious target for reform. A yellow fever epidemic in 1878 devastated New Orleans and Memphis, and another serious epidemic struck in 1898. Endemic diseases such as malaria and tuberculosis also gained ground. Poor urban blacks were particularly vulnerable to unhealthy living conditions.[20]

But the South was not a friendly environment for conservationism or urban reform, since it had a smaller scientific community than the North and its political culture was less progressive. There was in fact little southern involvement of any kind in progressive environmentalism. Nevertheless, after the turn of the century, advances in medical science made disease control more effective, and southern cities—aided by northern reformers—made dramatic progress in improving living conditions. Southern blacks did benefit from these initiatives, and black leaders endorsed them.[21] Conservation also gained ground in the South in the 1890s; the Populist influence provided support for restraining corporate exploitation of the forests, and the loss of forests, wildlife, and farmland drew the attention of southern politicians concerned about the long-term economic health of the region. Southern lawmakers therefore enacted a few conservation measures, creating state game or wildlife commissions and establishing a licensing system to preserve the supply of wild fish and game.[22] They even attempted to conserve the rapidly dwindling forests, although those efforts would have little effect until the demand for lumber produced by World War I made forest conservation more urgent.[23]

That black southerners showed little interest in these conservation efforts is due in part to the barriers to political participation they faced by the 1890s, including lack of resources, denial of voting rights, and vulnerability to political violence. But they had shown little interest in conservation even in the 1870s and 1880s, when they were participating in politics in larger numbers. This point suggests that conservationism did not serve their interests, or at least their understanding of their interests. Black southerners did not in fact fare particularly well under the new conservation measures in the South. Traditionally blacks, like poor whites, had supplemented their diet by hunting; the new restrictions on hunting interfered with those practices.[24] Blacks also faced stricter trespass laws and laws requiring livestock to be fenced, both of which were aimed at ending the customary practice of letting livestock run wild in the forest. Such progressive measures restricted traditional communal rights in order to protect landowners and were understandably more popular with the elites than with the masses.[25]

More generally, however, conservationism, preservationism, and urban reform were concerned primarily with the use of public spaces and public resources. Blacks were of course interested in gaining access to public spaces like parks, but for most black theorists in the late nineteenth century, the chief problem facing the black community was rebuilding the black *private* sphere. Slavery, they argued, had destroyed the black home, leading to a host of social problems that could be addressed only by recreating a vital, healthy black family life. As we will see, it was Progressives' efforts to reform the home rather than the environmental movements that most attracted black theorists, and it is in this domain that progressive ideas about the value of natural beauty had the greatest impact on black thought.

Progressive agriculture reformers, in comparison, were concerned with private spaces and private stewardship: They aimed at diffusing scientific and technological knowledge to farmers, in the hopes that better-educated farmers using the most advanced methods would increase agricultural productivity and promote soil conservation.[26] Scientific agriculture reform evolved from a small segment of the intelligentsia in the early nineteenth century to an influential force in public policy by midcentury. Reformers founded the United States Agricultural Society in 1852, and subsequently several states created agricultural colleges and departments of agriculture.[27] The movement received further support in 1862, when Congress established the Department of Agriculture, with the mandate to promote scientific knowledge to increase agricultural productivity, and granted public lands to states for the purpose of establishing colleges of agriculture and the mechanical arts.[28] By 1887, when the Hatch Act provided federal funds for agricultural experiment stations, scientific agriculture was institutionalized in the nation's universities and agricultural science had become a recognized discipline.[29]

Republicans embraced scientific agriculture reform as a means of advancing the interests of small farmers; as discussed in the previous chapter, during the antebellum period reformers were generally sympathetic to the philosophy and goals of democratic agrarianism. But agriculture reformers had always been less interested in the political and economic issues that animated antislavery advocates—namely, how an unfree labor system creates disincentives to private stewardship—than in promoting agricultural science and education. In fact, by the late nineteenth century, reformers did not uniformly favor small farmers, particularly in the South. Although they advocated diversified farming as a way for small farmers to achieve economic independence and conserve the soil, they did not effectively address the economic barriers to diversification. Instead, their reforms often involved reliance on expensive fertilizers and costly new equipment. Thus agriculture reform in the South was typically aimed at helping the more prosperous farmers and was often promoted by large planters with conservative views. (For example, C. F. Morehead, president of the National Cotton Planters Association in 1882, argued that consolidation of small farms into large plantations relying on wage labor would lead to better, more efficient farming.) Elite reformers did give some attention to improving rural living conditions, but their advice focused on improving communication and transportation and instructing farmers how to create more attractive homesteads.[30] The link between the status of labor and stewardship was at best a submerged theme among agriculture reformers—and among progressive environmentalists in general—until the New Deal era.[31]

Nevertheless, there was support for scientific agriculture reform in the black community. Booker T. Washington enthusiastically embraced it; the reformers' conception of agriculture as a science calling for special training allowed him to argue that blacks needed a higher education to be efficient farmers, thus gaining white support for vocational schools like the Tuskegee Institute. Washington's program was controversial in the black community, of course; his critics argued that the curriculum at Tuskegee actually offered less scientific or industrial training than promised and did not prepare its students for other careers. Still, most black leaders supported scientific training in agriculture as a legitimate goal of black education. Agriculture reform was directly relevant to black farmers—at least those who could afford it—and Washington became an important voice for scientific agriculture in the South. He supported the work of black scientists such as George Washington Carver, held agriculture conferences for local farmers, and employed extension agents to travel to black farmers demonstrating new tools and techniques. His efforts apparently found an audience among the more prosperous black farmers.[32]

Less prosperous farmers found other advocates—notably, the radical agrarian movements of the late nineteenth century. National farmers' organizations such as the Grange and the Farmers' Alliance emerged in the 1870s and 1880s to express the concerns of farmers and evolved into the Populist Party in the 1890s. These movements aimed at improving the economic and political condition of farmers, advocating land reform, corporate regulation, and reform of the banking and money system as well as political reform to increase representation of the working class.[33] Radical agrarians' proposals were wide-ranging and did, in fact, embrace the progressive goal of scientific reform of farming methods. Both the Grange and the Farmers' Alliance promoted agricultural education and supported practical agricultural instruction at the primary and college levels.[34] But agrarian radicals had less faith than the progressive reformers that scientific knowledge alone—particularly the theoretical knowledge pursued by agricultural scientists—would improve farmers' conditions, and they worried that the reformers' focus on technical knowledge (aimed at changing farming methods) would come at the expense of economic and political knowledge (aimed at changing the agricultural economy). The radicals therefore gave less attention to advancing agricultural science than to improving farmers' incomes, political status, and educational opportunities.[35]

Many black theorists found the radical agrarians' proposals relevant and compelling, as did the black masses. Black southerners were strongly supportive of the agrarian movements of 1880s and 1890s; the Colored Farmers' Alliance organized throughout the South, and southern blacks periodically supported Populist candidates. That support was not always rewarded, however, and the radical agrarians never adequately addressed the problem of racism. Those failures eventually lost them the support of black farmers and led black theorists to venture beyond the radical agrarian critique of southern agriculture. Nevertheless, as we will see, the Populists left an important mark on black environmental thought.[36]

In sum, progressive environmentalists and the Populists presented to black elites in the late nineteenth century diverging approaches to thinking about agriculture. But the black tradition itself was growing more complex as well. Abolitionists such as former slave Frederick Douglass still provided intellectual and political leadership after Emancipation, but new voices—highly educated religious leaders, editors, and scholars—brought a wider range of philosophical and political perspectives to black politics (and reflected the growing gap between the elites and the masses). Influential leaders ranged from the Episcopal divine and black nationalist Alexander Crummell, to radical editor T. Thomas Fortune, W. E. B. Du Bois (whose intellectual profile defies any simple characterization), and the conservative Booker T. Washington.[37] Given this intellectual diversity, we should not expect black leaders' views of nature to be monolithic or a simple derivation from either Progressivism or Populism. Rather, black theorists drew selectively from both traditions, along with the black agrarianism inherited from the abolitionists, to address the unique problems faced by the black community.

Those problems were legion, ranging from civil rights to education, lynching, labor relations, emigration, and the condition of the black family. But the primary social issue for black Americans, from Reconstruction through the first decade of the twentieth century, was creating a prosperous and stable community out of the millions of black farmers in the South. Thus the state of southern agriculture continued to be an important topic in black political discourse and a primary vehicle for considering blacks' relationship to the natural world.

POSTWAR BLACK AGRARIANISM

"Forty acres and a mule": this was what freedmen expected from freedom. It was the unfulfilled promise of Field Order No. 15, the Port Royal experiment of leasing plantations to freedmen, the Radical Republican land distribution proposals, and the Freedmen's Bureau efforts to settle blacks on abandoned and confiscated estates—none of which resulted in the widespread land ownership that freedmen believed they deserved as reparations for centuries of slavery.[38] Even today the phrase evokes a sense of deep injustice, of legitimate aspirations to the status of free proprietorship unfairly denied. This sense of broken faith is a critical part of the background of postwar black thought. Importantly, however, that disappointment did not undermine the masses' desire for land ownership, nor the appeal of agrarian rhetoric.

Emancipation had left southern agriculture in chaos. Both white and black elites were unsure whether freedmen would work without coercion, and they were understandably nervous at the prospect of millions of black southerners fleeing the plantations into the cities. Freedmen, for their part, believed that owning productive land would give them the freedom to make a home, to exert some independent control over nature, and achieve a measure of autonomy. Thus democratic agrarianism, with its emphasis on the moral value of agricultural labor and the importance of property to citizenship, spoke directly to both the elites' fears and the masses' desires.

A primary use of agrarian rhetoric after Emancipation was to discourage blacks from migrating to the cities. Even before the war, black leaders were concerned about the concentration of blacks in northern cities and urged urban blacks to seek economic independence by going "back to the land." This "back to the land" (or, more precisely, "stay on the land") theme in black politics continued after the war; settlement of blacks in agrarian communities seemed to many the most promising path to their economic and political development.[39] Douglass's 1873 speech to the Tennessee farmers rehearsed what was by then a well-developed argument for pursuing agriculture. Agriculture, he claimed, is a "refuge for the oppressed. The grand old earth has no prejudice against race, color, or previous condition of servitude, but flings open her ample breast to all who will come to her for succor and relief." He thus counseled black farmers to stay where they were: "If you have a few acres stick by them. The sweat and toil you put into them will add [to] their value and enable you to buy more."[40]

Ironically, however, agrarian rhetoric was also prominent among those encouraging blacks to *leave* the land—this land, at any rate. Throughout the nineteenth century, colonizationists such as Martin Delany, Edward Blyden, and Alexander Crummell urged black Americans to emigrate to Africa. When Blyden told black Americans that "the Lord thy God hath set the land before thee: go up and possess it," the land he had in mind was Africa.[41] African colonizationists had an important influence on black thought by emphasizing the historical and racial ties between black Americans and Africans. Much of their rhetoric, however, derives from democratic agrarianism. Like the early

American colonists, African colonizationists claimed divine sanction for their project, citing the "Ethiopian Prophecy" (a passage from Psalm 68): "Princes shall come out of Egypt; Ethiopia shall soon stretch out her hands unto God," declared Martin Delany in his call for the colonization of East Africa.[42] The land belongs to the black race, and "all that is left for us to do, is to make ourselves the 'lords of terrestrial creation'" by possessing it. It is more than a right; it is the duty of black Americans to "civilize" Africa: "Africa is our fatherland and we its legitimate descendants."[43]

And civilizing Africa, for the emigrationists, meant transforming its landscape—"finishing Creation" by turning the wilderness into an agrarian paradise. Blyden, for example, described how the visitor to Liberia, encountering a lonely, unbroken forest, would wonder "when and how are those vast wildernesses to be made the scene of human activity and to contribute to human wants and happiness?" A few years later, however, the visitor might return to find roads and bridges. As Blyden imagined the transformation, "The gigantic trees have disappeared, houses have sprung up on every side. . . . The waving corn and rice and sugar-cane . . . have taken the place of the former sturdy denizens of the forest." These "wonderful revolutions" were all to be accomplished by the American Negro colonist, who would cause "the wilderness and the solitary place to be glad—the desert to bloom and blossom as the rose—and the whole land to be converted into a garden of the Lord."[44] In short, the emigrationists offered blacks the chance to make Africa into a perfected America, an agrarian republic of black Jeffersonian farmers.[45]

The use of agrarian rhetoric in mass appeals to black southerners suggests the pervasiveness of this ideology in black culture in the late nineteenth century. But black thought was not monolithic, and by the end of the century some black leaders were criticizing the "back to the land" program of racial development. Du Bois, in his 1899 work *The Philadelphia Negro*, cautioned that urban migration represents "the worldwide desire to rise in the world, to escape the choking narrowness of the plantation, and the lawless repression of the village, in the South. . . . It must be discouraged and re pressed with great care and delicacy, if at all."[46] Similarly, Charles Chesnutt, who wrote in 1882 that "the main hope of the colored people . . . lies in agriculture," declared in 1892 that a purely agricultural people cannot be "so intelligent or enterprising as a people among whom there is a considerable diversity of interests and employment."[47] Despite these cautionary themes, however, both the conservative and radical camps continued to draw on the theoretical framework established by black agrarianism to explore the economic, social, and political challenges facing black farmers in the South.

Booker T. Washington, for example, combined the principles of democratic agrarianism with scientific agricultural reform to create a blueprint for improving the condition of black southerners. According to Washington, black farmers trained in the science of agriculture would achieve both the moral and the economic benefits of agricultural labor promised by democratic agrarians. He offered his own story as a case in point: His 1904 autobiography, *Working with the Hands,* explains how he learned the moral value of agricultural labor on his first job, cleaning his employer's yard. When he realized that the well-groomed yard was "a creation of my own hands," he reported, his "whole nature began to change": "I felt a self-respect, an encouragement and a satisfaction that I had never before enjoyed or thought possible."[48] His mind was "awakened and strengthened" by the manual labor; he immediately began to plan his work and imagine improvements. Moreover, "this visible, tangible contact with nature gave [him] inspirations and ambitions which could not have come in any other way."[49] The value of contact with nature is an increasingly prominent theme in Washington's writings after 1900: "There is something about the smell of the soil," he suggested, "a contact with a reality that gives one a strength and development that can be gained in no other way." He even claimed to feel "a nearness and kinship" to the plants in his vegetable garden.[50] But the point of this contact is not so much spiritual as educational: the pleasures of nature stimulate interest in the natural world, which leads to useful knowledge. For these reasons he favored outdoor work over factory work; working in a factory turns the worker into "little more than a machine."[51] The proper goal of manual labor is to create self-reliant, intelligent, and creative men and women.

This much is consistent with the slave narrative tradition, which also proposed that agricultural labor could serve as a source of pride and self-respect. But Washington's further reasoning begins to undermine that argument, calling into question whether agricultural labor, under current economic and political conditions, can be a source of racial pride. According to Washington, not all manual labor leads to a stronger sense of self: slaves, he insists, had not enjoyed the full benefits of the labor they performed. They had never known "voluntary incentives to toil"; the work they performed was not truly theirs, so they did not feel the sense of pride and agency that Washington enjoyed.[52] Slavery therefore degraded manual labor and led to poor farming. But similar problems, he argued, plagued southern agriculture under the sharecrop system. The primary problem, according to Washington, was tenancy: "Because the man who tilled the land did not own it, his main object was to get all he could out of the property and return to it as little as possible." The result was dilapidated farms, poor, eroding soil, and poorly tended livestock. He concluded that "no country can be very prosperous unless the people who cultivate the soil own it and live on it."[53]

Washington was not the first to worry about the effect of tenancy on agriculture; Adam Smith had warned of the dangers of short-term leases more than a hundred years earlier, and nineteenth-century policymakers were similarly concerned about the rising rates of tenancy in the South.[54] But is Washington's reasoning sound? After all, he claims that *he* learned good work habits and achieved the moral benefits of manual labor by working for other people. Why couldn't a tenant identify with his landlord's interest, and experience the same self-respect, encouragement, and satisfaction that Washington felt upon cleaning his employer's yard? Why isn't his story an argument *against* the conventional assumption that stewardship depends on widespread land ownership?

Of course, Washington wanted blacks to acquire property for reasons unrelated to stewardship. Capital accumulation, he believed, was important to the development of the race, and he also endorsed the Gilded Age belief that wealth itself conferred moral benefits. One might also argue that owning land would allow the farmer to secure the credit he needs to make improvements in his farming practices; lack of capital was, after all, one of the major barriers to adopting better farming practices. But these goals would not necessarily lead one to invest in land. Although land might be the most obvious investment for a farmer, one could build wealth by investing in other enterprises. Washington's argument concerning stewardship, however, has less to do with building wealth than with securing the conditions for free labor: he implicitly assumes that without their own land, most black farmers will not experience the favorable working conditions that he did.

According to Washington, the two factors motivating good stewardship are pride in one's labor, and economic incentives. But farmers have little incentive to invest in the farm's productivity unless they believe that they will reap the economic benefits of their labor. Washington's unspoken assumption is that the credit system made that belief implausible for sharecroppers. Similarly, they have little reason to take pride in their labor unless they actually have the authority to make critical decisions about what and how to farm; the credit system and labor contract (as Washington implicitly recognizes) typically took such decisions out of their hands. Of course, this lack of incentives and authority might not impair stewardship if the landowner forced the farmer into sustainable farming. But, as mentioned earlier, the landowner typically did not, in part because requiring the farmer to adopt more intensive farming methods would require greater supervision of the farmer's work.[55] It was hard enough to supervise plantation slaves when they engaged in complex tasks; sharecroppers and tenants were even harder to monitor. Thus the peonage system left the farmer relatively free from direct supervision (creating the illusion of freedom)—but it also left him or her without the incentives and the authority that might motivate responsible, careful farming.

And without those incentives and authority, under Washington's reasoning, neither the farmer nor the land was likely to benefit from manual labor. Tenants who are dominated and exploited, who have no reasonable hope of accumulating wealth through their labor, will not feel that they are working for themselves. They will not experience the pride or sense of ownership that would lead to good stewardship, and will thus be deprived of the moral and psychological benefits of labor—benefits that derive primarily from the sense of agency that labor creates and from the worker's experience of the economic consequences (positive or negative) of his actions. In short, Washington suggests that sharecropping and tenancy hurt agriculture for the same reason slavery did, by preventing the emergence of a truly free agricultural labor force—a labor force with the means, authority, and incentives for improving their economic condition by improving agriculture.

Granted, Washington often insisted that a diligent black farmer of good character would be treated fairly by the white elites, and he blamed some of the problems of black farmers on their own moral defects. But those moral defects, under his reasoning, should be cured if farmers were in fact working for themselves; free labor, unlike forced labor, should build character. Moreover, he did on occasion explicitly admit that some black farmers faced unscrupulous employers and had a reasonable fear of falling into peonage.[56] For all his optimistic rhetoric, it appears that Washington fully understood that for a black farmer in the South in the late nineteenth century, facing the host of laws and social practices that restricted blacks' contract rights, the best way to ensure that you were working for yourself was to own your own farm.

Even owning one's own land, however, did not guarantee that one would have the freedom to choose how to farm or that one's labor would be rewarded. According to radical agrarians, from the Farmers' Alliance of the 1880s to the Populists and their successors, small farmers faced not only declining prices and unstable markets but the anticompetitive practices of railroads, credit institutions, producers of farm machinery, and buyers of agricultural commodities.[57] These economic conditions kept them in servitude to creditors, preventing them from profiting from their labor and building wealth—which in turn would have given them more freedom to diversify their crops or try different farming methods. Washington largely overlooked these problems; like many proponents of scientific agriculture reform, he assumed that if farmers could only be encouraged to work more efficiently and intelligently, they would prosper. The radical agrarians, in contrast, argued that corporate regulation and reform of the nation's banking and transportation systems were necessary to make agricultural labor economically rewarding. Some black activists found their arguments persuasive.

W. E. B. Du Bois, for example, was also concerned with the degraded condition of black farmers in the South. His essay on Georgia's Black Belt in *The Souls of Black Folk* follows the analysis developed by black abolitionists, arguing that the situation of black farmers was the natural consequence of slavery. Although the Black Belt was initially quite fertile, by the Civil War the "hard ruthless rape of the land began to tell": "The harder the slaves were driven the more careless and fatal was their farming." Thus the land was devastated by the "wasteful economies of the slave regime," "devitalized by careless and exhaustive culture."[58] Freedom did little to improve the situation, however. Black farmers were burdened by crushing debt; with no hope of acquiring land, they had no incentive to work well. Referencing the eighteenth-century agrarian Arthur Young on the evils of serf labor, Du Bois insisted that these modern serfs "are careless because they have not found that it pays to be careful. . . . Above all, they cannot see why they should take unusual pains to make the white man's land better, or to fatten his mule, or save his corn."[59] Washington saw no solution to this situation except for farmers to lift themselves, one by one, into the class of landowners. For Du Bois, the situation called for more dramatic social and economic reform.

Du Bois and a few other radical activists, such as T. Thomas Fortune, contemplated widespread land reform in the South. In his 1911 novel, *The Quest of the Silver Fleece*, Du Bois analyzed the economic, social, and political forces that prevented black farmers from acquiring land or competing in the marketplace, including blacks' lack of capital and education, white resistance to black economic advancement, and the anticompetitive practices of monopolies that oppressed all small farmers. His solution was for the black community to organize: to pool their resources, buy land, and operate it collectively.[60] T. Thomas Fortune, even more sympathetic to radical agrarians, went further. He agreed that peonage "makes desolate fields that once bloomed 'as fair as a garden of the Lord.'" Peonage, however, resulted not only from racial injustice but from the monopoly of productive land. Indeed, Fortune explicitly placed his critique of race relations within the agrarian tradition discussed in Chapter 2 (referencing Pliny and the theory that the *latifundia* caused the downfall of Rome). Drawing on arguments that were also being deployed against the landed aristocracy in Europe concerning the inefficiencies and injustice of large landholding and absentee landowners, Fortune argued that the South, also, was burdened by an idle, grasping aristocracy. Moreover, on large estates, machines were replacing the muscles and brains of workers; small farmers were turned into tenants (or slaves), and thousands were being forced out of the countryside for the city. In fact, the concentration of land in the South had actually extended slavery to poor whites. Thus Fortune advocated confiscation and redistribution of the large southern plantations. His goal, too, was to secure the conditions for free labor; the man who owns the soil, he argued, dictates to and owns the men who work it.[61]

Few other black leaders supported such radical reform, but they did agree that improving the situation of black farmers would require broad reforms aimed at combating racism and protecting civil rights. The abolitionists had argued for civil and political equality partially on the grounds that the degraded status of agricultural workers led to contempt for labor. This argument was less prominent after the war,[62] but black leaders did insist that lack of protection for civil rights threatened freedom of labor. Even Washington recognized the importance of civil rights to protecting the worker's freedom. Du Bois and his fellow travelers were more explicit: racial oppression and political inequality made property and contract rights insecure— and therefore prevented blacks, as individuals and as a race, from establishing a long-term relationship with the natural world based on truly free labor.

Threats to blacks' property and contract rights were legion. Even if the law recognized such rights, white Americans often did not. Charles Chesnutt highlighted this issue in his novel, *The Marrow of Tradition*, where the hero—a black doctor—is deprived of not one but two legacies because the families of the white testators refuse to produce the wills. The novel points out that marriage rights are also important to protecting property; we are assured that the doctor's claim to his father's estate would not be legally enforceable even if the will were produced, since his white father's marriage to his black mother was illegal.[63] Ironically, in Chesnutt's story this disrespect for rights frustrates white men's ability to dispose of their estates. But the doctor suffers a more serious infringement of his property rights when a white mob burns down his hospital. The story reminds us of the extent to which an individual's ability to acquire and use property depends on the support of the community.

Blacks' degraded political status also undermined their property and contract rights. "Is it possible, and probable," Du Bois asked, "that nine millions of men can make effective progress in economic lines if they are deprived of political rights?" Workers and property owners, he pointed out, cannot defend their property rights without the suffrage. The farmers he observed in the Black Belt suffer in part from poor soil and poor markets, but also from the fact that without political power, they had little recourse when whites cheated them out of their rightful earnings and their land.[64] *The Quest of the Silver Fleece* dramatizes the problem: the white landowner—normally an honorable and trustworthy man—feels no compunction about cheating blacks out of their land because he can't envision them as landowners. In his world, blacks are economically, socially, and politically subordinate. When he attempts to renege on a contract with the heroine, she does successfully defend her contract rights in court—but only because she is able to exploit her own subordinate position to win the community's pity, and to take advantage of a factional conflict among the white elites.[65] Normally, blacks lacked the political power to put their own representatives on the bench and therefore could not be sure of a fair hearing. Thus for Du Bois, property and contract rights depend critically on political rights and social status.

This reasoning suggests that political rights and status are also critical to developing a sustainable and morally beneficial relationship with the natural world. Indeed, at this point, I think we can extrapolate some broader theoretical points from nineteenth- and early twentieth-century black agrarian discourse. Agrarians began from the premise that a positive relationship with the natural world arises out of an agriculture in which farmers have the authority, the means, and the incentives to stewardship. Under such ideal conditions, farming would truly be free, a creative interaction with the natural world by responsible and relatively autonomous agents; this much is certainly implied by the ideal of the Jeffersonian yeoman farmer. Good farming under these conditions would confer a host of moral, economic, and spiritual benefits—including (for black theorists) a sense of self-respect and racial pride. Under slavery and peonage, however, farmers are denied authority over and the economic rewards of their labor. They therefore feel coerced and are less likely to identify with the landowner's long-term interest in the land's productivity (which is also less pressing to the landowner than his interest in controlling his unfree labor force). Feeling no sense of ownership of their labor, they will work less carefully. They will also probably take less pleasure in their work and in studying the natural world to develop better farming methods (which they might not be able to adopt in any case). Charles Chesnutt put it concisely in his 1904 essay "The Race Problem": the South, he argues, should have been the garden spot of the nation. Instead, it remains in a "semi-barbarous condition." Southern whites expend their energy on keeping black labor in line, while immigrants shun a land where "life is held cheap, where labor is despised, and where opportunities for education are limited."[66]

To rectify this situation, according to theorists like Du Bois, workers must enjoy freedom of contract and be assured that the economic system will reward their labor. That may require radical reform of the economic system, but at the very least it requires that their rights be recognized by the community and enforced by the legal system—which in turn means they must have political and social equality. In sum, without a healthy agricultural economy, civil rights, and equality for black farmers, agriculture suffers, the land deteriorates, and workers are deprived the moral benefits of "working with the hands."

It is an elegant theory—but, as the previous chapter discussed, theories necessarily oversimplify. Farmers may in fact face a more complicated set of economic incentives than the theory suggests, and individuals may react differently to oppression or find other ways to develop a positive relationship with the natural world. Washington's claims notwithstanding, many slaves did find in their forced agricultural labor a source of pride and self-respect, leading to good stewardship; there can be little doubt that freedmen did as well. Nevertheless, the theory illuminates an otherwise obscure connection between stewardship and social justice: if free labor is even somewhat conducive to good stewardship, then full political and social equality for agricultural workers may also be important. In some circumstances, securing the conditions for free labor might even require widespread land ownership or collectivization. To take the argument further, a truly free agricultural labor force might require access to educational and economic opportunities, so that those who work the land do so out of choice and not economic necessity or social pressures, and are not so constrained by circumstances that they can't make real choices about how to farm. In short, postwar black agrarianism suggests that the best foundations for a productive, sustainable agriculture are freedom of labor, an economic system that rewards agricultural labor, and social and political equality for farm workers.

BLACK HOMES AND GARDENS

Undermining the voluntariness of agricultural labor is only one way that racial oppression affected blacks' relationship with nature, however. The abolitionists had argued that slavery could distort blacks' spiritual and aesthetic relationship to the natural world, thus alienating them from the land. That concern became more prominent in black thought after the war. By the end of the century, black theorists were drawing on progressive ideas to explore how racial oppression affected blacks' emotional connection to the American landscape and their ability to forge a spiritual relationship with nature—in other words, how lack of freedom and equality interfered with blacks' efforts not only to *make* a home but to *feel* at home on the American landscape.

The concept of home holds a critical place in black thought; one of the more persistent themes in this tradition is the claim that racial oppression creates in blacks a sense of homelessness, a sense that they don't *belong* anywhere. Frederick Douglass echoed many other fugitive slaves in claiming that under slavery, "the ties that ordinarily bind children to their homes were all suspended." His home "was charmless; it was not home to me; . . . I looked for home elsewhere."[67] He elaborated this theme in an 1894 speech against colonization: colonization schemes, he complained, weaken blacks' hold on one country without giving them reasonable hope of another. "It forces on him the idea that he is forever doomed to be a stranger and a sojourner in the land of his birth, and that he has no permanent abiding place here." "Permanent location," Douglass claimed, "is a mighty element to civilization. . . . There is a powerful motive for the cultivation of an honorable character, in the fact that we have a country, a neighborhood, a home."[68]

Under slavery, Douglass contended, "the full effect of this motive has not . . . been experienced by our people."[69] This homelessness was a contradiction produced by slavery; under the principles of democratic agrarianism, blacks' right to citizenship should not have been in question. Most activists—even those calling for African colonization—insisted that blacks had a right to a home on the American continent. Delany called America "our destination and our home," arguing that their presence here was God's providence, that they were more closely related to the Native Americans than white people were, and that the labor of slaves had earned them a right to the land.[70] Alexander Crummell agreed that "three centuries' residence in a country seems clearly to give any people a right to their nationality therein without disturbance" and, in addition, that blacks had "made large contributions to the clearing of their country; they have contributed by sweat and toil to the wealth thereof; and by their prowess and their blood they have participated in the achievement of its liberties."[71] None of this would have been questioned, they argued, if not for race slavery and racial prejudice. Racial oppression had prevented blacks, as a group, from securing the status of citizens, and therefore from establishing an emotional bond to the land and the nation—a bond of affection and belonging that in addition to being valuable in its own right, could motivate good stewardship.

The persistent language of homelessness in black discourse suggests that most black theorists considered property ownership and citizenship rights to be critical to creating an emotional bond to the land. The connection makes sense: citizenship rights constitute formal recognition of membership in the body politic—the community that asserts collective authority over and responsibility for the land. Similarly, property rights allow one to exercise individual authority over and responsibility for the land, and they help a community develop a sense of *enduring* connection to a place. Importantly, secure property (and marriage) rights allow owners to plan their own and their children's futures. This in fact is a central problem in Chesnutt's *The Marrow of Tradition;* in that story, insecure property rights made it difficult for parents to provide for their children (through estate planning) or to create institutions like hospitals that would benefit the community. The intergenerational transfer of wealth is one of the chief means by which a community achieves a sense of continuity with the past and future, and passing on the land itself can be a particularly effective means for a community to develop a deep connection to place. Secure citizenship and property rights are thus important to fostering a sense of connection to and responsibility for the land and one's community.

Of course, many blacks did develop a connection to a particular place and fought fiercely for their homes and communities. After Emancipation they seized the opportunity to build homes and villages; they not only desired land, they desired to own the land on which they had lived and worked—their *homes.* Freedmen often actively resisted postwar attempts to remove them from the plantations they claimed for themselves, and when they abandoned their homes, it was in order to establish new, more secure homes somewhere else.[72] This attachment to place even in the absence of state-protected rights points toward a less state-centered dynamic (discussed in Chapter 1) in which black Americans' connection to the land arises out of the customs and practices of slave culture—perhaps through grassroots resistance to oppression rather than state-created rights and status. That sense of entitlement is captured by the phrase "40 acres and a mule"; freedmen clearly felt they had a right to the land by virtue of their labor. Nevertheless, there is also evidence in postwar black southern culture of the sense of homelessness that Douglass referred to, exhibited for example in the periodic surges of interest in emigration.[73] The persistence of this desire to find or make a home suggests that racial oppression could in fact undermine blacks' sense of connection to the land. From the perspective of black Americans, such a connection could not be assumed; it had to be consciously created and fought for.

Equally damaging, however, was the effect of racial oppression on the individual black home—which, according to a growing body of experts, was supposed to play an important role in relating humans to nature. This concern is rooted in the "cult of domesticity," an ideology that took shape in the 1830s and was pervasive in black and white elite discourse by the late nineteenth century. The cult of domesticity idealizes the home and family—and particularly the mother—as the primary agents of moral uplift. The home is supposed to be a sanctuary and the mother the "angel of the house," using her moral and spiritual gifts to guide the development of the child into a virtuous citizen. The economic system might require that men compete with each other in the workplace; it might degrade the physical landscape and elevate economic over aesthetic and spiritual values. But the private home could serve as an antidote: a good wife could create a home to which men could retreat and enjoy the moral and spiritual benefits of sympathy, affection, and beauty—including the beauty of nature.[74]

The notion that natural beauty had important spiritual benefits was not new, of course; early agrarians had argued as much. But in the late nineteenth and early twentieth centuries, it was most closely associated with the progressive preservation and urban reform movements, both of which aimed at preserving natural beauty through the creation of public parks, and rural reform, which included efforts to beautify rural homes.[75] There was an affinity between these movements and the cult of domesticity: if preserving the natural beauty of public lands should be a national priority, then surely it is equally important for housewives to preserve natural beauty in their own yards. Thus advisers on domesticity insisted that a good home should include a good garden; a neat yard ornamented with flowers was evidence of civic as well as feminine virtue.[76]

We need only turn to the father of American landscape design, Andrew Jackson Downing, for confirmation of the spiritual benefit of gardens. Downing wished "to awaken [in Americans] a quicker sense of the grace, the elegance, or the picturesqueness" that can be produced by landscape gardening—"a sense which will not only refine and elevate the mind, but open to it new and infinite resources of delight." Quoting no less an authority than Goethe, Downing argued that

> if we become sincere lovers of the grace, the harmony, and the loveliness with which rural homes and rural life are capable of being invested, . . . we are silently opening our hearts to an influence which is higher and deeper than the mere *symbol*; and . . . if we worship in the true spirit, we shall attain a nearer view of the Great Master, whose words, in all his material universe, are written in lines of Beauty.[77]

For Downing, a lovely garden made the home a "sunny spot" where "social sympathies . . . grow and entwine trustfully with the tall trees or wreathed vines that cluster around, as if striving to shut out whatever of bitterness or strife may be found in the open highways of the world." A garden was a private retreat, a haven in a heartless world, even a "barrier against vice, immorality, and bad habits."[78] Thus gardening—and specifically *ornamental* gardening—was a means of bringing to the family the moral and spiritual benefits of contact with nature.

Black theorists in the late nineteenth and early twentieth centuries embraced the cult of domesticity. According to many black writers, a major challenge facing the black community was creating such a spiritually and morally uplifting home—a home that would (among other things) bring blacks into a proper spiritual and aesthetic relationship with nature. Alexander Crummell, for example, thought that Emancipation had failed to free black women; they would remain enslaved by a degrading social life until their homes were transformed by "neatness, taste, and beauty."[79] Du Bois agreed. Indeed, he thought the problem so important that he published in 1901 a five-part essay on "The Problem of Housing the Negro," which explains his views on the home. Slavery, he argued, had destroyed the traditional home of the displaced Africans. "Violently torn from the home of his fathers three centuries ago, he has not until this generation been allowed as a race to establish a strong, pure home life."[80] According to Du Bois, the disruption of the black home accounts for many of the moral defects of which the black community was accused. No other agent is as important to moral development as "the influence exerted on the growing child by the customs, morals and general situation of the family group into which it is born."[81]

Du Bois thought black home life defective in a variety of ways, but—like Crummell—he made a point of highlighting the lack of *beauty* in the home. This was not a new theme for Du Bois; in an earlier work, *The Philadelphia Negro*, he had also emphasized the importance of the physical environment to the social development of the race.[82] In the 1901 essay he elaborated on the point. Echoing Downing, he noted that "it is manifest that the sense of harmony and beauty receives its first training at home." Sadly, he lamented, southern districts are "bare, dull, unlovely places," and an unlovely home produces "minds without . . . adequate appreciation of the beautiful world in which they live."[83] In a later essay, he complained that the South was growing "hopelessly ugly" as the result of industrialization: "We are going to see this land, the natural beauty of which might rival that of any part of the country . . . transformed into all the ugliness of factory civilization . . . unless some one tries to make the South not simply rich, but good to look upon and decent to live in."[84] That concern could have led to an argument for preserving forests and other wild places, but Du Bois did not pursue that program; his brief for natural beauty was tied to his agenda for reforming the black home.

Nor was he alone. Although Du Bois's emphasis on natural beauty—a persistent theme in his writings—is somewhat unusual, progressive ideas about the value of natural beauty are not uncommon among black theorists. They typically appear, however, in discussions of black homes and gardens, not in discussions of the wilderness. Booker T. Washington, for example, also argued that the challenge facing the black community was rebuilding the black home, the fount of the "health, strength, morals and happiness of the family." He therefore worried about the effect of the ugly farms in the South on blacks' moral character. At Tuskegee, female students were taught how to beautify yards as part of their instruction in homemaking, and male students were also instructed in floriculture in order to develop in them a sense of beauty and to see that "more of nature's beauty shall pervade the home and its surroundings."[85] The National Association of Colored Women, an early twentieth-century progressive reform organization, also endorsed this theory of the home, which became the basis of its urban environmental reform efforts—including city beautification, securing access to green space, and various public health campaigns.[86]

Clearly, for many black leaders, natural beauty provided an alternative to agricultural labor as a basis of black selfhood. Even while Washington and Du Bois were questioning whether labor could serve as a source of racial pride, they were also considering how surrounding black families with natural beauty could create in them a stronger sense of self. However, they offered different accounts of how beautifying the home would have that effect. For Washington, gardening was valuable because, like farming, it offered the opportunity to create and execute plans. The gardener could enjoy the pleasures of independent agency, along with the pleasurable "sense of newness, of expectancy" derived from watching the plants develop from day to day.[87] Moreover, beautifying the home was a way to combat racial prejudice through assimilation to white middle-class standards. "We strive to have our students understand," he explained, "that no possible prejudice can explain away the influence of a Negro living in a nicely painted house, with well-kept flower yards, gardens, farm, poultry and live stock."[88] The more black homes look like white middle-class homes, the less reason whites (or blacks) will have to believe in black inferiority. Gardens were to bring black children into a proper relationship with nature, but the key point for Washington was that this relationship be the *same* as it was for white children.

George Washington Carver shared Washington's enthusiasm for gardening and even proposed that it be taught in primary school, as a method of practical nature study. Like Washington, he hoped that children could learn lessons from their gardens that could be applied to farming and business. But gardening, he hoped, would also beautify the school grounds, which would appeal to the children's aesthetic natures and teach them "order and system."[89] Carver advocated the aesthetic and scientific study of nature not only for the practical benefits to be realized, however, but for the spiritual insight that contact with nature offered. Carver's intense spiritual life centered on the concept of God as the "Great Creator" of the natural world. His scientific studies began with intuitions received through a kind of communion with the natural object under investigation, and he derived further intimations of God's benevolence and power from aesthetic appreciation of natural beauty. This eloquent passage from a letter written in 1927, reminiscent of the more ecstatic writings of John Ruskin, captures Carver's spiritual relationship to the natural world:

> As I sat in my little "den" reading . . . nature came to my relief when I was attracted by a strangely mellow light falling up on the paper. I looked up and out of the window toward the setting sun, which was just disappearing behind the horizon leaving a halo of never to be forgotten glory and beauty behind it. It seems as if I have never been conscious of such beauty and sublimity. The variety, brilliancy of color and arrangement were awe inspiring.
>
> As I sat there unconscious of everything except the scene before me, behold, before my very eyes it changed from the marvelous rainbow colors to the soft, ethereal "Rembrandtian" browns and the midnight blues of Maxfield Parrish. But the most marvelous of all was the pristine light which came from behind those strangely beautiful clouds; the light was like unto bright silver dazzleing [sic] in its brightness, and weird in the manner of its diffusion.
>
> As I came to myself I said aloud, O God, I thank Thee for such a direct manifestation of Thy goodness, majesty and power.[90]

But Carver was no passive spectator of nature; he was a scientist, actively intervening in natural processes. We can gain insight into the significance of such activities for Carver from a later passage, written in 1940. Reflecting on a gift of dahlias, he recalled the saying that "flowers were the sweetest things that God ever made and forgot to put a soul into." Carver ventured that God put a soul into humans instead, so that man—"copartner with him in creating some of the most beautiful and useful things in the world"—could express that soul in cultivating more beautiful strains of flowers.[91] For Carver, actively manipulating the natural world (as gardeners do, for example) was a way to come into contact with God and to express one's spirituality.

Du Bois, as mentioned, was similarly sympathetic to the spiritual and aesthetic value of nature, but he related the spiritual dimension of home beautification more explicitly to the project of creating a distinctive racial identity. Whereas preservationists wanted the public spaces of national parks to express "American" ideals, Du Bois argued that the private space of the home should embody the ideals of life peculiar to the race: "A real home is a way of thinking, a habit of doing . . . an insight into the beauty of things." The homemaker's function is therefore primarily spiritual: to "interpret life and the world" to the family.[92] Slavery, in destroying enslaved Africans' home life, deprived them of an important means of expressing and passing on to their children spiritual ideals; it left generations of blacks spiritually bereft, undermining an important basis of selfhood. Thus rebuilding the black home meant expressing blacks' own ideals of life. Under this view, domestic activities like gardening should not be aimed at mimicking the white middle class; rather, they should be means to develop and teach to the family black ideals of life, including "their interpretation of sunshine and rain and human hearts."[93] Du Bois often suggested that black ideals of life would be more sensitive to natural beauty than white ideals; indeed, he criticized white Americans for their failure to appreciate spiritual and aesthetic values.[94] But his point was that rebuilding the black home would make possible the articulation of these ideals, whatever they turned out to be. Under this reasoning, homemaking and gardening, because they had important spiritual and aesthetic dimensions—and because they pertained to private spaces under black control—were means to express and reinforce a distinct racial identity.

Du Bois's conception of homemaking and gardening was probably not widely shared among black southerners. Although rural blacks in the South did keep gardens, they were more skeptical than the elites of the cult of domesticity and its narrow conception of women's role, and their interpretation of the domestic landscape differed from that of black theorists.[95] Their gardens were utilitarian, a way to increase self-sufficiency by growing vegetables and keeping livestock. They viewed the yard as a work space and a living space—essentially an extension of the kitchen—rather than in the ornamental terms suggested by progressive reformers.[96] As Dianne Glave has shown, however, the educational efforts of Washington and others did bring progressive ideas to rural blacks, and by the 1920s, they were even competing in garden contests.[97] For some, improving one's garden was probably a means of assimilation and social advancement; some may have shared Carver's view of gardening as a spiritual pursuit (which is apparently a common theme among southern black gardeners today). But we have little evidence that early twentieth-century blacks made a connection between gardens and racial identity.[98] For our purposes, however, what is significant about Du Bois's reasoning is that he begins to outline a theory concerning the effect of racial oppression on blacks' aesthetic and spiritual relationship to nature—a theory that he and others would develop in the coming decades. On one hand, to the extent racial oppression made it difficult for a community to express its collective ideals aesthetically, it interfered with the community's ability to give its own meaning to the landscape. The destruction of the black home, like slave agriculture and peonage, deprived blacks of the authority and the means to respond creatively to the natural world, and so to establish a morally and spiritually beneficial relationship with nature. On the other hand, aesthetic and spiritual interaction with nature, as through gardening, could also be a means to resist the effects of racial oppression on blacks' sense of self, offering a new basis for racial identity.

CONCLUSION

After the war, black environmental thought evolved from a relatively unified conversation into a more complex and fragmented collection of arguments and sometimes idiosyncratic perspectives. Nevertheless, the continuity between pre- and postwar black thought is suggested by a passage in Du Bois's *Souls of Black Folk:* "I have seen a land right merry with the sun, where children sing, and rolling hills lie like passioned women wanton with the harvest. And there in the King's Highway sat and sits a figure veiled and bowed, by which the traveller's footsteps hasten as they go."[99]

The contrast between the beauty of the pastoral landscape and the ugliness of racial injustice echoes Henry Bibb's narrative, which similarly describes a landscape stained by human injustice. The image underscores black theorists' continuing emphasis on the importance of freedom and equality to achieving a healthy relationship to nature. Exploitive agricultural labor systems, they argued, alienate their victims from the natural landscape and scar the land itself; they create disincentives to stewardship and prevent the oppressed from establishing a secure, long-term interest in and sense of attachment to the land.

This tradition thus diverges from progressive environmentalism in its focus on how social structures—laws, rights, and social and economic systems—mediate a group's relationship to the natural world. It highlights in particular how such structures, by undermining freedom of labor and property rights, can undermine independent agency and thus interfere with a community's *creative response* to the land—its ability to accept and exercise responsibility for the land and to express its aesthetic and spiritual ideals by manipulating the natural world. The experience of black Americans, as understood by black theorists, suggested that this ability to respond creatively to the natural world is critical to a community's ability to form bonds of affection for and interest in the land. Thus this tradition makes freedom—encompassing freedom of labor, secure rights, and full membership in the political community—central to establishing a positive relationship to nature.

The black tradition also differs from progressive environmentalism in its concern with *private* space and private property. Modern environmental theorists have been much less enthusiastic than black agrarians about private property rights. In keeping with the progressive distrust of private ownership, environmentalists worry that strong protection for property rights can defeat government efforts to restrict destructive uses of private land. But contemporary environmentalists usually assume that the community in question already enjoys the capacity for independent action and decision-making—for free labor—as well as social and political equality and a sense of responsibility for the land. The black tradition highlights the importance of property and other civil rights to achieving this capacity for individual and collective stewardship. True, one could draw on these arguments to oppose environmental regulation, claiming that regulation interferes with the individual's creative interaction with the natural world, impeding innovation and preventing the community from developing a sense of responsibility for the land. But the black tradition suggests that support for property rights can also *legitimate* government regulation to protect the environment. Theorists like Du Bois emphasized property rights in order to support wide-ranging social and economic reform that would make those rights meaningful, and to create an agricultural economy that would encourage creative, responsible farming. That legacy informs the contemporary environmental justice movement, which seeks government action aimed at empowering minority communities to protect their property from environmental harms.

Still, contemporary environmentalists might be concerned that in this tradition, the moral benefit of agricultural labor lies in its ability to give the worker a sense of mastery or dominion over nature. It is precisely this celebration of domination, environmentalists have argued, that leads to unlimited exploitation of natural resources and the failure to recognize moral duties to nonhumans—as well as reinforcing a problematic conception of masculinity as involving "mastering" feminine nature.[100] It's a reasonable concern; many black theorists have suggested that mastery of nature through labor is an important foundation of selfhood and racial pride. For theorists such as Booker T. Washington, the chief means of achieving individual autonomy is to impose one's will on the natural world, and most of the benefits of manual labor derive from the experience of successfully mastering nature.

But black theorists are also keenly sensitive to the fact that mastering nature usually involves mastering other humans; that was, after all, the chief lesson of plantation agriculture. Thus it is not surprising that in the black tradition, a legitimate "dominion" relationship is not imagined as merely an exercise of naked power. George Washington Carver, for example, agreed that humans can and should manipulate nature, even to the point of developing new strains of plants and animals. But he saw humans as "copartners" with God in the creation—and junior partners at that, whose scientific study of nature is inspired and guided by God and justified by its charitable purpose of relieving human suffering and uplifting the human soul. For Carver, humans' right to exert some control over the natural world was contained by a moral and spiritual framework in which nature has independent value as God's creation.

For Du Bois, too, nature was not merely a material resource to be exploited; as his discussion of homemaking suggests, our relationship to nature is an integral part of our aesthetic and spiritual life. Interaction with nature should be not a blind mastery but a creative *response*, attentive equally to the aesthetic, spiritual, moral, and economic dimensions of the world we inhabit. This emphasis on responsiveness in turn suggests a conception of masculinity centered less on power than on responsibility, care, and stewardship. Indeed, it is significant that Du Bois and Washington both valued sensitivity in men and strength in women. (Washington, recall, gave his male students instruction in flower-arranging). They both insisted that a proper relationship to nature—for men and women—involved physical labor but also engaged the moral, aesthetic, and spiritual dimensions of one's personality.

This conception of nature as a source of artistic and spiritual inspiration in fact became the dominant theme in black environmental thought after the turn of the century. As new ideas about race and nature became prominent in American culture in the early twentieth century, black theorists would further explore how oppression and exploitation of agricultural labor can distort a community's aesthetic relationship to nature. Their arguments, however, increasingly went beyond black agrarianism to draw on Romantic intellectual currents, including vitalism, primitivism, and scientific racism. Black theorists' encounter with these Romantic ideas would complicate their understanding of the relationship between nature and human culture—and bring into question the very possibility of free, creative interaction with nature.

CHAPTER FOUR

RACE NATURES

———•◦•———

The title of W. E. B. Du Bois's 1903 book, *The Souls of Black Folk*, announces a new theme in black environmental thought: the Romantic conception of southern blacks as a peasant community with an organic connection to the land. Ironically, that conception emerged just as southern blacks were leaving the land in greater numbers, moving to cities and into industrial occupations. Du Bois's characterization of blacks as a "folk" can be read as a response to this modern movement away from the land, an attempt to express what was valuable about southern black agrarian life even as it dissolved under the forces of modernization.

For Du Bois and many others, what was valuable about that life was its connection to nature, in the rich Romantic sense of that term. Nature, for Romantics, is not a clocklike mechanism but a living, creative power, and the organic connection to nature enjoyed by "primitive" peoples like peasants (the folk) is the chief source of cultural vitality. The folk are supposed to enjoy an intuitive connection to nature's vital power, created through daily interaction with the natural world. Modern urban communities, in contrast, have lost their creative energy and sunk into a cultural malaise—a malaise all too apparent to Romantic critics of fin de siècle European society. If creative energy is derived from nature, they argued, only a people with an intuitive connection to the natural world can develop a folk culture sufficiently vital to inspire a great civilization. Under this view, the revitalization of European culture requires a return to the land and a revival of each nation's folk culture.[1]

But where could a young and largely immigrant nation like the United States look for cultural renewal? Du Bois was one of several theorists, black and white, who proposed that southern blacks were America's true "folk."[2] As such, they could serve as a source of cultural vitality, using their artistic gifts to inspire an industrializing American civilization. This argument, of course, conflicts with the black agrarians' claim that slavery alienated blacks from nature by impairing their bond to the land. But that tension was already present in nineteenth-century black thought. As discussed in the previous chapters, agrarians often insisted that despite the obstacles they faced, black slaves *were* able to develop a sense of belonging to the land; that argument supported their claim to citizenship and equality. For twentieth-century black theorists, the concept of black Americans as a folk was similarly appealing, allowing them to turn black Americans' alleged underdevelopment and "backwardness" into a cultural asset—a source of cultural vitality for white Americans and the groundwork of a stronger and more resilient sense of self for black Americans.

Nevertheless, claiming the title of America's folk posed challenges for black Americans. First, as Du Bois himself recognized, the black folk community did not arise out of a simple harmonious relationship with nature; it was the product of injustice and violence. The suffering entailed by that oppression continued to shape the collective memory of black Americans, complicating their relationship to their agrarian past. Second, the concept of folk is hard to disentangle from nineteenth-century primitivism and racial ideology, both of which reinforced problematic stereotypes—including the notion that blacks were biologically and culturally alien to America. Much of early twentieth-century black environmental thought centers on these two problems. I will address black theorists' confrontation with primitivism in the next chapter, along with their exploration of the relationship between black artistic creativity and the collective memory of slavery. This chapter lays the groundwork for that discussion by examining black theorists' critique of scientific racism.

Scientific racism challenged the democratic agrarianism that had informed environmental thought since the eighteenth century. Drawing on Darwinian evolutionary biology, scientific racists created a highly deterministic account of the relationship between nature and human culture: like the "folk" concept, scientific racism granted to each race a cultural uniqueness derived from its relationship to its natural environment. But it also ordered those cultures hierarchically (with whites on top) and denied that blacks could improve their standing in the scale of civilization. On the contrary, scientific racists argued that black Americans had no capacity for cultural creativity at all and therefore lacked the ability to forge a meaningful connection to the American landscape. Under their view, blacks were incapable of the autonomy and creativity that black agrarians thought essential to a proper relationship to nature.

Black theorists, happily, were able to respond to this challenge. Drawing on the work of anthropologist Franz Boas, theorists such as Du Bois and Alain Locke attacked scientific racism by offering an account of race formation that emphasized history over natural environment. Their historico-cultural understanding of race, like black agrarianism, affirmed the importance of individual agency and creativity in cultural development. But it also raised troubling questions about how nature is related to culture and how their culture relates "black folk" to the natural world.

THE RISE OF RACE

Even as white Americans were discovering the "black folk," the economic and social forces driving southern blacks from the land were intensifying. From 1890 to 1920, southern farmers continued to suffer the environmental and economic problems experienced during the late nineteenth century. Despite improving prices for cotton and other commodities—a trend that brought technological change and unparalleled prosperity to other American farmers—southern agriculture remained highly labor-intensive and troubled by unstable markets, rising rates of tenancy, poverty, and lack of education. True, this era did finally witness some movement toward agricultural reform, largely due to the spread of the boll weevil in the late 1890s. Cotton's vulnerability to the pest forced southern farmers, finally, into some of the practices promoted by the United States Department of Agriculture Extension Service, including crop diversification. The agency's efforts to combat the weevil helped it to become an agent of change in the South, promoting mechanization and the use of chemical fertilizers and pesticides. But only the more educated, aggressive, and prosperous farmers were able to adopt the capital-intensive methods advocated by scientific agriculture reformers. The small-scale farmers remained locked, by poverty and debt, into their traditional farming methods.[3]

If the situation of southern farmers in general was difficult, the situation of southern blacks was growing desperate. Not only did they suffer from periodic crises in the agricultural economy, they also experienced a dramatic decline in their social and political status and an increase in interracial violence. Never before had white supremacy had such a pervasive influence on public policy, scientific opinion, and mass culture. Southern politicians such as Ben Tillman and James K. Vardaman offered the most lurid examples of racist rhetoric, promoting fears of "amalgamation" and "negro domination" among southern voters. But the ideology gained legitimacy even among progressive elites, due in part to developments in evolutionary biology that purported to give a scientific basis to racial hierarchy. The new science of race, claimed white supremacists, demonstrated that blacks' cultural capacity is limited by their biology and that racial antipathy is natural and ineradicable. Of course, not all those who believed in the biological concept of race endorsed white supremacy; as will be discussed, some black theorists were willing to accept the premises of scientific racism but not its conclusions. Nor did white supremacists need evolutionary biology to support an ideology that already had a central place in American political culture. Nevertheless, the theory helped to put the stamp of scientific authority on racial hierarchy and was therefore an important part of the intellectual terrain for black theorists.[4]

For most blacks, however, white supremacy was less a theory than a collection of practices aimed at excluding them from public life. The defeat of the Populists in 1896 put an end to efforts to create a biracial politics in the South, and during the 1890s the triumphant Democrats spearheaded efforts to exclude blacks from electoral politics through legal disenfranchisement. Lynching of blacks increased during this period as well, tolerated and even actively promoted by the more radical white politicians.[5] As race relations deteriorated, race riots grew more frequent and bloody. And the 1890s also witnessed the spread of legal segregation—a wave of laws formally establishing segregation in public accommodations and reinforcing the informal patterns of segregation that had developed in the South (and persisted in northern cities) after Emancipation.[6]

Segregation's effect on blacks' relationship to nature, although undoubtedly significant, remains largely unexplored. Historian Joel Williamson points out that black schools, churches, and neighborhoods first arose in the South during Reconstruction, either by choice or by default. Segregation in other arenas of public life developed more slowly. Most southern blacks lived in the countryside and had neither the opportunity nor the means to use hotels, restaurants, trains, and other public accommodations, so the question of segregating them seldom arose during the early years of freedom. As for the countryside, Williamson contends that rural landscapes and living patterns were difficult to segregate because they were difficult to control.[7] Nevertheless, as discussed in Chapter 1, even before the Civil War efforts to control black labor had charged the rural landscape with racial meaning, and those meanings probably persisted after Emancipation—

although they may have been transformed by the breakup of the plantation system. The rise in racial terrorism during this period may also have influenced the meaning of the landscape to blacks. For example, it may be a legacy of this post-Emancipation period that trees in black American culture are typically associated not with liberty (as they are in white American culture) but with lynching and vulnerability to white violence.[8]

The meaning of urban landscapes was similarly complex. Cities were already highly managed and therefore more amenable to racial regulation than the countryside, and segregation in public accommodations reached its highest form in such urban settings. Thus one impact of segregation, often noted by blacks (if not by white environmentalists), was to deny or at least make difficult blacks' access to urban parks. More subtly, however, this racial apartheid connected the social control of blacks more tightly to control of the landscape, which in turn connected the meaning of the landscape to racial identity. To be black was, in part, to be confined to a particular space, a black world created through and as a means of racial oppression. As Du Bois explained in *Darkwater*, blacks could not find relief from social injustice by escaping to the local Walden Pond or Bar Harbour. Trying to do so only made racial oppression more salient by subjecting them to the indignities of Jim Crow.[9] Such experiences of escaping to "pristine" nature were largely reserved for whites, who could afford to forget (or simply couldn't see) the complex social system that made it available to them.

Blacks could, however, escape the poverty and oppression in the South by heading north. Southern blacks had been trickling into northern cities for decades, but during the second decade of the twentieth century black northern migration increased significantly. They were responding in part to the social and political conditions in the South, but also to new economic opportunities in the North; the United States' entry into World War I created a demand for industrial workers, just as conditions in Europe reduced the stream of immigrants from that source. As a result, between 1915 and 1930, about one-tenth of the black population (90 percent of which lived in the South in 1910) shifted to the North.[10] Numbers alone can't capture the psychic impact of the Great Migration, however. For white southerners, it dramatized their dependence on black labor and even led to some self-criticism and efforts to improve race relations. For blacks, in contrast, the migration was another step on the road to freedom. The journey north had long been associated with escape from oppression in black culture, and for the early twentieth-century migrants, the North was still the "promised land."[11]

But the migration north was also a migration to cities; it was part of the larger pattern of urbanization that transformed rural America in the early twentieth century. Thus an important result of the migration was the growth of black urban communities. Between 1910 and 1920, the black population in Chicago increased from 65,355 to 109,458, and New York, Philadelphia, Detroit, and Cleveland showed similar dramatic increases. Overall, the proportion of blacks living in cities (North and South) increased from about 27 percent in 1910 to 43 percent in 1930.[12] Black elite culture was already largely the product of urban blacks, but mass black urbanization made cities—and the transition from agrarian to urban life—a central subject of black thought and literature. During this era, black writers began to explore their relationship to the land in terms of their relationship to an agrarian *past*. Blacks' relationship to the land would therefore become involved in their relationship to their history; a key question for twentieth-century black writers would be how an industrial, urban black community could maintain a connection to a land they left behind—a land that both shaped and scarred them.

White Americans, also leaving the land in ever-larger numbers, were facing a similar question. Concerns about white urbanization and industrialization were often expressed (most famously by Brooks Adams) as anxiety about the loss of Anglo-Saxon cultural "vitality"—a pervasive theme in late Victorian American culture. The early twentieth-century rural reform and wilderness preservation movements were both promoted as efforts to retain (white) Americans' connection to nature's "vital power" in an increasingly urban, industrial world. For blacks, the meaning of urbanization was more complex, because the transition to the city represented not only a search for better economic opportunity but political freedom and possibly even integration into American society. At the same time, however, they experienced a similar sense of loss and longing for the southern agrarian life—a longing complicated but not diminished by the suffering that life had inflicted. In short, both blacks and whites were struggling to understand the significance of urbanization and industrialization for their relationship to nature. And ideas about race would figure prominently in the efforts of both groups.

Race was in fact growing in importance not only in blacks' social experience but as an analytic category in black thought. Racism, of course, was not a new theme; color prejudice was an important issue in black politics even before Emancipation and became even more central in the twentieth century. In the midst of segregation and a political climate suffused with white supremacist ideology (and the conciliatory rhetoric of Booker T. Washington), Du Bois and his allies organized the Niagara Movement, calling on radical black leaders to protest more forcefully the abridgment of civil rights and inequality of economic opportunity that resulted from racial discrimination. Although the movement itself lasted only a few years, it led to the establishment of black journals—the *Moon*, the *Horizon*, and finally the more successful *Crisis*—and inspired the formation of the National Association for the Advancement of Colored People (NAACP) in 1910.[13]

But race itself—not just discrimination but race consciousness and solidarity as a driving force in history—was also becoming a more important category in black thought. The 1890s witnessed among black elites an increased interest in African ethnology and African survivals in black culture; encouraging this interest, Alexander Crummell founded the American Negro Academy in 1897 to promote the creation of an Afro-American civilization.[14] The rise of scientific racism further reinforced blacks' race consciousness, as did U.S. adventures in imperialism, which, beginning with the annexation of Hawaii and the Spanish-American War over Cuba in 1898, contributed to the acceptance of white supremacy among American political elites; they justified white rule as a means to bring the benefits of democracy to the less-advanced races.[15] But such policies also prompted black theorists to consider black Americans' relationship to other colored peoples.[16] Du Bois, for example, became a spokesman for the Pan-African movement; by 1920, he was arguing that the improvement of black Americans' condition required efforts to improve the condition of persons of African descent around the world. In this (if in little else) he agreed with Marcus Garvey, the Jamaican immigrant who founded the Universal Negro Improvement Association and led the popular Pan-African movement from 1918 to 1925. Garvey's message of racial solidarity and separatism reached thousands in the United States, Latin America, the Caribbean, and Africa. His and Du Bois's stature in the black community are measures of the expansion of racial consciousness among blacks during this period.[17]

In sum, black political thought during the early twentieth century began to focus on blacks' relationship to an agrarian past and on race as a central force in social life. As we will see, these two issues were intertwined; black Americans' relationship to the land was inextricably bound up in their racial identity. They were not unique in this respect, however. White Americans, too, had to reexamine their relationship to nature in light of scientific racists' central claim: that human culture is the expression of a biological heritage shaped by the race's aboriginal natural environment.

RACE AS AN ENVIRONMENTAL THEORY

Early twentieth-century race theory was part of a centuries-old debate in western thought: one side claims that natural environment determines the shape of human culture, while the other argues that culture is influenced less by nature than by social institutions, history, and individual creativity.[18] Scientific race theorists emerged by the end of the nineteenth century as proponents of a distinctive version of environmental determinism.

The idea that human races evolved as a result of centuries of interaction with a specific natural environment was not new. By the eighteenth century, the belief that the physical environment determines the habits, dispositions, and the physical characteristics of national groups was commonplace.[19] It was elaborated in particular by the German Idealists, whose understanding of race would shape black thought in important respects. Johann von Herder's account of the origin of national differences, for example, rejects the idea that humans are divided into permanent races but argues that the physical environment shapes culture and character and affects (to a degree) the "living organic power" that forms organisms. For G. W. F. Hegel, a race was defined by its spirit, its *volkgeist*, which is in turn the product of its natural environment.[20] Many German theorists, however, recognized the complex historical process of national development and argued that the cultural groups arising from these environmental factors are fluid and dynamic. Thus the Hegelian Heinrich von Treitschke—whose lectures would influence W. E. B. Du Bois—argued that it was nations, which are constantly mingling and changing, rather than the relatively stable biological races that drive history.[21] This idealist tradition, with its focus on culture and history rather than biology, would inform not only Du Bois's thought but the critique of scientific racism developed by Franz Boas.

American race theory developed in a different direction. In the early nineteenth century, a group of American ethnologists, the polygenists, proposed that human races were not the product of environmental influences but were divinely created as separate (and permanently distinct) species. Polygenism enjoyed a brief popularity in the United States but rapidly lost adherents as biologists refined their understanding of the evolution of species. By the late nineteenth century, race science had incorporated the new evolutionary biology, which returned environmental factors to their central place in explaining human physical variation.[22] Nevertheless, polygenism left its stamp on American race theory by focusing inquiry on the biological rather than the cultural process of racial development.

There were many versions of turn-of-the-century scientific racism, and a full appreciation of them would require more careful attention to their qualifications, nuances, and debates than I will offer here. However, the various theories (as elaborated by Nathaniel Shaler, Frederick Hoffman, Joseph Le Conte, Henry Fairfield Osborn, William McDougall, Madison Grant, and Lothrop Stoddard, for example) were similar enough to constitute a school of thought whose contours we can describe in general terms. The foundations of this biological, evolutionary account of race were laid by the eighteenth-century anthropologist Johann Blumenbach. He postulated that organisms develop by virtue of a "formative force" (*nisus formativus*) that gives determinate form to matter. However, this force reacts to external stimuli, which can over many generations lead to its "degeneration." This degeneration accounts for the variety we see in members of the same species, such as the human races. Lamarck's 1809 work on the origin of species, *Zoological Philosophy*, similarly argues that an organism's response to the external environment could lead to physiological changes that could be inherited; some "power in nature," Lamarck suggested, preserves in new individuals all the changes in organization acquired by their ancestors as the result of their life and environment.[23] This school of race theory thus proposed that human races are the product of an internal vital force reacting to the external natural environment.

Charles Darwin's theory of natural selection offered a more elegant way to explain the origin of human races, eventually allowing biologists to dispense with Lamarck's hypothesis that traits produced by an organism's reaction to the environment could be inherited. In the 1880s, August Weismann challenged Lamarck by proposing that "germ plasm" alone is inherited—and that germ plasm is not directly affected by or responsive to external stimuli. According to Weismann, germ plasm (genes, rather than a responsive formative force) determine the physical characteristics on which natural selection operates, thus resulting over many generations in the adaptation of organisms to their natural environment.[24] As we know, the scientific community eventually lined up behind Weismann—but that was a twentieth-century development, and it never entirely eliminated the influence of Lamarck and

Blumenbach on American scientific racism. Even those race theorists who accepted Darwinian natural selection would nevertheless persist in describing the process of race formation as a dynamic interaction between an internal vital power and the external environment.

Specifically, American scientific racists in the late nineteenth and early twentieth centuries argued that environmental factors determine climate, diet, and mode of life, which in turn shape groups of humans biologically. Whether they endorsed Darwinian natural selection or Lamarckian adaptation, they agreed with Madison Grant: "The laws which govern the distribution of the various races of man and their evolution through selection are substantially the same as those controlling the evolution and distribution of the larger mammals." Although man now has more control over his physical environment than other organisms do, thus diminishing the force of natural selection, "nevertheless, the various races of Europe have each a certain natural habitat in which it achieves its highest development."[25] The natural environment does not only create physical differences between races, however. Scientific racists argued that mental processes are also directly determined by racially differentiated biological processes—in other words, the mind is the product of the brain, and brain structure varies (quite a lot) by race. Darwin himself proposed that mental faculties, being rooted in biology, are heritable. This accounts for cultural differences between races—and (according to Darwin) the superior intelligence, moral disposition, and even aesthetic sense of "civilized" races.[26]

This claim that the mind is determined by biology was among the most controversial aspects of race theory in the late nineteenth century, and its troubling philosophical implications would be of particular concern to black theorists.[27] It challenged the view, most famously associated with Des Cartes, that the mind could be understood as a causal agent distinct from the body but nevertheless influencing its behavior. The "materialists" proposed instead that the mind should be understood as a bundle of nervous reflexes or chemical reactions, operating mechanically. Under this view (which William James would call the "conscious automaton" theory of mind), external forces stimulate brain cells, which react in a predictable fashion, leading to behavior. Consciousness merely experiences these operations; it doesn't direct or cause them. James himself criticized this model, arguing that mental activity may be caused but it also *causes* behavior. Moreover, he suggested that only *some* operations of the mind have survival value and can therefore be explained as the product of natural selection. In particular, he attacked the evolutionists by pointing out that logical, aesthetic, and moral ideas often have no obvious relationship to the survival of the species.[28] As we will see, this insistence that not all mental activity can be explained by evolutionary imperatives was shared by Boas and by the black theorists he influenced.[29]

But the racists were nevertheless drawn to the power of the materialist model to account for cultural differences among national groups. As William McDougall explained, the physical environment affects the mental qualities of a people not only by directly influencing the mind and occupations of each generation, but also by molding the mental constitution through natural selection.[30] Assuming that human races all descended from "one original stock," the causes of their divergence are "differences of physical environment" and "spontaneous variations in different directions of the innate mental qualities of individuals, especially of the more gifted and energetic individual of each peoples." Those mental qualities that help individuals in their "struggle for existence with the physical environment" are transmitted to the next generation. However, any innovations created by these gifted individuals are also made available to the rest of their community, who will adopt them through imitation—thus raising the whole group on the scale of civilization.[31]

Race theory thus offered a powerful way to explain the relationship between nature and human culture. It was troubled by a number of difficulties, however, including lack of consensus on how to define a race or the historical processes producing the current distribution of races, lack of reliable data to support its claims, and some persistent theoretical inconsistencies. In particular, the evolutionary biology on which the racists relied assumed a mechanistic model of nature—the view that nature is best understood as a machine and can be wholly comprehended through rational analysis of its component parts.[32] But as suggested above, race theorists also persisted in using vitalistic language. Vitalism was the chief alternative to mechanistic models of nature during the nineteenth century, and it was particularly favored by Romantic philosophers. Vitalists such as Johann Wolfgang von Goethe argued that mechanistic theories of nature fail to explain either the phenomenon of life itself—the movement and growth of animate beings—or the orderliness of nature. Vitalists postulated a force, variously called a "plastic principle," "vital principle," or "anima mundi" (spirit of the world), that imposes form on and animates living organisms (including humans) and also directs inanimate moving objects such as planets.[33] Nature in this view is not merely an order one can observe but a force working actively on human beings, giving form to their growth and development. Blumenbach's *nisus formativus* can be read as one version of the vital force, as can Lamarck's "power in nature."

Several nineteenth-century developments in biology and neurology—including Weismann's genetic theory—made it possible to explain biological evolution without relying on this mysterious vital force. For race theorists, however, internal vital power would remain critical to explaining racial development. Le Conte referred to "resident forces" driving the development of races—although he attempted to distance himself from vitalists by insisting that such forces were a form of electrical or chemical energy.[34] William McDougall also emphasized the innate tendencies of the more "gifted and energetic" members of race as an important force driving racial development, and Madison Grant wrote of the Aryan race's "vigor" or "energy," its "inherent capacity for development and growth."[35] Many racists in fact clung to Lamarckianism precisely because it made the vital force central to racial development: it suggested that those races that respond to their environment with vigor (that is, that have more of this vital force) will be rewarded by seeing the traits acquired by such efforts passed on to their offspring.[36]

The persistence of this vitalist language in race theory was not simply due to confusion or carelessness. Rather, vitalism seems to be inseparable from nineteenth-century discourse about culture. Even though most natural scientists were moving away from vitalism by the late nineteenth century, it continued to inform social theory well into the twentieth century—particularly theories of cultural development and artistic creativity. Romantic philosophers posited that the vital force of nature accounted not only for biological development but for the creative power of the human mind; the vital force is what gives a race the energy to create great art as well as nations and empires. This theory may have conflicted with the racists' materialist model of the mind, but it was widely influential and became central to the concept of race. As historian Ivan Hannaford explains, race theorists understood race not just as a biological category but as a *folk*, a group sharing a dynamic, creative spirit, derived from nature, that drives their cultural development.[37] Under this view, races that have more of this vital energy—that are in this sense "closer to nature"—are more creative and powerful.

But Madison Grant was no William Wordsworth. For the racists, gaining access to nature's creative power wasn't a matter of communing with nature's beauty. Rather, they argued that dominating a harsh natural environment (and other races) during a race's early history made a race vital. The American geologist Nathaniel Shaler elaborated this point in his discussion of the "cradle lands." Humans, he argued, evolved originally in one place, but then spread out into environmentally diverse niches. As they adapted to these "cradle lands" over the course of many centuries, they developed into distinctive races.[38] For Shaler (as for virtually all the scientific racists), the environmental conditions of northern Europe made it the cradle of "strong peoples" because its climate was harsh enough to require vigor and industry but not so harsh as to discourage effort. In contrast, warm climates such as Africa would not produce great peoples because (according to the standard nineteenth-century view) tropical climates are easy to live in. Thus the races cradled in these lands never developed civilization; in fact, they barely have the capacity for culture at all.[39]

Harsh conditions, then, were favorable to racial development; natural beauty was not. In fact, it might have negative effects. French writer Émile Boutmy, for example, contended that the beauty of the landscape could adversely affect a race's intellect. The English, he argued, are given to introspection and analysis because their bleak landscape affords them little sensual pleasure; they are forced to turn inward and detach their thoughts from the material world around them.[40] Similarly, the influential English historian Henry Thomas Buckle argued that that peoples living in severe environments—among high mountains, great rivers, or endless deserts—are stimulated by the scenery so that they become more imaginative and less analytical, and are also rendered passive by the sheer enormity of the natural forces they face (thus neatly accounting for the widely recognized artistic and spiritual achievements of Indians and other Asians without threatening Aryan superiority).[41] Although Buckle did not consider these differences to be rooted in biology, William McDougall drew on the new evolutionary biology to argue that at least some such environmentally determined mental differences could become hereditary.[42] He reasoned,

> The physical environment stimulates the imagination, and it represses the tendency to control imagination and superstition by reason and calm inquiry after causes; acting thus upon successive generations of men, it determines the peculiarities of the religious systems and of the art and literature of the people. Individuals in whom the same tendencies are innately strong will then flourish under such a system. . . . Thus the social environment, working through long ages, may have constantly determined a certain degree of selection of the innate tendencies congenial to it.[43]

Thus races favored by austere, bleak, unremarkable landscapes develop civilizations characterized by a high degree of rationality and energy.

What did this theory imply for racial development on the American continent? Perhaps very little. While the racists gave primacy to natural environment in the formation of races, they discounted the *continuing* influence of environment on contemporary cultures. Indeed, most American racists asserted that the racial characteristics developed during the millennia preceding the advent of civilization were relatively stable. Some argued that the "lower" races had actually hit an evolutionary dead end—that they lacked the capacity for further evolution despite environmental pressures.[44] For example, Shaler argued that Africans lacked literature, religion, and social polity, demonstrating "that the folk for all their ethnic variety had, in their African life, come to a state of arrest in their development." Madison Grant called blacks a "stationary species" that "do not posses the potentiality of progress or initiative from within."[45] Under this view, the lower races either never developed or had lost (through disuse) the vital power to develop the higher faculties necessary for civilization. Others, like Josiah Nott, were willing to concede that all races had the capacity to evolve but argued that such evolution takes not decades or centuries but millennia. Thus the races as we know them are relatively stable; we shouldn't expect to see any changes as they move to different environments because significant evolution would take thousands of years.[46] In fact, some scientific racists contended that even for the Caucasian race, natural selection was no longer operative. Le Conte, McDougall, and Grant reasoned that environmental factors, such as competition for food, don't influence human reproductive choices once a race has developed a complex civilization. For the civilized (that is, the white) race, social selection—the selection of persons with socially desirable traits—replaces natural selection.

That the natural environment was no longer actively forming races, however, did not mean that the white race's relationship to nature was no longer a matter of concern. Race theorists tended to conceptualize a race's vitality as a reservoir formed during the early period of racial development. But reservoirs can be depleted. Thus, while Joseph Le Conte might celebrate civilization as the triumph of human reason over nature, others worried that the creative power of the civilized races—an inheritance from their primitive origins—could dissipate as the race mastered nature and no longer faced the harsh conditions that created it. Granted, American white supremacists tended to focus more on amalgamation as the primary threat to the race.

Nevertheless, they also expressed concern over the impact of urbanization and industrialization on the white race—a concern that led many to support wilderness preservation. Urbanization and industrialization, according to Madison Grant, was adversely affecting the Nordic race. "Heavy, healthful work in the fields of northern Europe enables the Nordic type to thrive," he claimed, "but the cramped factory and crowded city quickly weed him out." Mediterraneans, he argued, thrive in ghetto conditions. So the increase in urban conditions favored Mediterraneans in the struggle for survival—leading to the "fading of the Nordic type."[47] Preserving rural and wild places would give Nordic types the environment they needed to flourish, thus giving them a competitive advantage over the other races flooding into the United States. Historian Stephen Fox notes that such concerns were shared by many American conservationists, including George Bird Grinnell, Abbott Thayer, George Dorr, Theodore Palmer, and Henry Fairfield Osborn.[48] President Theodore Roosevelt, a conservationist, was almost obsessively concerned with maintaining the vigor of the American race and suggested that hunting and fishing in the wilderness could prepare American boys for the "strenuous life" of racial domination and imperialism.[49] Even Robert Marshall, whose liberal credentials are impeccable, used the language of racial development to justify wilderness preservation, citing the "soundness, stamina and élan" as well as the independence and competence that come from escaping the "artificial edifice raised by man" into the wilderness.[50]

If the white race's fortunes on the American continent depended on preserving the American wilderness, the black race's future in America was less clear. There was considerable speculation after Emancipation and again in the 1890s that the black race, deprived of the "protection" of slavery, would simply die out, a victim of its natural inferiority to the white race and its maladaption to the American environment.[51] In contrast, a long tradition of proslavery thought held that blacks, being a tropical race, were well suited to the hot, humid South. Joseph Tillinghast, for example, speculated that "the northern states of our Union present so great a contrast for people of tropical origin, that it is possible they may never thrive there. But we have no reason to suppose that the transfer to our southern states had, so far as climatic influence is concerned, other than beneficial effects on the health of the negro." He suggested that the climate in the American South, more temperate than that of West Africa, encouraged more vigorous activity, and "the variety of season, with its successive changes of natural background and associated activities . . . must have exerted a mild and helpful stimulus, particularly to the psychic life."[52] Tillinghast even implied that such improvements might be inherited—in other words, that the natural environment was still shaping American blacks, encouraging their further evolution and biological adaptation to the American continent. Such optimism about blacks' capacity for evolution was the minority view among scientific racists,[53] but they did usually agree that blacks were biologically adapted to subtropical climates. In fact, nineteenth-century white supremacists worried that blacks' superior fitness might lead to a race war erupting over control of the South.

That concern was less salient by the second decade of the twentieth century, however.[54] Madison Grant and Lothrop Stoddard argued that the black race was simply too inferior to seriously threaten white civilization, and Grant insisted that even in the South blacks required the direction and protection of whites to flourish.[55] Whether they flourished or not, however, most scientific racists insisted that blacks' success on the American continent had nothing to do with their own efforts and shouldn't be taken as evidence of their capacity to develop further. Under their reasoning, blacks were and would remain essentially African; the immediate natural environment, social environment, and history (including the history of slavery and oppression) had little influence on blacks' culture and capacity compared to the overwhelmingly determinative force of their biological heritage. Scientific racism thus challenged the theoretical framework created by black agrarians, in which the relationship between a people and the land centered on the individual agent's creative response to the natural world—a response that should, under ideal conditions, result in a morally, aesthetically, spiritually, and materially rich culture. According to the scientific racists, the black race has virtually no capacity for such independent, creative agency. Therefore, giving them control over their own labor would make little difference to their relationship to the American landscape or the natural world in general. Behavior, mentality, and spiritual traits are already determined by racial biology.

BACK TO AFRICA?

Scientific racism provided black theorists with a powerful new language with which to talk about their relationship to nature, and many of them embraced it. To be sure, most of them rejected the claim that blacks were biologically inferior to whites and lacked the inherent capacity to create a culture. Moreover, they tended to favor the romantic racialism of German Idealists, which emphasized the value of cultural diversity rather than the inevitability of race conflict. These differences made their approach to race more compatible with black agrarianism; rather than displacing the older tradition, black race theory merely gave a different inflection to discourse about man's relationship to nature and blacks' connection to (and alienation from) the land. Ultimately, however, the strong environmental determinism inherent in the biological concept of race was too limiting for the more progressive black theorists.

Not surprisingly, race theory found its strongest proponents among nineteenth-century emigrationists and early twentieth-century black nationalists, who used it to explain Africa's role in world civilization and black Americans' relationship to Africa. Alexander Crummell, for example, proclaimed in an 1877 speech the "destined superiority of the Negro," predicting that they would be responsible for the next great advance in the progress of mankind. He argued that the black race was distinguished by its "vitality, plasticity, receptivity, imitation, family feeling, veracity, and the sentiment of devotion"—all characteristics of a "strong race" destined for greatness.[56] Edward Blyden agreed; in an 1890 speech he explained race as "the outcome not only of climate, but of generations subjected to environments which have formed the mental and moral constitution." Citing the example of diversity in nature, he argued that each race was "the unfolding of a new bud, an evolution; the development of a new side of God's character and a new phase of humanity. . . . As in every form of the inorganic universe we see some noble variation of God's thought and beauty, so in each separate man, in each separate race, something of the absolute is incarnated." Thus the development of world civilization required the development of each race.[57]

And according to the black colonizationists, development of the black race required the development of Africa. Thus while white supremacists urged preservation of the American wilderness as a means to regenerate the white race, colonizationists encouraged blacks to "regenerate" the African wilderness by bringing to it the benefits of western civilization. Martin Delany, for example, described central Africa as a tropical jungle: undeveloped, unpossessed, and inhabited by savages. His plan for cultivating this jungle, he declared, was "the first voluntary step that has ever been taken for her regeneration."[58] Blyden, too, compared Liberia favorably to two iconic American wildernesses—the Rocky Mountains and Yosemite Valley—but urged black Americans to transform this wild landscape to "a garden of the Lord" by bringing it under cultivation.[59] Indeed, Africa needed not only physical but moral transformation. The wildness of the landscape, they argued, was evidence of moral corruption; enlightened, civilized people would cultivate the land. Regenerating the land thus involves enlightening the "benighted heathens" as much as transforming the landscape.

To be sure, after the turn of the century black elites would question this view of Africa as spiritually degraded and in need of regeneration. Du Bois, for example, had a more favorable view of traditional African culture, and he argued that the moral corruption that Crummell condemned was the result of white imperialism and the slave trade.[60] In fact, as the next chapter will discuss, some black theorists by the 1920s would be looking to the heathen cultures of Africa to regenerate American civilization. Regardless of which way the regenerating energy flowed, however, according to black race theorists it traveled by means of black Americans' racial tie to Africa.

Black Americans' tie to America, in comparison, was the focus of considerable debate. Edward Blyden, for example, argued that black racial development could not occur in the United States, where blacks are under Anglo-Saxon domination. "[The black man] can serve *man* here. He can furnish the labor of the country, but to the inspiration of the country he must ever be an alien." Sounding a familiar theme, he argued that slavery had impaired blacks' agency and thus prevented the black race from expressing its distinctive spirit through free action. "It is by God in us," he declared, "where we have freedom to act out ourselves, that we do each our several work and live out into action, through our work, whatever we have within us of noble and wise and true." Slavery had prevented the race from expressing its aspect of the divine through its own free labor. Moreover, the persistence of racial prejudice made it unlikely that blacks would ever enjoy the freedom to express their racial identity in the United States.[61]

Some twentieth-century black nationalists agreed with Blyden. Marcus Garvey, for example, also insisted that racism made it impossible for blacks to flourish in the United States; only strong African states, he argued, would provide the political and social environment in which black culture could develop.[62] Importantly, however, neither Blyden nor Garvey rested their argument on the claim that blacks aren't biologically adapted to the American environment. Rather, it is racial oppression and prejudice that prevents blacks from adapting culturally to the United States. To be sure, Garvey did contend that race conflict is inevitable when two ambitious races occupy the same territory and compete for the same resources; in this he echoed

Lothrop Stoddard and other white supremacists. Garvey believed that such conflict could be avoided by separating the races geographically; Africa in his view was the logical place to create a black civilization because it was already a largely black continent.[63] But nothing in his reasoning suggests that blacks couldn't thrive on the American continent if only it were cleared of white people.

In fact, Garvey was much less concerned than the white supremacists with whether the race "fit" the natural environment. Skeptical of the scientific racists' environmental determinism, he emphasized instead the importance of developing the capacity for free thought and independent agency—which required not the right natural environment but the right social and political environment. This emphasis is consistent with the general tendency in black thought to focus on the conditions promoting creative, independent agency; Garvey echoed a familiar theme when he proclaimed that "God and Nature first made us what we are, and then out of our own *creative genius* we make ourselves what we want to be."[64] Nature, for the black nationalists, was not necessarily destiny. Despite their pessimism about the prospects of blacks in America, neither Blyden nor Garvey denied that blacks had the capacity to create a vital culture on American soil or argued that alienation is the inevitable result of removing a race from its aboriginal environment. Blyden's view even implies that under the right social conditions, different races might thrive together in the same environment.

W. E. B. Du Bois developed that cultural pluralist vision, arguing that blacks could develop as a race on the American continent. Du Bois's concept of race, as we will see, evolved significantly over the course of his career, but his early writings strongly echo Alexander Crummell and Edward Blyden. Exposed to the scientific racism of Nathaniel Shaler at Harvard University, he also encountered the romantic racialism of the German Idealists such as von Trietschke at the University of Berlin.[65] These influences are apparent in his famous 1897 essay, "The Conservation of Races." He put this understanding of race to quite different uses than did Shaler and von Trietschke, however. For Du Bois, the language of race suggested a new ground on which black Americans could establish a secure sense of self; race, rather than agricultural labor, could be the core of civic personality.

Du Bois began by acknowledging that we typically divide humans into races according to physical differences but pointed out that these differences do not explain all the differences in their histories, and that physically, humans are more alike than different.[66] But he then suggested that there are differences . . . which have silently but definitely separated men into groups. While these subtle forces have generally followed the natural cleavage of common blood, descent and physical peculiarities, they have at other times swept across and ignored these. At all times, however, they have divided human beings into races, which, while they perhaps transcend scientific definition, nevertheless, are clearly defined to the eye of the historian and sociologist.[67]

Each race, he argued, is characterized by certain "ideals of life" for which they struggle. Thus the English nation stands for constitutional liberty and commercial freedom, the German nation for science and philosophy, and so on. Like Blyden, Du Bois asserted that the African race has its own ideal of life to deliver, an ideal that would grow out of its artistic creativity. Negroes "are that people whose subtle sense of song has given America its only music, its only American fairy tales, its only touch of pathos and humor amid its mad money-getting plutocracy."[68] This is the claim supporting Du Bois's conception of blacks as a "folk." It challenges the white supremacists' view that the "vigor" of the Nordic race gives it superior creative capacity, but it follows Buckle and McDougall in attributing greater imaginative power to tropical races. It implies that Africans' imaginative capacity gives them better access to the creative, vital force of nature—a claim supported by artistic primitivism and related intellectual currents, which we will explore in the next chapter.

Du Bois's understanding of black Americans as members of a young, vital race on the verge of world-historical importance had tremendous rhetorical power; it turned the arguments of the racists against them, making a virtue of blacks' alleged racial difference and underdevelopment. But Du Bois went further, insisting that black Americans had an important contribution to make not just to world civilization but to *American* culture. Under his reasoning, black Americans' African identity is precisely what gives them a strong claim to full participation in American society. It is both possible and desirable, he claimed, for blacks to develop their own racial ideals in the United States: if "there is substantial agreement in laws, language and religion; if there is a satisfactory adjustment of economic life, then there is no reason why, in the same country and on the same street, two or three great national ideals might not thrive and develop."[69]

But Du Bois himself recognized that developing black racial ideals in America would be difficult. For example, in his essays on black homemaking (discussed in Chapter 3), Du Bois argued that racial oppression had destroyed black homes and prevented blacks from expressing their racial ideals by modifying their physical environments. These writings seem to support Blyden's position that racial oppression alienated blacks from the land; specifically, Du Bois's reasoning suggests that the constraints of such oppression prevented blacks from expressing their African racial spirit through manipulation of the natural world.[70] Of course, there are natural constraints on such expression as well; it wouldn't be easy to recreate a tropical landscape in Ohio. But that probably wasn't what Du Bois had in mind. He apparently believed that the African spirit would take a different form in the United States, as African aesthetics were applied to a different material world. The landscape needn't be African, merely *Africanized.* The more it reflected African "ideals of life," the more black Americans would feel a connection and sense of belonging to the land. Under this view, racial oppression alienated black Americans from the land by preventing them from bringing an African worldview to bear on the American landscape.

This emphasis on alienation is not the only theme in Du Bois's writings, however. There is in "The Conservation of Races" and *Souls of Black Folk* a suggestion that blacks *had* found ways to express their racial spirit—that slavery had not in fact prevented them from developing at least a rich body of music and folk tales. Of course, it may be that slavery interfered with only some forms of expression, diverting rather than suppressing blacks' creative energy. Still, Du Bois's celebration of black folk culture doesn't seem entirely consistent with his argument that slavery's impact was wholly destructive. This problem is of course another expression of the question first posed by the black agrarians: Did slavery alienate blacks from the land, or were they able to forge a connection to the natural world despite (or even *because of*) the restrictions and cruelties they suffered? Or (from a more strategic perspective), how can slave culture serve as both a standing indictment of racial oppression and a source of racial pride?

One promising approach to this problem appears in Kelly Miller's 1908 work, *Race Adjustment.* Miller shared considerable ideological common ground with Du Bois, and his treatment of blacks' relationship to the American landscape reflects the influence of both scientific and romantic racialism. Blacks, he argued, were not alienated from the land. On the contrary, he insisted that the black man was biologically suited to the South; in fact, because "the climatic conditions of the North are not congenial to his tropical nature," he is destined to remain in the South—and even to push out the whites. "Like flora and fauna, that race variety will ultimately survive . . . that is best adapted to its environment."[71] Miller further insisted that black southerners enjoyed an emotional bond to the land and were able to express their racial ideals. He cited the black spirituals as evidence; this music, he argued, "is the spontaneous expression of the race soul" in a new and depressing environment. "Its racial quality is stamped on every note," but "these songs are not African, but American." The "scene, circumstances and aspirations" reflected in the spirituals "are not adapted to some distant continent, but to their new environment in a land, not of their sojourn, but of their abiding place."[72]

According to Miller, then, blacks did enjoy enough independence and freedom to develop a vital folk culture in the South. This is not to suggest that racial oppression was irrelevant to cultural capacity, however. It did not prevent the emergence of a folk culture, but it was preventing the emergence of a highly developed artistic and intellectual tradition. Such traditions, Miller argued, are the products of genius. Every race has the capacity for genius, but "capacity is potential rather than a dynamic mode of energy. Whatever native capacity the mind may possess, it must be stimulated and reinforced by social accomplishment before it can show great achievement." Great achievements depend on "environment and social stimulus"—an environment and stimulus not available to blacks in a racist society.[73]

Miller's argument thus explained both blacks' organic bond to the land—a product of their biological fitness for warm climates and their creative capacity—and the harmful impacts of racism on their further development. This theory demonstrates the versatility of the language of race: even granting that racial characteristics are determined by the race's aboriginal environment and relatively stable, Miller could still describe blacks as creative agents in their relationship with the natural world, and even capture some of the complexity of blacks' relationship to Africa and America. Nevertheless, Miller's reasoning was ultimately unsatisfying to progressive theorists like Du Bois. Miller's cultural history seems plausible, but his claim that blacks are biologically adapted to the South is less so—particularly in light of the Great Migration. And his insistence that blacks enjoyed an unproblematic relationship to the southern landscape, untroubled by the slavery and violence they experienced, is equally unconvincing.

In fact, by 1908 intellectual forces were already at work that would render Miller's arguments archaic, at least to black progressives. Progressive theorists continued to explore blacks' relationship to nature and to the American and African continents. But by the second decade of the twentieth century, they were questioning the biology underlying the nineteenth-century concept of race and focusing more attention on the role of history—particularly the history of slavery—in forming racial identity. Drawing on a new historico-cultural theory of race developed by Franz Boas, these theorists developed a dramatically different, and differently problematic, account of the relationship between nature and culture.

THE BOASIAN DIVIDE

In 1938 Franz Boas published a revised edition of his 1911 work, *The Mind of Primitive Man*. This work summarized the understanding of race he had been developing since 1895, rejecting the scientific racists' biological concept of race in favor of a historico-cultural understanding of racial difference. This extraordinarily influential critique of scientific racism took several decades to mature, but its basic outlines were already evident—and already making an impact on black intellectuals—when the German-born and -educated anthropologist began teaching at Columbia University in 1899.[74] Du Bois discovered Boas's "new anthropology" in 1906; he was deeply impressed and invited Boas to deliver the commencement address at Atlanta University.[75] This invitation brought Boas into contact with the young Howard University professor Alain Locke, who would become the principal architect of the philosophy informing the New Negro movement during the 1920s.[76] Through Boas, Du Bois and Locke were exposed to the cultural relativism that supplanted scientific racism.

Boas was not entirely dismissive of the physical anthropology on which the scientific racists rested their case; even in 1911, he was willing to entertain the possibility that blacks on average suffered some genetic inferiority to whites.[77] However, he was always skeptical of the data on which those judgments rested and was more interested in challenging than in confirming them. The revised edition of *The Mind of Primitive Man* summarizes these challenges: racial categories, he argued, are based on mere phenotypical differences. There is in fact more genetic variability within races than scientific racists usually recognize, and most modern populations are far too diverse to be characterized as races in any case.[78] Therefore, race conceived as a biological category can explain very little about social phenomena. In general, he contended that while individual humans may have different capacities and talents, *groups* of humans are on average similar, and even the races characterized by white supremacists as inferior do have at least roughly the same biological endowment—including mental capacity—as civilized peoples. The "mind of primitive man," it turns out, is the same as the mind of civilized man, neither less rational nor more intuitive (and therefore not in that sense "closer to nature").

In addition, Boas argued that culture is not directly determined by adaptation to the environment. Importantly, he did not refute the evolutionary view of human development or the notion that mental activity is a physiological operation of the brain. However, he did (like William James) argue that culture is not as directly determined by biological imperatives as scientific racists would have us believe. Although our mental capacities are the product of natural selection, once they have developed we can use them for activities that have no relation to reproductive success. Thus there is no necessary relationship between a group's natural environment and the symbolic forms it produces. He pointed out that although two societies may have access to the same resources, they will not necessarily use those resources or use them in the same way. This also applies to intellectual resources; different cultures may share similar myths and symbols, for example, but interpret them very differently. We can therefore expect to find considerable cultural diversity among peoples in very similar environments.[79] In fact, "it may even be shown that ancient customs, that may have been in harmony with a certain type of environment, tend to survive under new conditions, where they are of disadvantage rather than of advantage to the people." In general, the natural environment can only modify a preexisting culture; the environment itself has no creative power. "However rich in ore a country may be, it does not create techniques of handling metals; however rich in animals that might be domesticated, it will not lead to the development of herding if the people are entirely unfamiliar with the uses of domesticated animals," he wrote.[80]

For Boas, it is not nature but history that creates culture. Specifically, cultural development is the work of individuals who develop the practices they learned from the previous generation (or from outsiders). Boas elaborated on this process of cultural development in his 1927 work, *Primitive Art*. There he argued that art and other advanced forms of cultural production evolve when some groups in a society have the resources and leisure to pursue the "playful development" of techniques they originally devised for pragmatic purposes.[81] Boas was a bit vague on what drives or guides this "play," but clearly it is not determined by the natural environment; nature itself does not impress on us formal aesthetic ideals. He did suggest that "the feeling for form is inextricably bound up with the technical experience." The artist's

mastery of technique gives him the opportunity for "imaginative development of form"—which may or may not draw on the natural environment for
inspiration.[82] But he leaves this "playful" and "imaginative" element of
artistic production largely unexplored. As the next chapter will discuss,
black theorists were particularly interested in the concept of creativity and
would explore it in more depth. But for Boas, art is merely the product of the
free play of our faculties, drawing on the myths and symbols inherited from
earlier generations. Thus each social group develops its own culture out of
the creative use of its traditions—which are transmitted through social
learning, not genetics.

This theory does not entirely erase the influence of natural environment
on culture, but under Boas's view mental activity is underdetermined by both
biology and natural environment. Cultural forms are best understood as the
result of the free play of mental faculties working on inherited traditions
within multiple environmental contexts, rather than the uniform operations
of a physiology shaped by uniform responses to a single, stable environment.

Boas's theory had some obvious attractions for black theorists. It suggests
that blacks are, as a group, substantially equal in biological endowments to
other races and that Africans have complex histories and cultures that are the
product of centuries of development[83]—both claims that black theorists were
happy to embrace. Du Bois's article on the First Universal Races Congress in
1911 reported the Boasian view approvingly. He noted that most of the participants rejected the ideas that there are "vast and . . . unbridgeable differences between the races of men" and that whites have higher cultural capacity
than other races. Moreover, they insisted that races are not static and emphasized the importance of social factors in accounting for differences among
groups of humans. According to Du Bois, the scientific evidence showed that
one cannot argue from differences in physical characteristics to differences
in mental characteristics, that physical and mental characteristics of racial
groups are not static, and that the status of a race offers no index to its innate
capacities.[84]

Du Bois's 1915 work, *The Negro*, reflects his evolving understanding of
race: "The darker part of the human family," he asserted, is "separated from
the rest of mankind by no absolute physical line, but . . . nevertheless
forms, as a mass, a social group distinct in history, appearance, and to some
extent in spiritual gift." He proceeded to explain African history as the product of geography and the European slave trade rather than of black racial

characteristics.[85] Moreover, he attributed racism ("modern color preju-dice") to slavery and the slave trade. Africans, he argued, were originally en-slaved because they were not Christians; only later did color prejudice develop to justify the practice.[86]

Clearly, Du Bois was developing a historical and political understanding of race. Importantly, however, he continued to embrace the romantic idea that races are characterized by their spiritual and artistic gifts—an idea that would remain central to black cultural politics and to black environmental thought. Alain Locke also embraced this historical concept of race, develop-ing it in a more specifically political direction while retaining its connection to the idea of cultural creativity. In a series of lectures delivered at Howard University in 1915 (subsequently published as *Race Contacts and Interracial Relations*), Locke described not just racism but race itself as the product of a history of imperialism and oppression. When the modern man talks about race, he explained, "he is not talking about the anthropological or biological idea at all. He is really talking about the historical record of success or failure of an ethnic group." Indeed, "the conception of 'inferior' races . . . and 'su-perior' races largely comes from the political fortunes and political capacity of peoples. . . . The people that have not been successful in acquiring domi-nance . . . will be called the inferior people"—regardless of how much they have actually contributed to civilization. He noted that modern European imperialism is economic in nature but no less effective at creating "inferior races" out of the non-European peoples of the world.[87]

According to Locke, racial ideology in the modern world typically serves the economic interests of the dominant class. But he suggested that subordi-nate races could also benefit from developing a "secondary race conscious-ness"—essentially, a pride in race that could stimulate collective action and facilitate cultural assimilation.[88] Assimilation did not require erasing racial difference, however; like Du Bois, he insisted that blacks had a vital folk cul-ture and a distinctive contribution to make to American culture—particu-larly through their artistic expression. Indeed, for Locke, artistic expression served an important political purpose: it could be the prologue to political recognition and full participation in the "joint civilization" of a multiracial society. Thus instead of racial domination and subordination, he advocated a "politics of creative individuality and cultural reciprocity."[89]

In sum, Du Bois and Locke offered a cultural and political concept of race that emphasized both its historical dimension and its creative role in cultural development. To be sure, not all black leaders would embrace this concept, but those who did necessarily took a different view of the relationship between nature and culture than did the scientific racists. Under Du Bois's and Locke's view, culture is not fully determined by a group's original natural environment and innate biological capacity; rather, it grows out of a group's historical experience with the natural and social world—an experience that is in turn structured by law and social practices. Moreover, this view also preserves some room for individual creativity, for the "free play" of the mind. Both history and individual creativity (when it is allowed to operate) account for cultural development. This point in turn suggests that black Americans' history on the American continent, including the history of slavery and racial oppression, is critical to explaining black American culture and in fact continues to shape that culture. As Boas argued, historical experience influences culture by being encoded in cultural forms—in art, literature, music, religion, even family and economic behavior. Importantly, blacks take this cultural legacy with them even as they leave the South and slavery behind, so that their agrarian past continues to serve as an artistic, moral, and spiritual resource.

This theory of race therefore allows black theorists to explain the significance of blacks' distinctive experience with the American landscape to black culture and identity. But it also problematizes the nature/culture link in a new way. First, under this view the individual's relationship to nature is determined in large part by one's relationship to one's cultural group. But membership in a cultural group can no longer be considered simply a matter of biology; group identification might admit of different degrees, or one might identify with more than one group. Such questions of racial identity are therefore implicated in one's relationship to nature.

But even those who identify fully with black culture may be troubled by how that culture relates them to the natural world. History may be a resource, but it may also be a burden; to the extent that modern black culture consists of forms inherited from slave culture, blacks who participate in that culture are constantly confronted with the collective memory of slavery. To "get back to nature" is to get back to violence and oppression. As we will see, this becomes a central concern of Alain Locke and an enduring problem in black thought: black artists who choose to forget the South are left with only alien cultural forms on which to exercise their creative intelligence (and inferior cultural forms at that, derived from a decaying and enervated Anglo-Saxon culture). But black artists concerned with exploring the race's relationship to the American landscape must confront the extraordinarily painful memories of slavery.

Even without the problem of slavery, however, Boas's understanding of race suggests that there is a much deeper divide between nature and culture than the scientific racists recognized. The racists had argued that human culture is the product of nature—specifically, the inner vital power of nature interacting with the external natural environment during the race's formative stage. To be sure, many racists argued that civilized man, by gaining control over nature, was now relatively unaffected by natural selection—and perhaps for that reason out of touch with the creative force of nature. But under Boas's view, *all* human culture is disconnected from nature in this sense. There is little room for a concept of "cultural vitality" in his conceptual framework, or for the Romantic concept of nature as the force driving cultural development. For Boas, nature figures in cultural production primarily as scenery, and even as scenery it has only a weak connection to culture. The scenery does not fundamentally shape the actor's mentality, as Boutmy and Buckle had argued. Rather, it is merely a source of images or conditions for the human actor to make use of or not, as he or she chooses. Thus nature, for Boas, plays an entirely passive role in cultural production. It has no creative power at all.

Under this view, there is no particular advantage to cultural development in enjoying an aesthetic or spiritual relationship to the natural environment; the forces driving cultural development are history and economic resources. His theory therefore poses difficulties for black theorists concerned with explaining blacks' cultural contribution to American society. Du Bois, we will recall, claimed that blacks had superior artistic creativity by virtue of their relationship to nature. Indeed, the philosophy behind the New Negro movement would be based largely on this concept of blacks as a folk, a cultural group enjoying superior creative energy based on their connection to nature. In developing that argument, black theorists would not only have to grapple with issues of racial identity and collective memory but would have to go beyond Boas to consider more deeply the relationship between nature, history, and artistic creativity.

CONCLUSION

Black Americans, said Marcus Garvey in 1924, "are strangers in a strange land."[9] In the midst of the rising tide of scientific racism and white supremacy, legal segregation, and the Great Migration, it's not surprising that black Americans responded to his message. Racism, according to black nationalists, not only estranged blacks from white Americans but also estranged them from the land itself. Denied by an oppressive social and political system the opportunity to act independently, to express their aesthetic and spiritual ideals through their own work, black Americans lacked the opportunity to form a meaningful bond with the American landscape. Africa, under this view, offered more promising social conditions for the development of the race.

Not everyone agreed with this diagnosis, however. Du Bois and Locke, among others, believed that black Americans in the South had something of value to offer to American culture—that slavery had not extinguished all traces of creative capacity and agency, and that black southerners had become under the pressure of slavery a true folk with a vital connection to the land. That was not a simple claim to make, however; it required a close analysis of the meaning of race, including black Americans' relationship to Africa and more generally the relationship between nature and culture. For Du Bois and Locke, the biological determinism of scientific racism did not effectively capture the complexities in black Americans' relationship to Africa and to the United States. Franz Boas's understanding of race, in contrast, was considerably more promising. Boas proposed that our relationship to nature is always mediated by historically determined social structures. We come to the natural world as members of a group, and our relationship to nature is necessarily structured (and complicated) by that membership. The laws and customs of the community affect how the individual interacts with the natural world—determining, for example, whether he or she will respond to the natural world as a slave carrying out another's will or as an independent, creative agent. Boas's theory of race in fact complements black agrarianism, explaining how a history of slavery continued to shape black Americans' relationship to nature even as they left the South and moved into urban communities.

Nevertheless, Boas may have gone too far in rejecting the concept of black folk as a uniquely creative force in American culture. For activists like Du Bois and Locke, there were political as well as philosophical reasons to retain that understanding of black folk culture, even while rejecting the racial ideology supporting it. Drawing on both artistic primitivism and more progressive ideas, they would develop a new understanding of the sources of artistic creativity and the effect of racial oppression on blacks'—and whites'—relationship to the natural world.

CHAPTER FIVE
BLACK FOLK

———•◦•———

By 1925 the conception of the black folk as children of nature was common-place—so much so that some could see their primitive spirit even in the highly educated, city-dwelling artists of the Harlem Renaissance. The New Negro artist, announced art collector Albert Barnes, "has made us feel the majesty of Nature, the ineffable peace of the woods and great open spaces."[1] The previous chapter considered the theories of race implicated by that view; this chapter explores how black theorists drew on artistic primitivism and related ideas to elaborate and critique it.

During the early twentieth century, primitivism—the idea that "primitive" peoples are close to nature and therefore a potential source of cultural vitality—became a major theme in black environmental thought, reaching its height during the Harlem Renaissance period. Some black intellectuals found primitivism useful for supporting blacks' claim to full membership in American society, as well as making sense of their relationship to nature in an increasingly urban, industrial environment. But primitivism was also in-timately associated with scientific racism and racial essentialism; it would require some revision to make it compatible with the Boasian, social con-structivist understanding of race that was becoming popular among black progressives. That revision, accomplished most successfully by philosopher Alain Locke, is the focus of this chapter.

Alain Locke was a principal interpreter of the Harlem Renaissance by virtue of his 1925 anthology, *The New Negro*, his promotional activities, and his extensive writing on black music, art, and literature. From this vantage, he played a key role in reframing black intellectuals' conversation about race and nature in terms of the progressive cultural pluralism developed by philosophers such as William James, John Dewey, Josiah Royce, and Locke himself. Drawing on the pragmatism of James and Dewey, Locke developed an account of the value of black folk culture that went beyond Romanticism and scientific racism: he argued that the chief source of cultural vitality is the group's collective *experience* with the natural world, rather than a "racial essence" in harmony with nature. It is intense experience that inspires great art—and the crucible of slavery, he argued, provided the black community with a surfeit of such experience.

By reorienting primitivism from racial essences to racial experiences, Locke offered a progressive argument for preserving black folk culture, as well as a theoretical framework for understanding the problems for cultural production raised by racism and black urbanization. But beyond that, he encouraged black artists to explore the actual historical experiences of the race with the American landscape—to replace the myths, stereotypes, and propaganda about black folk with the voices of the black folk themselves. This project, he suggested, would revitalize American culture by helping Americans, white and black, to "see more understandingly" the world they inhabit.[2]

THE NEW NEGRO

Alain Locke insisted there was nothing new about the New Negro; he was in fact the old Negro shorn of the worn-out stereotypes and preconceptions that had for generations rendered him invisible.[3] But there *was* something new about the development of black culture in the early decades of the twentieth century. Between 1903, when *The Souls of Black Folk* was published, and 1930, the beginning of the end of the Harlem Renaissance, black Americans developed new urban communities, political organizations, economic institutions, and an extraordinary body of literature, visual art, social theory and criticism, and music. They shared—not fully, but significantly—in the twentieth-century birth of modern American culture.

The symbolic and to a large extent economic and political center of this renaissance was Harlem, New York. Neighborhoods like Harlem emerged out of the early twentieth-century urban migration of rural black Americans, which meant that for the first time in U.S. history, the representative Negro—the New Negro—lived in the city. Thus the transition from country to city—a profound transformation in the black migrants' relationship to the American landscape—was a central theme of the social theory and literature of this period. Moreover, black urban communities were growing more complex, experiencing greater class differentiation and (as West Indian immigration increased) cultural diversity. As we will see, that complexity is reflected in the evolving understanding of racial identity at work in black political thought and literature, and in black theorists' understanding of the relationship between nature and culture.

The social processes that gave rise to black Harlem were complex as well. There were many black enclaves in New York even before 1900, but between 1890 and 1910, the black population in New York grew dramatically—just as the real-estate market in Harlem collapsed, a confluence of events that created, for the first time in New York, a large, self-contained black neighborhood.[4] At the same time, New York began to attract leading members of the black intelligentsia. W. E. B. Du Bois moved from Atlanta to New York when he began working for the NAACP in 1910. James Weldon Johnson arrived soon thereafter, as did Charles S. Johnson (becoming director of the Urban League and editor of *Opportunity*). Marcus Garvey would also make Harlem his American headquarters. Northern migration during this period had increased black urban populations in general, and other cities—particularly Chicago—were also important to the Negro renaissance. But Harlem, according to James Weldon Johnson, was by 1930 "the recognized Negro capitol," the Zion of the New Negro.[5]

The New Negro phenomenon had several dimensions. From one perspective, it reflected broad changes in American culture during the early decades of the twentieth century, such as the support for artistic and literary production made possible by postwar changes in the broader publishing establishment. Historian George Hutchinson points out that the Harlem Renaissance followed not only the Great Migration but the emergence of a new set of "white" liberal, reform-oriented magazines centered in New York, including the *Nation*, the *New Republic*, and the *Seven Arts*.[6] These magazines promoted an aesthetic, social, and cultural reform program that resonated with the main themes of the Harlem Renaissance. Another contributing factor was the development of the economic base of urban black communities like Harlem; the concentration of blacks in these neighborhoods fueled the rise of black businesses, from realty companies to beauty salons to cabarets.[7]

But the New Negro was not just an economic phenomenon. He also represented a growing political and race consciousness among the black masses. Political organizations such as the NAACP, the Urban League, and Marcus Garvey's Universal Negro Improvement Association (UNIA) flourished, and the number of black newspapers in New York doubled between 1912 and 1921, covering a broad range of political viewpoints.[8] More generally, the rise of black nationalism created (particularly among whites) the perception of a new assertiveness—a perception strengthened by the return of black soldiers from Europe after World War I. Indeed, David Levering Lewis begins his history of the Harlem Renaissance with the 1919 parade of black soldiers up New York's Fifth Avenue to Harlem—a striking spectacle for both white and black observers, representing, it seemed, a more militant attitude and a determination to claim full citizenship.[9]

Finally, the evolution of black popular culture was central to the Harlem Renaissance. Southern and West Indian immigrants to Harlem brought with them a variety of cultural forms and artistic traditions, resulting in the rich bohemianism, the ragtime and jazz culture associated with 1920s Harlem nightlife. That bohemian pop culture attracted white elites to Harlem as well—and reinforced the long-standing association in white culture between blacks and primitives. To white observers, Harlem could look like an urban jungle, the expression of a tropical, savage racial temperament. Such images would proliferate in descriptions of Harlem and other black urban neighborhoods (by both black and white writers) during this period.[10]

But, importantly, the cabaret was not the sole source of white interest in black culture. The Harlem Renaissance was essentially interracial, owing much to the white writers, publishers, and audiences that patronized the emerging black literary community. Many historians attribute that interest to the same longing for the "primitive" that filled Harlem's nightclubs, but George Hutchinson points out that white intellectuals had many other reasons for involving themselves in black culture—and black intellectuals had many reasons for welcoming their involvement.[11] Black and white intellectuals were involved in a common conversation about cultural pluralism, drawing from a common intellectual tradition that encouraged such interracial communication. As we will see in this chapter and the next, black theorists associated with the Renaissance were strongly influenced by white theorists of cultural pluralism and pragmatism such as William James, Franz Boas, John Dewey, and Josiah Royce.[12]

But pragmatism and cultural pluralism were not the only philosophical influences on black social theory during this period; the next chapter, for example, will discuss the influence of John Ruskin and William Morris, whose ideas on the relationship between art and labor were important to black theorists' evolving conception of the "Beloved Community."[13] Even more central to the Harlem Renaissance, however, were artistic primitivism and literary regionalism. Indeed, one could say that these traditions posed the problem to which pragmatism would supply the answer. Primitivism and regionalism provided an attractive language with which to defend the value of black American culture—but they were underwritten by scientific racism and a problematic understanding of racial identity. They would therefore require some pragmatic reconstruction to be useful to black activists.

PRIMITIVISM AND REGIONALISM

Artistic primitivism and literary regionalism permeated discourse about the relationship between humans and nature during the early decades of the twentieth century. Like scientific racists, primitivists and regionalists suggested that culture should grow out of the folk's relationship to the land. But while American racists usually celebrated the highly developed state of western civilization, primitivists and regionalists reinforced their lingering fears that civilized peoples had evolved too far from the sources of creativity—namely, the organic connection to nature enjoyed by more "primitive" peoples.

Artistic primitivism evolved primarily out of the symbolism and Art Nouveau of the 1890s.[14] But it drew on philosophical primitivism, a long-standing theme in western thought concerning humans' relationship to nature. This ancient tradition teaches that "primitives" are closer to nature and for that reason enjoy a moral innocence unavailable to civilized peoples.[15] What it means to be both "primitive" and "close to nature," however, has changed considerably, particularly over the course of the nineteenth century. For eighteenth-century primitivists, "primitives" were simply at a lower stage of cultural development than civilized peoples and were "close to nature" in the sense that because they lacked well-developed political institutions, they were governed largely by natural law. By the late nineteenth century, however, evolutionary biology, scientific racism, and anthropology had transformed the intellectual terrain, giving new meaning to primitivism.

Edward Tylor's *Primitive Culture*, published in 1871, was particularly significant. Tylor was the first to describe the belief systems of "primitive" peoples as "animism"—that is, so-called primitives believe that nature is inhabited by spiritual forces and therefore live in an animated world of nature spirits. Moreover, although he insisted that primitive religions are in their own way quite rational, Tylor also suggested that primitives were less fully developed psychologically and therefore more childlike and emotional than civilized peoples.[16] In the intellectual milieu of the late nineteenth century, of course, to feel a spiritual kinship to the natural world and to be childlike and emotional were not necessarily undesirable. On the contrary, for

Romantics, those features of primitive psychology meant that such peoples enjoyed a less analytic and more intuitive relationship to the vital force of nature than do civilized peoples. Indeed, when this view was combined with the scientific racists' claim that modern "primitives" were evolutionary cul-de-sacs—examples of arrested cultural development—one could conclude that the culture of modern tribal peoples (and even their descendants in civilized countries) was prerational and therefore a direct, unmediated expression of nature's vital force.[17]

And this, according to artistic primitivists, was exactly what western art needed. Western civilization, they claimed, was languishing, devitalized by its increasing alienation from nature. Ironically, their major evidence for this devitalization was the nineteenth-century academic school of painting, whose disciples clung to a naturalistic aesthetic that valued faithful representation of the social and natural world. Indeed, the nineteenth century was the era of great landscape painting, producing those works we now associate with the Romantic appreciation for natural beauty. But many artists and theorists nevertheless considered the western artistic tradition out of touch with nature—alienated from the sources of creativity and weighed down by its obsession with technique and with conventional themes (like landscapes). What was needed was a closer—or at least different—relationship between the artist and the vital force of nature. Artistic creation should be *production*, not reproduction: the product of the artist's spirit, resonating in harmony with the spiritual force animating nature.[18]

Artists turned for inspiration in several directions, including the folk art of Europe (a popular source for the Art Nouveau movement), prehistoric cave paintings, and childrens' art, looking always for products of "pure perception": what we see unmediated by what we know.[19] But primitivists also looked for inspiration to the art of modern "primitive" non-Europeans—usually the peoples of Africa, Oceania, and the Americas. Primitivists reasoned that such "primitive" peoples lacked the traditions that were suffocating western art, and that their animistic belief systems enabled them to interact with nature in a nonscientific, nonanalytic way. Under this reasoning, "primitives" experienced a more direct, unmediated relationship with the vital forces animating nature, a sympathy with nature that was reflected in their art. "Are not savages artists who have forms of their own as powerful as the form of thunder?" asked August Mack, of the Blau Reiter school. "Each genuine form of art," he insisted, "emerges from a living correlation of man to the real substance of the forms of nature."[20] That such art might be less technically sophisticated or less concerned with naturalistic representation than western art was not important; under this view, art is not a matter of imitating the forms of nature but an attempt to produce in the audience the *feeling* that the artist experiences when communing with nature. According to Wassily Kandinsky, for example, the virtue of primitives was that they were "pure artists" who "sought to express only inner and essential feelings in their work."[21] What Kandinsky and his fellow travelers hoped for from primitive art was a direct if crude expression of that feeling, which would then inspire the western artists' more sophisticated and technically superior art.

Primitivism stimulated interest in African art among Europeans and Americans. By the mid-nineteenth century, European museums had begun developing collections of the artifacts of African and other tribal cultures; European imperialism in Africa during the 1880s and 1890s increased the stream of artifacts from Africa to European museums (including the famous Benin bronzes), and several exhibitions in Europe included such artifacts.[22] For some German primitivists the value of African art even became a *justification* for imperialism. Leo Frobenius, for example, justified German expansionism on the grounds that the German character needed an infusion of energy from the nature-folk of Africa: "Our youth demands nature. The rediscovery of the oldest simple ties with nature, a return to naturalness. Art calls for simplification."[23] But most primitivists were looking merely for inspiration, not empire. And apparently they found it. The direct influence of African and other tribal art on western artists is difficult to document, but historian Colin Rhodes argues that artists began to use primitive artifacts for inspiration around 1900 in France and Germany and "discovered" African sculpture around 1906—at which point we begin to see its stylistic influences in the work of Matisse and Picasso, for example.[24]

Americans, too, showed interest in the art of primitives, and the black artists and intellectuals of the Harlem Renaissance shared the Europeans' fascination with African sculpture. They were encouraged in this interest by Albert Barnes, who became a patron and interpreter of the Harlem Renaissance. Barnes saw in the art of African Americans the same regenerative potential that he saw in the art of Africans, and he brought this primitivist interpretation of the Renaissance to his 1925 essay on "Negro Art and America," in Alain Locke's *The New Negro*. Indeed, this remarkable synthesis of primitivism and romantic racialism is worth quoting extensively; it represents a set of ideas from which Du Bois and Locke would struggle to distinguish themselves.

The American Negro, according to Barnes, belongs to "a primitive race." Their art "comes from a primitive nature upon which a white man's education has never been harnessed." To understand Negro art, one must understand "the psychological complexion of the Negro as he inherited it from his primitive ancestors and which he maintains to this day." Indeed, "The outstanding characteristics are his tremendous emotional endowment, his luxuriant and free imagination and a truly great power of individual expression. He has in superlative measure that fire and light which, coming from within, bathes his whole world, colors his images and impels him to expression. The Negro is a poet by birth."

The white man, in contrast, "cannot compete with the Negro in spiritual endowment." Centuries of civilization have "attenuated his original gifts and have made his mind dominate his spirit." Having wandered too far from "the elementary human needs and their easy means of natural satisfaction," the "deep and satisfying harmony which the soul requires no longer arises from the incidents of daily life." Barnes concludes that "when art is real and vital it effects [*sic*] the harmony between ourselves and nature which means happiness."[25]

It's hard to say what's more striking about this essay—Barnes's confident mastery of primitivist rhetoric, or his blindness to the actual mentality of the modern, urban New Negro artist. But Barnes was not unique; few white primitivists questioned the racist assumptions underlying primitivism. According to one enthusiast, "These Africans being primitive, uncomplex, uncultured, can express their thoughts by a direct appeal to the instinct. Their carvings are informed with emotion."[26] Marius de Zayas, who staged an exhibit of "African Negro Art" in New York in 1914, claimed that the degree of development of art toward naturalism is in direct relation to the intellectual development of the race; citing the biology of the scientific racists, he concluded that the African Negro was the least developed of races and therefore produces the most expressive art.[27] Since these racial differences were supposed to be relatively stable, such qualities should also characterize the art of black Americans. Indeed, Elie Faure suggested that "even when transported in great numbers to places like North America that have reached the most original . . . degree of civilization . . ., the black man remains, after centuries, what he was—an impulsive child, ingenuously good, and ingenuously cruel." Faure therefore sought in Negro art "that still unreasoned feeling which merely obeys the most elementary demands of rhythm and symmetry. . . . Brute nature circulates in them, and burning sap and black blood."[28] To be fair, not all white primitivists relied on these racial stereotypes. But the underlying motive of the movement was to discover an art produced through an untutored, almost instinctual process free of culture, history, and tradition: an art that was virtually organic, the product of nature itself. Many primitivists thought they found such an art among Africans—and their descendants in the United States.

Primitivism, like scientific racism, reached its height in the early decades of the twentieth century, just as a related current in literary criticism was fostering a broader interest among the American intelligentsia in the artistic potential of black Americans. Although less dependent on scientific racism than was primitivism, regionalism was associated with the organic theories of identity and nationalism that were thriving in the United States and Europe at the beginning of the twentieth century.[29] Regionalists expressed the familiar anxiety that modern life was increasingly characterized by artificiality and alienation from nature, particularly the unique natural environment—the German forest, the English countryside, the American wilderness—that was supposed to give each nation's folk its distinctive character. Thus primitivists and regionalists shared a common goal: to revitalize western civilization by creating a more "natural" culture, a culture that would grow organically out of a community's direct experience with the natural environment.

That goal also links regionalism closely to the strain of American environmentalism that focuses on developing a "sense of place," which culminates in contemporary bioregionalism.[30] The connections between literary regionalism and early American environmental thought are strikingly evident in William Dean Howells' regionalist manifesto, *Criticism and Fiction*. Howells argues for developing a distinctive American literature by faithfully depicting the lives of ordinary Americans in their local habitats. Throughout the essay, Howells uses organic metaphors that suggest an ecological perspective: The writer, he argues, should find "nothing insignificant; . . . nothing that God has made is contemptible." Writers should be like naturalists who study to understand all organisms, no matter how ugly or minute, viewing each one as equally important.[31] Science, he points out, has taught man that in nature there is neither great nor small; all are equally subject to the same laws, equally beautiful because equally divine.[32]

The consonance of Howells's views on literature with the philosophy of the environmental movement reflects the direct influence of evolutionary science on both, but also their common roots in organic theories of the folk—particularly the idea, discussed in the previous chapter, that the natural environment of a people shapes its genius, which is displayed in its art, its way of life, and its mode of thought.[33] Howells echoes this notion, describing literature as "a plant which springs from the nature of a people, and draws its forces from their life."[34] More precisely, literature *should be* as a plant which springs from the nature of a people; his complaint about American literature is that it tends not to do so, but merely to imitate English models. It is therefore (like so much of modern life) artificial, lacking vitality and creativity. His advice to American writers is to turn their attention to the material at hand and describe the corner of the world they inhabit. Such literature, he insists, will more faithfully express the spirit of the American people.

Primitivists, of course, might question the regionalists' goal of "faithful depiction," if that means the sort of representational art they were attempting to move beyond (although regional literature need not consist of simple reportage, as Du Bois and Jean Toomer would demonstrate). Nevertheless, both regionalism and primitivism encouraged artists to look to the lives of ordinary folk—particularly the folk who worked the land—for their themes and subjects. They therefore fostered interest in black Americans. Regionalists like Hamlin Garland, for example, praised Joel Chandler Harris's retelling of folk tales told by black southerners, declaring that "the Negro" was the most interesting part of southern fiction and would soon become "an artist in his own right."[35] The postwar "lyrical left," including Randolph Bourne, Waldo Frank, Robert Frost, and Van Wyck Brooks, also saw in black Americans the potential to regenerate a decaying Anglo-Saxon culture. Eugene O'Neill's 1920 staging of *Emperor Jones* was one of the more notable expressions of this interest, as was Sherwood Anderson's 1925 novel *Dark Laughter*, which was inspired by the work of Harlem Renaissance writer Jean Toomer.[36]

Regionalism and primitivism thus helped to legitimate black Americans as artists and subjects of art. Indeed, more than that, they implied that blacks may be the *only* people qualified to produce a truly American art. If artificiality and conformity to convention—in short, distance from nature—were preventing the emergence of an American art, then one could argue that blacks were the only remaining Americans with a sufficiently direct, primitive, and organic relationship to nature to speak with its voice. Black theorists, however, suspected that the relationship between black culture and nature in a racially oppressive society was more problematic than that. Their engagements with primitivism explored several pathologies suffered by victims of racial injustice—from overdeveloped class consciousness to underdeveloped race consciousness—that might muffle nature's voice.

BLACK PRIMITIVISM

Black intellectuals had a troubled (not to say tortured) relationship with primitivism and regionalism: they were drawn to the notion that black folk had something distinctive and valuable to contribute to American culture, but they struggled with the movement's conception of those folk. Consider, for example, Charles Chesnutt's 1899 masterpiece, *The Conjure Woman.* Written at the height of popular interest in black folk tales, *The Conjure Woman* raises two key questions about the regionalist project: Can black artists draw inspiration from a land haunted by the ghosts of slavery? And are black folk actually the simple, natural peasants that primitivists assume them to be?

The Conjure Woman is a collection of stories concerning a white Northerner who buys a plantation in the South after the Civil War. Like most of the plantations we have encountered in this tradition, it is "exhausted" and "decaying" (no doubt the result of the bad cultivation characteristic of slavery). Even worse, however, the Northerner is informed by the former slave Julius that the plantation is also "goophered" (cursed).[37] According to Julius, the place is teeming with the ghosts of dead slaves, victims of cruelties perpetrated by the slave system. If Julius is to be believed, these ghosts pose a serious obstacle to the Yankee's attempts to revive the plantation. Indeed, his stories suggest that nature itself is cursed by the injustice of slavery—that the ghosts of slavery continue to haunt the woods and fields, impairing their fertility and making them hostile to human projects. The suggestion calls into doubt not only the Yankee's ambitions for the plantation but the regionalist project of drawing artistic inspiration from one's immediate locale. Can a sensitive artist seeking to describe the South adequately render its painful and conflicted history? What sort of inspiration can one receive from a land cursed by injustice?

The Yankee, however, is not particularly sensitive, and he is inclined to dismiss Julius's ghost stories. As it turns out, he is wise to do so. In Chesnutt's book, very little is what it appears to be. To begin with, *The Conjure*

Woman appears to be a conventional example of regionalist literature, similar to Joel Chandler Harris's Br'er Rabbit stories. But the stories are not
black folk tales; although based on such tales, they are Chesnutt's own invention.[38] That point alone raises a host of questions about what constitutes
folk culture and what is valuable about it. But the book also raises questions
about primitivism. To be sure, Chesnutt appears to follow the conventions of
primitivism: The Yankee's wife, for example, is enervated by some mysterious illness; this highly civilized couple has come to the rural, underdeveloped South to improve their vitality. Julius's stories contribute to their
revival, and Julius himself is described by the Yankee as a primitive, enjoying a "simple life" that had "kept him close to nature." But he also comments
that Julius is not "altogether African" and is in fact quite shrewd.[39] The Yankee remains suspicious of the former slave, noting that the old man appears
to be as entrepreneurial as any Northerner.

Julius in fact has economic motives for discouraging several of the Yankee's planned projects—from reviving a vineyard (from which Julius may
have been making money) to cutting down a stand of trees (which contained
a bee-tree that Julius may have been using). Nor is it clear that Julius believes any of the stories he tells, or that he is even troubled by the cruelties
they recount. Julius is in fact less a primitive than a trickster, like Br'er Rabbit himself—morally ambiguous, cunning, and deceptive.[40] For example, in
the chapter titled "The Conjuror's Revenge," Julius advises the Yankee to
trust what he sees and what he hears: "ef a man can't b'lieve w'at 'e sees, I
can't see no use in libbin—mought 's well die en be whar we can't see nuf-
fin."[41] But when the Yankee follows that advice and buys a healthy-looking
horse (recommended to him by Julius), he discovers that the horse is rid-
dled with disease. The lesson is for the reader as well: these "primitive"
black folk are not what they appear to be. The folk culture southern blacks
present to the white world may be nothing more than a sophisticated mask
intended to obscure rather than reveal their true nature.[42]

Chesnutt's doubts about regionalism and primitivism would continue to
surface among black writers, even those apparently working within their
conventions. Du Bois, for example, frequently used the language of regionalism and primitivism to explain blacks' unique capacity to contribute to
American culture. *The Souls of Black Folk* is in fact precisely the kind of regional literature Howells was calling for. Du Bois's announced aim in *Souls* is
that of regional literature generally—to help make each part of the nation
known to all other parts, or "to depict a world as we see it who dwell

therein."[43] More specifically, he tells us that *Souls* was inspired by the Negro spiritual, which he describes as "sprung from the African forests" and "intensified by the tragic soul-life of the slave" until it became "the one true expression of a people's sorrow, despair, and hope."[44] There are primitivist moments, as well, in *Souls:* Du Bois describes the enslaved Africans as "endowed with a tropical imagination and a keen, delicate appreciation of Nature." The African, he claims, lived "in a world animate with gods and devils, elves and witches; full of strange influences." Although slavery suppressed many of these beliefs, "that vein of vague superstition which characterizes the unlettered Negro even to-day was strengthened." Despite his exposure to civilization and Christianity, the slave remained a primitive, and "like all primitive folk, the slave stood near to Nature's heart." This nearness to nature is the source of two of the Negro's "gifts" to American civilization: his music and his spirit.[45]

This all seems quite conventional. But *Souls* is not a simple expression of primitivism; its primitivist moments are accompanied by antiprimitivist themes and observations. For example, the simple rural community Du Bois describes in the essay "The Meaning of Progress" is filled with warm, earthy black folk—but is also hemmed in by limited opportunity, ignorance, and poverty. The small southern town he imagines in "The Coming of John" is even less idyllic, riven with class and racial conflict.[46] As literary critic Houston Baker points out, *Souls* is not just *about* black American culture; it *is* a cultural performance—a sophisticated presentation of a cultured black man. Du Bois's use of primitivism, he argues, is strategic, a device to mollify and gain the attention of his white audience before moving them to his more sophisticated view of black culture and of racial identity.[47] Moreover, as suggested in the previous chapter, Du Bois is also speaking to black audiences, using a careful, qualified language of primitivism and regionalism to develop a concept of racial identity that can serve as a foundation for black personality in a racially oppressive society.

That strategy seems to be at play as well in Du Bois's 1911 novel, *The Quest of the Silver Fleece.* The story follows Zora, a black girl born in rural Georgia, through her struggles to educate herself and find her place in the world. Over the course of the novel, she leaves Georgia to attend school, then travels to New York and Washington, D.C., becomes politically active, and finally returns home. Du Bois presents this as a journey from primitive to civilized. Zora begins her life in the primeval muck: in a swamp that Du Bois describes as a dark "sinister and sullen" place of "strange power." Daughter of the reputed witch Elspeth, she is "a heathen hoyden"; when we first encounter her she is dancing in the firelight to "wondrous savage music." Du Bois underscores her primitive vitality and spirit; she glows "with vigor and life." She is also a child of nature, "steeped body and soul in wood-lore" but disdainful of white folk: "They just got things,—heavy, dead things. We black folks," she insists, "is got the *spirit*."[48]

But Zora does not remain a primitive. Under the tutelage of the northern schoolteacher, Zora's savagery diminishes; she becomes "a revelation of grace and womanliness." Without losing her energy and spirit, she develops into "a brilliant, sumptuous womanhood; proud, conquering, full-blooded, and deep bosomed—a passionate mother of men." She also begins to speak "better English," drifting into "an upper world of dress and language and deportment."[49] She continues her education in politics and economics in the North but eventually returns to Georgia, intent on improving the economic and social condition of the black farmers. Her plan is "a bold regeneration of the land": she encourages the farmers to clear the swamp and establish a collective farm.[50] The result is a transformation akin to Zora's own evolution. The farmers create a thriving communal cotton plantation on the site of the swamp. The swamp does not wholly disappear, however. Its vital energy persists in the fertility of the soil, and the swamp remains in Zora's memory—not "cold and still" but "living, vibrant, tremulous."[51]

The story thus draws on primitivism, albeit a primitivism modified by what commentators variously call Du Bois's Victorian, elitist, or civilizationist views.[52] They are referring to his understanding of the relationship between high culture and folk culture. Du Bois's views on this relationship are easily misunderstood; his point is *not* that folk culture is to be rejected in favor of high culture. True, he seems to value high culture—the cultural products of elites—more than folk culture. But, like the primitivists, he insists that high culture should be rooted in folk culture; high culture is in fact a way to *preserve and elaborate* folk culture. Folk culture provides inspiration and the basic themes and images that inform great works of art. It does take a superior intellect or talent to refine those themes and images into high art, of course; hence the importance of the "Talented Tenth," the intellectual and artistic elite. But it takes a vital folk culture to produce and inspire such talented individuals—who in turn owe a duty to the folk that created and nurtured them. They are in essence cultural custodians for the black community. The relationship between folk and high art, like the relationship between the masses and elites, is supposed to be an organic and reciprocal one. Du Bois thus turns the conventional Romantic artist into a political figure: a race leader, a political and cultural resource for the black community.

Du Bois illustrates this relationship between folk and high culture not only in Zora herself—the primitive who is transformed into a race leader—but also in the fate of the land. Although the swamp for Du Bois is a reservoir of nature's creative energy, that energy is not necessarily positive. It is essentially amoral—or even immoral. The swamp seems to corrupt its inhabitants; Zora's mother, for example, prostitutes her daughters to the wealthy white landowners (a reference perhaps to Africa's exploitation by Europeans as well as Americans' exploitation of black slaves), and Zora also initially has an underdeveloped moral sense. Thus the land must be transformed through human labor into a productive pastoral landscape. This is of course in accord with black agrarianism, which also informs this novel: it is the task of humans to "finish Creation"—to make the wilderness more hospitable to human purposes. Even transformed, however, the wild, natural energy of the swamp is not lost. Instead, it remains under Zora's feet in the fertility of the soil, as well as in cultural representations of the swamp—the community's collective memory of this original wilderness. Most important, it remains within her, in her racial consciousness and memory, as the foundation for further action.

For Du Bois, then, racial consciousness served as a link to the primitive sources of culture—to the folk and, through the folk, to nature itself. Thus it is tempting to conclude that his primitivism relied on racial essentialism—that he posited a primitive racial "essence" that links Zora to her folk in spite of the changes she undergoes. But there is evidence that by 1911 Du Bois was already beginning to question essentialism in favor of a Boasian understanding of race. For example, not all of the characters in the novel enjoy Zora's strong race consciousness; many have chosen to mimic the white upper class, even choosing to "pass" as white. One confused southern black man, confronted with these deracinated cosmopolites, felt he had "slipped and lost his bearings, and the characteristics of his simple world were rolling curiously about."[53] Du Bois in fact describes racial identity as unstable and even arbitrary at times. Zora's race consciousness is more of an achievement, the result of her intelligence and strong will, than an automatic expression of her nature. It is something that must be constructed out of the limited resources available to the oppressed in a racist society.

Nor was Du Bois alone. For many black writers, primitivism became (somewhat paradoxically) a vehicle for exploring the problem of constructing a viable racial identity.[54] Consider, for example, James Weldon Johnson's

1912 novel, *Autobiography of an Ex-Coloured Man.*[55] Johnson, like Du Bois, drew on Romantic ideas of art, nature, and the folk, but he focused in particular on the problems of racial identity raised by this complex of ideas. Indeed, the title itself announces that race is contingent; it is not determined by biology but chosen or, in many cases, imposed. Johnson's protagonist is sufficiently light-skinned to pass as either a white man or a black man; this choice is the central problem in the novel. As a musician, the protagonist appreciates the vitality and creativity of African American culture, but he also longs for the sophistication of European artistry. He therefore wanders from the American South to New York, and then to Paris and London, seeking to develop his art. But he is drawn back to the South to find inspiration in "black rural folk." Their folk music, dances, and stories may be a "lower form of art," but "they give evidence of a power that will some day be applied to the higher forms." Indeed, he criticizes those who disdain blacks' popular music; in his view, it represents the "heart of the people," which is the only true source of art. He is eager to begin the project of creating classical pieces based on ragtime music and spirituals.[56]

Unfortunately, our protagonist is disappointed by the "dull, simple people" of the South. Like Charles Ball and other earlier critics of southern agriculture, the narrator describes the landscape as ugly: instead of "lush semi-tropical scenery," he finds "the red earth partly covered by tough, scrawny grass. . . .The muddy straggling roads, the cottages of unpainted pine boards, and the clay-daubed huts imparted a 'burnt up' impression." The poverty of black southerners discourages him, along with their poor diet and general ignorance.[57] He is nonetheless still inspired by their folk music: "There is sounded in them that elusive undertone, the note in music which is not heard with the ears." But his enthusiasm dies when he witnesses a lynching. This savage killing convinces him that he can't remain in the South; in fact, he can't remain a black man at all: "I understood that it was not discouragement or fear or search for a larger field of action and opportunity that was driving me out of the Negro race," he explains. "I knew it was shame . . . shame at being identified with a people that could with impunity be treated worse than animals." In abandoning his race, however, he also abandoned his art. He is left at the end with only some "fast yellowing manuscripts, the only tangible remnants of a vanished dream, a dead ambition, a sacrificed talent."[58]

Clearly Johnson's novel relies on the Romantic concept of the folk. Without ignoring the poverty and violence they suffer, he nevertheless depicted southern blacks as a people whose daily interaction with the natural world gave them access to nature's vital, creative energy. But Johnson also rejected racial essentialism and the biological concept of race. Like Du Bois, he described racial identity as a choice—not a costless choice, to be sure, but a difficult process of claiming or rejecting membership in a historically determined group. In fact, the central problem in both Du Bois's *Quest* and Johnson's *Autobiography* stems from the fact that the folk's relationship to nature is *not* shared by those members of the race who don't participate in the folk life. For Du Bois and Johnson, the black artist's relationship to nature is determined by his or her relationship to the black folk.

Two dimensions of that relationship are particularly salient in these novels: class and history. Both Du Bois and Johnson are at pains to point out that class barriers are not easily overcome. On the contrary, the novels' protagonists both express a distinct distaste for the folk's rude manners and way of life. Johnson also points to deeper problems, such as the stigma resulting from association with lower-class persons and the oppressive communalism and violence of folk life. Those barriers, he suggests, are made even more daunting by racial oppression. Racism raises the stakes of social mobility; black elites must work harder than white elites to escape the ignominy associated with lower class, since blacks will suffer more (from racial violence and oppression) if they slip back into it. Thus racism encourages the "talented tenth" to abandon their folk roots. In doing so, it interferes with black elites' relationship to the creative power of nature.

History, too, can create barriers between the black artist and folk. By the second decade of the twentieth century, most black artists and intellectuals would be seeking inspiration from a folk life that lies in the past. To be sure, it may simply lie in one's personal past—in which case one might actually return to it, as did Zora. But black elites increasingly would conceptualize the true folk life of the race as located in the more distant past, in the American South or even Africa. Du Bois's swamp, for example, seems to be located not only in Zora's personal past but in the history of the race; although it appears in Georgia, it is contiguous with the African jungle by virtue of cultural continuity between American rural blacks and their African forebears (represented by the witch Elspeth). Thus Zora's return to Georgia is, in a sense, a return to Africa as well—a return made possible by the survival of African influences in the collective memory of the folk. But racial oppression can interfere with this sort of return as well. Racism can lead to distorted versions of history in which the actual accomplishments of the oppressed are erased, to be replaced with mythical pasts that support the official racial ideology—such as the version of history that denied that Africa had ever produced a civilization or that slaves had contributed anything to American society. From Du Bois's perspective, of course, it is a chief task of the artist and intellectual to rectify these distorted versions of the past. But if the collective memory of the race is too distorted—if too much has been forgotten or suppressed—that project of recovery may be impossible. Indeed, it may not even suggest itself. The artist may learn not to look to the folk's history for inspiration and may therefore remain permanently alienated not only from her past but from nature itself.

In sum, Du Bois's and Johnson's novels suggest that, particularly in a racially oppressive society, the relationship between nature and high culture may be complicated by class relations and by the vagaries of personal and collective memory—complications that can interfere with the organic, reciprocal relationship that should exist between the cultural production of the elites and the masses. This diagnosis of the pathologies created by racial oppression, however, suggests a more contingent and conflicted concept of racial identity than that proposed by the white primitivists. It suggests, in fact, that behind their primitivism lay a Boasian, social constructivist understanding of race. Under Boas's view, group identity—and therefore personal identity—is always socially constructed and therefore always vulnerable to social and economic forces, including racism.

But is that view of racial identity really compatible with the assumptions about nature and culture underlying primitivism? After all, if there is no racial essence to carry one unproblematically over the divide between nature and culture, then *all* humans (including the folk) must create a relationship with the natural world out of their (possibly maladapted) traditions and their own free, conscious choices. What then makes "primitives" closer to nature than "civilized" persons—or black folk more creative than white elites?

BRIDGING THE BOASIAN DIVIDE

Boasian anthropology does not fit comfortably with conventional primitivism. Not only does Boas reject the Romantic concept of nature as a source of artistic creativity, but his understanding of culture challenges primitivist assumptions in important respects. First, primitivists claim that "primitive" cultures are closer to nature because they lack well-developed traditions; they are innocent of history. As explained in the previous chapter, Boas firmly rejects that claim; all modern cultures have traditions and histories. No culture is in this sense closer to nature than any other. Second, under Boas's view, black Americans do not necessarily have an "African" culture; their traditions are determined not by a biological race nature but by a history that removed them from African influences long ago. Boas's view therefore raises some troublesome questions for black primitivists: if African art is the product of well-developed traditions, in what sense is it more vital than western art? Indeed, if one rejects the Romantic concept of nature, what does it mean for an artistic tradition to be "vital"? Similarly, if culture is not a biological inheritance, what connection can black Americans claim to Africa? What claim do they have to be primitives at all?

Alain Locke attempted to answer these questions in his contributions to the 1925 anthology *The New Negro*. His essays are among the most successful attempts by a Harlem Renaissance theorist to synthesize the Boasian concept of race with artistic primitivism. This synthesis allows Locke to explain the significance of black artistic production—in particular the literature of the Harlem Renaissance—in a way that differs in important respects from traditional primitivism (as represented by Albert Barnes's essay in the same book).

Locke begins with the familiar language of regionalism and primitivism: the new generation of black writers, he declares, is embracing a "lusty vigorous realism." They are finding "vital originality of substance" by digging deep "into the racy peasant undersoil of race life." In short, they are turning for inspiration to "our instinctive and quite matchless folk-art. . . . Here for the enrichment of American and modern art . . . in a people who still have the ancient key, are some of the things we thought culture had forever lost."[59] This art, according to Locke, exemplifies "a return to nature, not by way of the forced and worn formula of Romanticism, but through the closeness of an imagination that has never broken kinship with nature."[60] Thus far, he sounds much like Barnes—although it is significant that black artists have to "dig deep" into peasant life for inspiration. Such inspiration is not, apparently, the automatic efflorescence of their racial psychology.

In fact, Locke rejects the theory of race underlying white primitivism. Black slave culture is a genuine folk culture for Locke, but not because it is the product of a primitive race. On the contrary, Locke insists "there is little evidence of any direct connection of the American Negro with his ancestral arts" except for some African musical influences. Slavery, he claims, "uprooted" most of the technical traditions of the slaves' former culture; the transplanted Africans retained at most "an emotional inheritance of deep-seated aesthetic endowment" (whatever that might mean), but it "blossomed in strange new forms." We should not read Locke as denying some African influences in slave culture. Rather, his point is that

> what we have thought primitive in the American Negro—his näiveté, his senti-mentalism, his exuberance and his improvising spontaneity are . . . neither characteristically African nor to be explained as an ancestral heritage. They are the result of his peculiar experience in America and the emotional upheaval of its trials and ordeals. . . . They represent essentially the working of environmental forces rather than the outcropping of a race psychology.[61]

In short, what Locke actually values about black American culture is not that it is primitive (meaning innocent of history and tradition). Rather, it is *authentic,* in the sense valued by regionalists: it is not merely an imitation of white culture but the product of the creative imagination and experiences of blacks themselves. To be sure, blacks borrowed freely from the culture of their captors, but Locke insists that they resisted cultural domination and used those borrowed cultural forms to express their own feelings and per-spectives. Clearly what Locke is concerned with here is maintaining the link between art and *experience;* what makes culture vital is that it reflects the ac-tual experience of the artist and his or her community. Thus it is experience rather than a racial essence that bridges the Boasian divide between culture and nature.

Locke's emphasis on experience reflects both his own intellectual orien-tation toward pragmatism and the influence of philosophical pragmatism on black progressivism and black environmental thought. We needn't conduct an in-depth exploration of early twentieth-century pragmatism here, but a brief overview will help to illuminate Locke's arguments. Pragmatists like William James and John Dewey claimed that experience validates belief and is therefore the chief source of meaning in human life. Under this view, meaning—indeed, truth itself—is something humans create out of their in-teractions with their external environment.[62] This idea resonates, of course, with the emphasis in the black intellectual tradition on freedom of will and creative interaction with the world. And it has important implications for humans' relationship to nature.

Pragmatists usually addressed that relationship most fully in their dis-cussions of art—discussions that were of great interest to the theorists of the Harlem Renaissance, given their interest in the social and political significance of art. Dewey's aesthetic theory, as represented in his 1934 work *Art as Experience*, deserves special attention in this regard. Dewey was inspired in part by the Harlem Renaissance and developed his views on art in close collaboration with Renaissance patron Albert Barnes. His essay on aesthetics offers a well-developed statement of a set of ideas circulating in Locke's and Du Bois's immediate intellectual milieu.[63]

Drawing on Darwinian evolutionary biology, Dewey argues that humans struggle to find an "equilibrium" with the natural environment. That struggle, according to Dewey, results not only in natural selection but in moments of temporary harmony—moments when one is fully alive and alert, experiencing a "complete interpenetration of self with the world of objects and events." Interestingly, he attributes to both "savages" and animals this unity of experience. But humans, unlike animals, go on to express this experience in artistic forms. Art thus reconstitutes on the plane of meaning the "union of sense, need, impulse and action characteristic of the live creature." Artistic expression is the consummation of one's experience with the external environment; the artist takes material from the common, public world and shapes it to express his or her individual experience of the things in that world.[64]

Clearly this is a very different understanding of the relationship between nature and cultural vitality than that endorsed by the scientific racists. Although cultural vitality is a central value for Dewey, he gives nature's "vital force" no role in cultural production. Rather, vitality is a quality of one's *experience* with nature; a culture is vital if the people creating it live intensely and faithfully express that intense experience. Nor did Dewey believe that intense experience should involve dominating other social groups. On the contrary, a chief social function of art is to facilitate cross-cultural understanding. Art under his view allows foreigners to enter sympathetically into the life of the group, and therefore enhances appreciation of the subjective worldview of the alien group. This assumes, of course, that the artist and the art are fully integrated into the common life of the group; for Dewey, popular art forms such as jazz and comic strips are the best examples of this kind of fully integrated artistic expression. Such "works of art are the only media of complete and unhindered communication between man and man that can occur in a world full of gulfs and walls that limit community of experience."[65]

Locke's argument is consistent with Dewey's understanding of art as experience; both would agree that black art, to remain vital, should express the consummation of the black folk's actual experience with the external world.[66] This claim is also consistent, of course, with literary regionalism and literary realism that permeated Locke's intellectual milieu, which similarly valued authentic experience over imitation. It thus resonates with the broader intellectual trends informing black progressivism. Nevertheless, it was problematic in one respect: Locke's theory conflicts with the claim (endorsed by Du Bois, among others) that the value of black folk culture lies in black folks' distinctive experience *with nature*—or, more properly, with Nature in the Romantic sense, the spiritual source of creativity. Locke talks about experience *per se* rather than experience with nature; under his reasoning, contact with the social or built environment is just as valid an experience, and therefore just as inspiring, as contact with forests and fields. If it is experience per se rather than experience with nature that gives rise to great art, then black Americans would seem to have no special claim to cultural vitality, and therefore no special grounds for claiming membership in American civilization.

Fortunately, the pragmatists provided alternative grounds for that claim. Dewey, for example, argued that white American culture lacked vitality because the living patterns created by industrial capitalism were too monotonous, routinized, and vicarious to produce the sort of intense experience that would inspire great art.[67] Locke voiced similar concerns, criticizing popular culture as derivative and commercial in comparison to the more pure, natural folkways of the southern peasant.[68] Under this reasoning, what makes black folk culture valuable is not that it arose out of blacks' contact with nature but that it arose out of a *particular kind* of contact with the world: it was the product of an intense, deep engagement with an extraordinarily challenging natural and social environment—the kind of engagement that is (arguably) less available in a mechanized and commercialized urban environment. In short, black folk culture has superior vitality because it is an authentic expression of a particularly intense collective experience. It is not, like white American pop culture, the product of a deracinated elite manipulating tired, conventional forms for a mass market.

This reasoning thus accounts for the value of black folk culture to American civilization without drawing on racial essentialism or the Romantic concept of nature. But replacing nature's vital power with the power of intense experience has further implications: Locke's argument also helps to legitimate *urban* black culture as a source of artistic inspiration. Mechanization and commercialization notwithstanding, black urban life would provide plenty of intense experiences for artists to mine. Following this logic, Charles Johnson would apply the principles of "folk realism" to the urban lower classes, publishing stories about this group in the pages of *Opportunity*.[69] As the next chapter will discuss, primitivist themes would find their fullest expression among the writers who depicted the black city, and the black urban folk would become a principal theme in black literature during and after the Harlem Renaissance. For Locke, however, the main function of primitivism was to turn artists' attention to their roots in the past—in slavery and the South.

SINGING THE SOUTH

Under Locke's view, the vitality of black folk culture derived from black folks' intense experience with the world. Unfortunately, slavery was central to that intense experience. Indeed, according to Locke, slavery was not merely destructive of African culture but was also uniquely creative: slavery was the chief factor in producing the race consciousness that must inform a vital black artistic tradition. "All classes of a people under social pressure are permeated with a common experience," he explained. "They are emotionally welded as others cannot be. With them, even ordinary living has epic depth and intensity."[70] Thus it is not race that produces culture and history, but culture and history—specifically a common history of suffering and oppression—that produces a race and the potential for a vital racial art.[71]

This is not to suggest that Locke believed racial oppression is good for art, however. Blacks may have had the resilience to create a rich folk culture even under slavery, but Locke worried that the degraded status of blacks threatened to prevent them from developing an original artistic tradition out of their folk culture. Kelly Miller had made a similar argument, claiming that racial prejudice denied black artists the social and economic resources they needed to produce great art. Locke pointed to a different problem, however: echoing James Weldon Johnson, Locke argued that racial prejudice makes black artists *ashamed* of the very culture that ought to inspire them. Consider Negro spirituals, for example, "suppressed for generations under the stereotypes of Wesleyan hymn harmony, secretive, half-ashamed, until the courage of being natural brought them out."[72] Here "being natural" does not mean breaking with tradition, as it usually did for the European primitivists; that would be inconsistent with the Boasian view that cultural production is working with inherited traditions. Rather, "being natural" means drawing from traditions that developed out of the group's *own* experience instead of mimicking the traditions of the dominant culture. According to Locke, racial disparagement has created a psychological barrier between blacks and their roots, resulting in a timid conventionalism—a tendency to imitate white models rather than creating original art out of their own experience. Howells had advised Americans to look to their native place and experience to create a distinctive American literature. Locke contended that this project was even more necessary to American blacks—they must "shak[e] off the psychology of imitation and implied inferiority."[73] The creation of an authentic black racial identity was both the precondition for and the result of a racial art that must grow naturally, like a plant, out of blacks' native environment.

And that native environment, for better or worse, includes the American South. In fact, for Locke, a truly southern literature would necessarily be a black literature:

> The Negro has been the peasant matrix of that section of America which has most undervalued him, and here he has contributed not only materially in labor and in social patience, but spiritually as well. The South has unconsciously absorbed the gift of his folk-temperament. . . . A leaven of humor, sentiment, imagination and tropic nonchalance has gone into the making of the South from a humble, unacknowledged source.[74]

Although black communities had of course developed in other parts of the country, for centuries the majority of American blacks had lived in the South. They had interacted with and bonded to a southern landscape. It was this southern environment that informed the cultural forms—the music, art, dance, literature, ways of thinking, and feeling—that blacks had brought with them to northern cities. Under this view, the vital elements of black American culture come from the folk culture originating in Africa but developed under the pressure of slavery in the American South.

The paradigm of this sort of art is Jean Toomer's 1923 *Cane*, one of the great works of American regionalism. *Cane*, a collection of stories and poems set primarily among the black peasants of Georgia, evokes the landscape and folkways of the black South with lyrical descriptions of the pine forests, the red clay, and the cabins and fields of the black folk. According to Waldo Frank, *Cane* not only describes the South, "this book *is* the South"; it is the "aesthetic equivalent to the land." Others saw in *Cane* the expression of Toomer's dawning (if fragile) race consciousness as well. According to Montgomery Gregory, it not only "IS the South, it IS the Negro."[75] It was written after a visit to Georgia during which Toomer first felt a strong connection to his black heritage after hearing "folk-songs come from the lips of

Negro peasants."[76] In Toomer's words, it was an attempt to capture the spirit of the lives of "a song-lit race of slaves."[77] Toomer's sojourn among southern black folk inspired him as northern urban life could not: "Georgia opened me," he wrote. "And it may well be said that I received my initial impulse to an individual art from my experience there. For no other section of the country has so stirred me. There one finds soil, soil in the sense the Russians know it,—the soil every art and literature that is to live must be imbedded in."[78] His lyrical and impressionistic prose seems designed not so much to explain the South as to reproduce in the reader an emotional connection to the South and its people—to create in them the sense of place he experienced in Georgia.

This, it seems, is what Locke had in mind by vital racial art: an art that captures the race's authentic experience with the natural and social world. But *Cane* also raises some questions about Locke's theory. The first harkens back to *The Conjure Woman:* How does a sensitive artist draw inspiration from a history of brutal oppression? Wouldn't he experience that history as an assault on his personality, his sense of self? Waldo Frank suggested that *Cane* offered a new, less critical attitude toward the South, celebrating its beauty rather than condemning its history. In fact, however, Toomer did confront the violence and terror of racism in the South, exploring in depth its psychological costs. Indeed, the first part of *Cane* ends with a terrifyingly graphic lynching.[79] But what was the emotional cost of that exploration to Toomer himself? Does artistic vitality really require artists to keep picking at the wound of slavery—and if so, is it worth it?

The second question is even more problematic: Toomer was not actually from the part of Georgia he described. He was born in Washington, D.C., and spent most of his life in northern cities; *Cane* was based on a mere two-month sojourn in Sparta, Georgia. In what sense, then, can we say that *Cane* reflects the artist's authentic experience? And if the artist does not have to draw from his individual experience, why should he be limited to drawing on the experiences of other members of his race? Indeed, how does he determine which race is his? This was a serious problem for the mixed-race Toomer, who struggled against and ultimately rejected a strictly defined black racial identity.[80]

Locke didn't address these questions directly, but to the first he would probably reply that confronting slavery is simply the price of artistic creativity. Intense experience is often painful, but it is such experience that shapes the consciousness of the race and inspires great art. Indeed, intense experience can itself be the foundation of a secure sense of self, particularly if that experience is shared among a community and can be given meaning through art. Such art, in turn, is the only hope for the true cross-cultural understanding that is essential to achieving racial justice.[81] To this extent, Locke was still very much a Romantic: it is the artist's calling to suffer for the race.

The second question is more complex. In parsing these issues of racial identity, it is important to bear in mind that, for Locke, race may be socially constructed but it is still *real*; it has a historical reality that can't be ignored. Membership in a race for most people will not be optional but a fact of the social reality they are born into. However, it doesn't appear that Locke intended black artists to *limit* themselves to their own experiences or the experiences of their race. He never denied that one might sympathize with another's experience; on the contrary, much of the political value of a racial art is its ability to allow others to understand the subjective reality of the race. Rather, his point is that a strong race consciousness allows one access to the experiences of one's race as embodied in its folk culture. In fact, race consciousness is useful for Locke precisely because it facilitates such sympathy, helping black artists to understand and draw on the experiences that shaped the race—particularly the painful ones.[82] In short, Toomer was able to speak from the experiences of black Georgians because his race consciousness helped him to understand their world.

Under this view, of course, sympathy with the black folk need not be limited to blacks. Anyone might draw inspiration from a living, vital black folk culture, provided one could fully sympathize with the way of life it reflects. Indeed, Sherwood Anderson and Eugene O'Neill claimed to have done so. To the extent they succeeded, their work may be concerned vital and even authentic—that is, true to the experience of the group whose lives they were exploring. And, logically, black artists also ought to be able to sympathize with the folk culture of white ethnic groups.[83] According to Locke, however, that is not likely to happen. It is not white *folk* culture that attracts black artists; they want to engage the products of high culture, which are already far removed from their folk roots. Indeed, black artists' shame about their own roots would probably make them equally unlikely to embrace the lowly folk culture of other groups. Thus, under Locke's analysis such cases of interracial sympathy are quite rare in a racially stratified society. In the oppressive atmosphere of early twentieth-century America, the person best positioned to draw effectively on black folk culture was a black artist with a robust racial consciousness.

Toomer's black race consciousness was not robust; notoriously, it disintegrated soon after he published *Cane*. Like James Weldon Johnson's protagonist, Toomer became an ex-colored man and, in an infamous example of life imitating art, apparently lost his creative energy.[84] Locke would have predicted that result. Under his theory, there should be an organic relationship between culture and nature; culture should grow out of a group's actual experience with its external environment. But drawing artistic inspiration from a group's collective experience requires one to identify or at least sympathize with that group, which may be difficult in a culturally diverse society divided by race and class hierarchies and troubled by a history of racial oppression. Moreover, racial injustice can impair the victims' personal and collective memories, alienating them from their own and their group's historical experience with the world. According to this analysis, Toomer tried to listen to nature's voice, but his sense of belonging to the black race was not sufficient to sustain his efforts. His fragile race consciousness didn't provide him the psychological resources he needed to continue drawing inspiration from the black folk's intense suffering on and with the American landscape.

This may be too simplistic an explanation of Toomer's individual psychology, of course. But the theory has certain undeniable strengths: it offers a persuasive explanation of both the proper relationship between culture and nature and the special vitality of black folk culture without relying on either racial essentialism or a Romantic concept of nature. It recognizes the black folk's unique history with the southern landscape without relying on the racial stereotypes associated with white supremacist ideology. Thus it seems a promising foundation for the Negro Arts movement.

Nevertheless, many black intellectuals remained wary even of this reconstructed primitivism. George Schuyler, for example, famously dismissed the whole Negro Arts project as "hokum," insisting that the products of black elites are squarely in the same European-centered tradition as those of white Americans.[85] Moreover, not all artists found southern folk culture inspirational; the picaresque tradition in black letters persisted as well, emphasizing the burden of slavery, the value of upward mobility, and the freedom of leaving the South behind.[86] Even those writers most famous for drawing on folk sources also warned of the danger of primitivist conceits. Zora Neale Hurston's "Drenched in Light," for example, brings together Isie, a rural black girl who dreams of travel and adventure, with a couple of white motorists who see her as a "shining little morsel" of primitive vitality.

They decide to "keep" her, a happy arrangement based on several layers of mutual misunderstanding.[87] Langston Hughes offers a similar critique in his 1934 collection, *The Ways of White Folks*. "Slave on the Block" gives us Michael and Anne Carraway, who "go in for Negroes." But not in a philanthropic way: "They saw no use in helping a race that was already too charming and naïve and lovely for words." They went in for the "Art of the Negroes" that was "so simple and fervent," so "real." So they collected Covarrubias originals: "Of course, Covarrubias wasn't a Negro [he was a Mexican caricaturist], but how he caught the darky spirit!"[88]

Hurston and Hughes did sympathize with the ideas underlying primitivism and regionalism; both found artistic inspiration and a special sort of vitality in black folk culture, urban and rural.[89] And their critique of white primitivism rests on the realist principle that one should carefully observe and describe what is there, rather than seeing the world through unexamined stereotypes. But they nevertheless invite us to wonder what, after all, is really there. Hughes's more satirical works echo Chesnutt's conjure stories, asking whether black folk culture truly expresses authentic experience—or whether it is merely a maze of masks and deception put on for white folk. Beneath that question, of course, lies the persistent ambiguity in black environmental thought: Did slavery create a vital folk culture—or did it destroy the conditions for authentic cultural production, leaving blacks with an impoverished and distorted relationship to the American landscape? How can any authentic culture—white or black—emerge from a land cursed by injustice?

CONCLUSION

In the end, black writers' reflections on primitivism suggested that neither black nor white Americans could look to their past to find a culture in harmony with nature; because of the legacy of racial oppression, such a culture has yet to emerge. So argued Du Bois, for example, in his 1926 essay "Criteria of Negro Art." Like Albert Barnes, Du Bois contended that black artists could yet make Americans feel the "majesty of Nature"—but not by virtue of their primitive psychology. Rather, black artists would reform Americans' relationship with nature through authentic expression based on an honest confrontation with their own history.

The essay begins by describing the beauty and peacefulness Du Bois experienced while visiting a Scottish lake: "You could glimpse the deer wandering in unbroken forest," he remembered, "you could hear the soft ripple of romance on the waters." But then a group of American tourists descended on him: "They poured upon the little pleasure boat. . . . They all tried to get everywhere first. They pushed other people out of the way. They made all sorts of incoherent noises and gestures so that the quiet home folk and the visitors from other lands silently and half-wonderingly gave way before them." The ugly Americans "struck a note not evil but wrong," he complained. "Their hearts had no conception of the beauty which pervaded this holy place."[90]

According to Du Bois, white Americans' insensitivity to natural beauty is the result of racial injustice. He reaches this surprising conclusion by reasoning that racial oppression has distorted American art: white artists as much as black artists are limited by the prevailing racial ideology. They cannot write from authentic experience because no one wants stories that reveal the dignity and humanity of blacks—or the "pitiful human degradation" revealed in the lives of many white folk. "In other words, the white public today demands from its artist, literary and pictorial, racial pre-judgment which deliberately distorts truth and justice."[91] Deprived of a vital art derived from true experience, white Americans lack the resources to develop a sensitive appreciation for the beauty of the real world.

It is a provocative argument, to be sure. However, it seems to challenge the more recent revisionist view that the love of natural beauty was primarily a white, middle-class value and even an integral part of white Americans' racial ideology. According to the revisionists, white middle-class Americans' privileged position allowed them to cultivate an appreciation for the non-instrumental value of nature—an appreciation that working-class Americans, including most black Americans, couldn't afford.[92] Du Bois's argument isn't necessarily inconsistent with that view, however; it is in fact an extension of it. His point is that white middle-class Americans—because of their privileged position and insistence on racial orthodoxy—developed an appreciation for a natural world that *didn't exist:* an imaginary, picture-postcard natural world in which all trace of human suffering and oppression was erased from the landscape. As a result, they hardly knew how to respond to an *actual* landscape (even a very pretty one).

Thus understood, Du Bois's argument in fact resonates with a long-standing theme in the mainstream tradition of environmental thought: that developing a proper appreciation for the value of nature involves learning to see what is actually there. We must carefully observe the world around us to appreciate its beauty and complexity. For the romantic, this attentiveness gives the artist access to nature's creative power; for the pragmatist, it results in the kind of intense experience that inspires great art. Under either view, however, it produces an art that can in turn educate the community to be more sensitively attentive to the world, to invest it with value and meaning. This process is in turn the key to cultural vitality. Black theorists like Du Bois and Locke contribute to this tradition by explaining how racial oppression cuts off that vital link between nature and culture. According to these theorists, one accesses nature through participation in a culture—ideally, a folk culture that develops out of and truly expresses intense, sustained experience with the natural world. Black folk may have such a culture, but racial oppression has suppressed the most authentic expressions of their experience and made accessing those experiences painful and costly. Indeed, white elites' relationship to their own folk culture is also affected by racism: to the extent the life of lower-class whites resembles that of blacks, whites will do their best to disassociate themselves from it and won't tolerate truthful depictions of it. Under this analysis, then, achieving a proper relationship to nature requires reforming race relations.

Fortunately, according to Du Bois, "we black folk may help for we have within us as a race new stirrings; stirrings of the beginning of a new appreciation of joy, of a new desire to create, of a new will to be." To realize that potential, black Americans must take hold of their past: "We thought nothing could come out of that past which we wanted to remember; which we wanted to hand down to our children," he admitted. But "suddenly, this same past is taking on form, color and reality, and in a half shamefaced way we are beginning to be proud of it. We are remembering that the romance of the world did not die and lie forgotten in the Middle Age; that if you want romance to deal with you must have it here and now in your own hands." The vitality of black art will come from depicting, with honesty and sensitivity, the authentic experiences and perceptions of the race—the suffering, cruelty, and despair as well as the hope and joy. This truthful depiction will be the starting point for "this great work of the creation of Beauty, of the preservation of Beauty, of the realization of Beauty."[93]

Du Bois's project, and indeed the Harlem Renaissance as a whole, has been criticized by later commentators as naïve, giving far too much significance to the political value of art.[94] But few of those commentators would dispute his and Locke's diagnosis of the problems of black artists and the effect of racism on white culture. Their solution may be partial, but it still has power to provoke and inspire: black artists, they insisted, must liberate their own minds from racial stereotypes and embrace their past, so that they can speak the truth about their race's experience with the American landscape. Their efforts will help to give a truer, more complete meaning to the landscape for both black and white Americans. Understanding that landscape—one of suffering as well as hope—could in turn be the starting point for envisioning more vital and healthy modern communities—communities, as Du Bois put it, "where men know, where men create, where they realize themselves and where they enjoy life."[95] The next chapter explores how that vision of community took shape as black artists and theorists turned their attention to the urban industrial landscape.

CHAPTER SIX

URBAN MONTAGE

———— ·•·•·· ————

Seventy years after Albert Barnes declared that black artists would invoke for us the "ineffable peace of the woods," Carl Anthony—at that time president of the Earth Island Institute—asserted that "we, as people of color, have had very little to say about nature."[1] As I've argued in these chapters, black Americans have in fact been talking about nature for over 150 years. But Anthony's statement reflects a widespread misconception, rooted in the twentieth-century development of the black urban consciousness. By 1930, nearly half of black Americans lived in cities. Accordingly, over the subsequent decades, the focus of black environmental thought would shift from the forest and fields of the rural South to the built environment of the urban North: the landscape of skyscrapers and tenements, streetcars and subways, streetlights and nightlife.[2]

The city is in fact one of the richest themes in twentieth-century black thought. That richness, however, defies any simple interpretation; the city has been a protean concept for black writers, carrying multiple and conflicting meanings. Indeed, the dominant theme in black writing on the city is ambivalence: the urban environment has many potentialities, represented in black literature by a montage of urban images in conversation and competition with one another.[3] The city can be a frontier promising individual freedom, a jungle bursting with primitive energy, an organic community growing naturally out of the lives of its inhabitants, a homeland embodying the common consciousness of the race, or a modern-day plantation withering—or exploding—under the pressure of racial oppression. Nevertheless, most black writers continued to link the character of the urban environment to the justice of the social order. In a land cursed by injustice, they warned, the city's best possibilities will seldom be realized, and the city will remain a particularly dangerous place for black Americans.

Black writing on the city therefore shares important continuities with the larger tradition of black environmental thought. It is those continuities that

I explore in this chapter. This exploration will take us a few years beyond the period I've promised to focus on, in order to highlight the connections between the foundational period and contemporary black environmental thought. Black writing on the city even today is in many ways an extension of black writing on slavery; after all, as was suggested in Chapter 1, the slave plantation itself was an industrial, mechanized, and tightly controlled order that shared many of the characteristics of the urban ghetto. Thus black writers used the city as they had used the plantation, to explore how oppression can inhibit creative and responsible interaction with the external environment, creating a landscape of racial barriers and distorting one's aesthetic and spiritual connection to the land. At the same time, though, the potentiality of the city—its apparent promise of escape from traditional ways of life—inspired many black writers to develop utopian themes, using the city to explore what freedom, equality, and community might look like in a reformed America. The city in black thought thus embodies both black oppression and black aspiration; it can be either a prison or a promised land.

A DANGEROUS ATTRACTION

The city that appears in early twentieth-century black literature has roots in a nineteenth-century discourse (developed by both white and black writers) about cities, civilization, and race. It is a predominately anti-urban, agrarian discourse, contrasting the unhealthful, dangerous city with the more wholesome countryside. A typical example is the 1860 short story "Life in the Iron-Mills" by white author Rebecca Harding Davis. "A cloudy day: do you know what that is in a town of iron-works?" she asks. The city air "is thick, clammy with the breath of crowded human beings." Across the street "a crowd of drunken Irishmen are puffing Lynchburg tobacco in their pipes." Indeed, the town is filled with smoke: "It rolls sullenly in slow folds from the great chimneys of the iron-foundries, and settles down in black, slimy pools on the muddy streets. Smoke on the wharves, smoke on the dingy boats, on the yellow river." About the "dull and tawny colored" river, Davis writes, "[it] drags itself sluggishly along, tired of the heavy weight of the boats and coal-barges." She fancies "a look of weary, dumb appeal upon the face of the negro-like river slavishly bearing its burden day after day."[4]

Such bleak descriptions of urban landscapes are common in late nineteenth-century and early twentieth-century American literature, particularly among the muckraking writers of the Progressive era. As one might expect, they reflect the class perspective of the writer (evidenced in, for example, Davis's patrician disgust with the crowd). Davis's description of the river as slavish and "negro-like" suggests the influence of abolitionist ideology as well, implying that industrial production enslaves nature as well as people. But her vision of the urban landscape also draws on the theory of social progress discussed in Chapter 2, in which the growth of large cities represents a civilization's moral decline from the agrarian ideal. The rise of great cities and the closing of the frontier in the late nineteenth century was to many Americans a sign that their republic was fast approaching the final stages of moral degeneracy; cities were becoming seedbeds of tyranny and moral decay—ugly, corrupted, and corrupting environments. The ugliness of the city should thus be read as both a cause and a result of this moral decay. Under the standard assumptions of nineteenth-century environmental thought (as discussed in previous chapters), a virtuous people would not let their environment degenerate, and urban dwellers deprived of the beneficial effects of natural beauty could be expected to suffer both spiritually and morally.

But how did such corruption infect a predominately agrarian, republican people? The degeneracy of American civilization could be blamed on white Americans themselves, of course. Much of the anxiety about urbanization in the late nineteenth and early twentieth centuries focused on the corrupting effect of luxury and wealth on the white race. But the influx of racially and ethnically diverse immigrants into the cities in the late nineteenth century seemed to many social critics to aggravate the problem. These new citizens, they reasoned, came from races that had not yet evolved enough to produce freedom-loving, virtuous republicans. Thus, these non–Anglo-Saxon immigrants contributed to the slavishness and corruption that infected the great cities.[5]

The racial ideology underlying this negative view of cities was of course problematic for black Americans, who (despite their 300-year history on the American continent) could still find themselves classed among the "aliens" responsible for degrading Americans' moral fiber. But the conventional view of cities also had some political value for blacks. During the nineteenth century and into the twentieth, most blacks were farmers living in rural areas; as was noted in previous chapters, they could claim for themselves agrarian and primitive virtues. Thus although there were black communities in many northern cities, black leaders did not necessarily encourage their growth. Martin Delany worried as early as 1852 that black

Americans were becoming a race of servants, due to their tendency to gravitate to cities.[6] Frederick Douglass agreed; like Delany, he advised blacks to turn to agriculture as a more virtuous calling. The service jobs they sought in the cities would not offer them true independence, since such jobs were founded on the "pride and indolence" of whites; servants were not providing any real necessities, so they could not count on continued employment.[7] These theorists saw some truth in the conventional, negative view of cities: they seemed to pose considerable moral risks, particularly to blacks.

That concern is reflected in the 1853 narrative of fugitive slave Solomon Northrup. Born a free northern black man, Northrup was the son of a slave who had been a paragon of agrarian virtues: respectable, industrious, frugal, religious, humble, and honest, he kept to "the peaceful pursuits of agriculture" and avoided the "menial positions" that Douglass and Delany disparaged.[8] Northrup initially follows his father's example but is lured to the city in the hope of improving his social status, whereupon he soon falls into "shiftlessness and extravagance."[9] He encounters a couple of con men who promise him work if he will travel with them to New York. Eager to see the metropolis, he agrees. Eventually, he imprudently accompanies them to Washington, D.C., where—after a heady tour of the city sights—he is plied with liquor and sold into slavery. The story of an innocent lured to the slavery of vice in the big city is familiar to readers of Gothic romances; Northrup's adventures highlight the special dangers of city life to blacks, who faced legal and not just moral slavery if they wavered from the path of virtue.

Solomon Northrup's story is a cautionary tale, but it highlights an important feature of the city as it appears in black literature. The reason the city is dangerous to blacks like Northrup is precisely because it is so *attractive* in comparison with the countryside. Whereas white writers often idealized rural communities as repositories of agrarian virtues, black writers could not ignore the reality of slavery, racial oppression, lack of economic opportunity, and the sheer drudgery of farm labor. Douglass's and Delany's concerns notwithstanding, that reality made the attractions of city life—its sensual appeal as well as its economic, social, and political advantages—a prominent theme in black literature and an important counterpoint to black agrarianism. Indeed, this ambivalence about the city is the other side of black writers' ambivalence about the effects of slavery: slavery may have made blacks a rural folk, but to the extent it alienated them from the land, it also made urban life particularly appealing.

That vision of the city as a "liberating space," an alternative to the oppressive conditions of rural life, is prominent in Frederick Douglass's autobiographies. Robert Butler's penetrating analysis of the *Life and Times of Frederick Douglass*, for example, points out that Douglass "praises the city as a new space, offering various forms of liberation for black people."[10] Douglass's native plantation is oppressive, rigidly hierarchic, and "desertlike," and the wilderness that surrounds it is even more hostile. In Baltimore, however, he has the opportunity to see himself as a person rather than a slave. The work he does in the city—housework and working in a shipyard—is more creative than field work, giving him more independence and leisure. He meets a broader range of people with varying views on slavery and equality, and even has the opportunity to learn to read. Moreover, the greater social control exercised in the city—the tendency of one's neighbors to observe and judge one's behavior—serve to increase slaves' freedom by protecting them from the worst physical abuses of their masters. And being in the city increases Douglass's mobility, putting him closer to the trains and ships that facilitate escape. In short, judging from Douglass's story, the city could serve for blacks the same function as the frontier did for whites: as a freer space in which one could better develop one's individuality.[11]

Another well-known narrative of urban slavery echoes Douglass's message. Harriet Jacobs also experienced some of the advantages of city life; specifically, her master's sexual advances were restrained by his fear that they would be made public. "It was lucky for me," she commented, "that I did not live on a distant plantation, but in a town not so large that the inhabitants were ignorant of each other's affairs."[12] But even urban spaces are not free for slaves, and Jacobs ultimately had to take refuge in a small, cramped attic above her grandmother's porch. She remained in hiding there for seven years. Confined, separated from her children and family, deprived of sunlight and fresh air (but not protected from the cold and rain), her situation vividly illustrates the sense of imprisonment that later generations of black Americans would experience in urban ghettoes.

Indeed, Douglass himself didn't conclude that urban environments *in general* are more liberating than rural communities. In his *Life and Times*, as elsewhere in his writings, he continues to pay tribute to the agrarian ideal. Butler considers this an inconsistency in his thought, but as argued in earlier chapters, blacks had reason to believe that in a truly just society, farming could offer the freedom, independence, and community that slaves were denied.[13] Moreover, as Northrup's narrative demonstrated, the city's promise of riches, anonymity, and freedom from social convention posed its own dangers to vulnerable blacks; Jacobs, in fact, points out that a larger city, where she and her master would enjoy a degree of anonymity, would be just as dangerous for her as an isolated plantation.

This view of the city as a place of dangerous attraction is a persistent theme in black literature. It received further elaboration after Emancipation in Paul Laurence Dunbar's 1902 novel, *Sport of the Gods*, which helped to shape the discourse about the city that we find in the literature of the Harlem Renaissance. Dunbar tells the story of a reasonably virtuous southern black family who moves to New York after the father is falsely imprisoned. The son and daughter are entranced by the city:

> To the provincial coming to New York for the first time, ignorant and unknown, the city presents a notable mingling of the qualities of cheerfulness and gloom. . . . If he have the right stuff in him, a something will take possession of him that will grip him again every time he returns to the scene and will make him long and hunger for the place when he is away from it. Later, the lights in the busy streets will bewilder and entice him.[14]

Eventually, "the real fever of love for the place will begin to take hold upon him. The subtle, insidious wine of New York will begin to intoxicate him."[15] The son and daughter both fall victim to the heady lure of New York's vices and end up thoroughly degraded. But the novel also highlights the freedom and opportunity that New York offered to blacks, in contrast to the oppressiveness of the rural South. Dunbar's, like Northrup's, is a cautionary tale, but he makes vivid the attraction of city life to the "untrained negro" seeking to escape the confines of southern rural poverty.

This vision of the city is summed up most eloquently in James Weldon Johnson's *Autobiography of an Ex-Coloured Man*, whose New York "sits like a great witch at the gate of the country, showing her alluring white face and hiding her crooked hands and feet under the folds of her wide garments—constantly enticing thousands from far within, and tempting those who come from across the seas to go no farther. And all these become victims of her caprice." Paris and London, too, are charming and alluring—but he warns that many bright, intelligent colored men "fall under the spell" of the low life of the city and cannot throw it off.[16] The writers of the Harlem Renaissance understood Dunbar's and Johnson's ambivalence. They, too, celebrated the city's beauty, its rich materiality, diversity, and vitality—but they also warned of its dangers. Primitivism, of course, was well suited to this task. Drawing on primitivist conventions, the writers of the Harlem Renaissance portrayed the city as a potential reservoir of energy and creativity that could revitalize American society—but also a confusing social world in which identity was slippery, violence was endemic, and the unwary black was particularly vulnerable.

MODERN MANMADE JUNGLES

Carl Van Vechten's 1926 novel, *Nigger Heaven*, is admittedly a controversial place to begin an exploration of the city in Harlem Renaissance literature. The novel was widely condemned by black intellectuals, who objected to the white author's arguably exploitive depiction of Harlem's low-life. But it was also widely influential; Van Vechten was immersed in the Harlem milieu, and his novel developed themes that would continue to engage other Harlem Renaissance writers—particularly the concept of the city as a source of vital energy that had the potential to regenerate American civilization.[17] The novel's main character, Byron, is a young black man who comes to Harlem to pursue his writing. For Byron, as for so many protagonists in black literature, the city is a place of opportunity and freedom, particularly when contrasted with the oppressive and provincial rural South. Byron's father (like the earlier generation of black intellectuals) is ambivalent about the promise of city life; he offers the usual warning about the dangers of the city, the temptations toward a life of idleness and sensuality.[18] But Van Vechten suggests that what is hindering Bryon's art is precisely his failure to appreciate the vitality and sensuality of Harlem social life, and to take advantage of the full range of freedom offered by city life. As a white editor tells him, "The low life of your people is exotic. It has a splendid, fantastic quality. And the humour! How vital it is, how rich in idiom! Picturesque and fresh!" Byron replies coldly, "I'm afraid I don't know very much about the low life of my people."[19]

He soon learns, however, seduced by the primitive vitality of Harlem nightlife. In contrast to Davis's bleak urban landscape, Van Vechten describes Harlem as a jungle of vivid color and savage passions. A colored ball is a "kaleidoscope of colour" and "fervour," where wild dancing displays "that exotic Negro sense of rhythm" and the participants behave like "primitives" and "savages." Nightclubs are jungle-like as well, filled with the throbbing of drums and exotic music, amber moonlight, and dancing women with painted faces, seething with "love, sex, passion . . . [and]

hate."[20] Importantly, this jungle imagery is not derogatory, at least not in any simple sense. For some characters in the novel (who may not be speaking for Van Vechten, of course), the wild, primitive aspect of Harlem is precisely its value. Mary, the female protagonist, laments that she has lost touch with this "savage" element in her own soul: "She had lost or forfeited her birthright, this primitive birthright which was so valuable and important an asset, a birthright that all civilized races were struggling to get back to."[21] Harlem offers Mary and Byron not just economic opportunity but the chance to recapture their primitive birthright, to bring them back into contact with the source of their creativity. Thus in Van Vechten's novel, as in Frederick Douglass's autobiography, the city—or, more precisely, the black urban neighborhood—promises to serve for blacks the function of a frontier: it is not only a liberating space but a place where nature's vital energy, accessed through one's racial consciousness, is uniquely available to black Americans. Going to Harlem is, in a sense, returning to Africa.

Other Harlem Renaissance writers similarly explored the theme of Harlem as a jungle—a "modern man-made jungle," in Joel Roger's words, whose distinctively urban social forms (free of the conventionality of rural and small-town communities) and diverse venues for artistic expression constituted "a safety valve for modern machine-ridden and convention-bound society." Rogers thought the jazz musicians of Harlem offered a "recharging of the batteries of civilization with primitive new vigor."[22] Claude McKay, in *Home to Harlem*, also described a "little Africa" in Harlem's nightclubs, where you "could turn rioting loose in all the tenacious odors of service and the warm indigenous smells of Harlem, fooping or jig-jagging the night away."[23] Just as Martin Delany had imposed an Old Testament landscape on the American wilderness, twentieth-century writers imposed a tropical landscape on New York. In Claude McKay's poem, the tropics appear suddenly in a New York market: "Bananas ripe and green, and ginger root / Cocoa in pods and alligator pears" bringing "memories / Of fruit-trees laden by low-singing rills."[24] Like Van Vechten, they described in Harlem an opportunity to connect to a primitive vitality that Western civilization had lost.

Not surprisingly, however, many black elites found these primitivist motifs problematic. Both Van Vechten and McKay seemed to promote (or perhaps simply expose) a troublesome racial essentialism: blacks' allegedly primitive culture is essentially African, the outcropping of a racial psychology on which (in Albert Barnes's words) a white man's education has never been harnessed.[25] In other words, it is because blacks are and have remained alienated from "modern machine-ridden and convention-bound" white society that Harlemites remain in touch with their own primitive nature. Under this reading, the jungle imagery not only reinforces the very racial stereotypes that were being used to justify white supremacy, it made a virtue of blacks' exclusion from the industrial economy. W. E. B. Du Bois, for example, worried that books like Van Vechten's valorized precisely those aspects of black urban life that whites considered evidence of a savage temperament, as well as depicting economic and social aspiration as a misguided rejection of one's "true" nature. Such concerns relate to class as much as race, of course; the black urban culture these novels celebrated was a lower-class culture, and well into the 1920s the black intelligentsia tended to see the working class as targets of moral uplift rather than bearers of their own distinctive culture.[26] But Du Bois's criticisms shouldn't be dismissed (as they often are) as mere elite fastidiousness. Du Bois claimed to be judging these works by the standards of literary realism, and by those standards he surely had a point: the more sensational novels weren't very realistic descriptions even of lower-class life. In contrast, he praised works like Toomer's *Cane* and DuBose Heyward's *Porgy*, which depicted the "low-life" of blacks with more insight and sensitivity.[27] It was the primitivist stereotypes that bothered Du Bois—and, as was discussed in the previous chapter, the younger and less elitist generation of black writers shared his concerns.[28]

In fact, even those writers who celebrated the primitive vitality of urban street life also expressed ambivalence about its moral value. Van Vechten's novel, for example, forces the reader to confront the savage and violent aspect of Harlem social life. Byron, the hero, ends up morally degraded, falling for a beautiful but heartless woman and finally shooting a man out of jealousy and despair. Similarly, Claude McKay's protagonist Ray in *Home to Harlem* fails to find a place for himself and his art in the jungles of Harlem, with its "brutality, gang rowdyism, [and] promiscuous thickness." His friend Jake is also disgusted by the violence that permeates Harlem social life.[29] Freedom from "convention-bound society," it seems, carries with it a high price in social disorder. Beneath the primitivist celebration of Harlem a cautionary theme persists: the city is a beautiful, vital, but also extremely dangerous place. Its primitive energy may rejuvenate one's artistic impulses, but it also threatens one's moral character and physical safety. In

James Weldon Johnson's words, the "dread power of the city" is as stimulating as "opium is to one who is addicted to the habit."[30]

Clearly the jungle imagery in the novels of the Harlem Renaissance is part of the broader conversation about the effects of industrialism on Americans' relationship to nature. Harlem is figured in many of these novels as an urban alternative to the wilderness—a place to escape from a machine-ridden society and come into contact with nature's vital power, the wilderness within the black racial consciousness. But even those black writers who experimented with this theme had reservations about it, questioning whether the vitality of Harlem could be—or should be—a model for American civilization generally. White tourists to Harlem might hope that such a project would result in a more authentic, more "natural" urban lifestyle. But the Renaissance artists never entirely lost sight of the danger, violence, and brutality that accompanied Harlem's much-vaunted vitality.

NATURAL HABITATS

The urban jungle is not the only image of the city we find in black environmental thought during the early years of the twentieth century, however. Accompanying this theme was the concept, developed by Alain Locke and others, of the urban neighborhood as a *homeland*—a land held in common and the ground of a group's common consciousness. This image emerges sometimes as a description but more often as an ideal, a utopian vision that serves as a standard for evaluating racial progress as well as illuminating the nature and causes of black Americans' continuing alienation.

The longing for a home, as we have noted in previous chapters, is a persistent motif in black thought. In the 1920s, Harlem looked like it might fulfill that longing. Harlem was, in James Weldon Johnson's memorable phrase, "the recognized Negro capital," a black city-within-a-city.[31] The concentration of blacks—particularly property-owning blacks—made Harlem a potential "homeland" for the race. "Never before has [the Negro] been so securely anchored, never before has he owned the land, never before has he had so well established a community life."[32] Rudolph Fisher's short story "City of Refuge" describes the reaction of a black man's first encounter with Harlem: "Negroes at every turn; up and down Lenox Avenue, up and down One Hundred and Thirty-fifth Street; big, lanky Negroes, short, squat Negroes; black one, brown one, yellow one. . . . In Harlem, black was white. You had rights that could not be denied you; you had privileges, protected by law. And you had money. . . . It was the land of plenty."[33] In Harlem, it appeared, blacks held political, social, and economic power, allowing black Americans to feel safely at home there.

That impression, however, is deceptive. Fisher's protagonist does not in fact find safe refuge in Harlem; he is swindled and eventually arrested for peddling drugs (although he takes some comfort in being arrested by a black policeman). Claude McKay's protagonists in *Home to Harlem* are also disappointed by the city, by the violence and sheer social density that undermines both community and individuality. Alain Locke captures this sense of unrealized hope when he suggests that Harlem is the "home of the Negro's 'Zionism'" where the "pulse of the Negro world has begun to beat."[34] He emphasizes the utopian element in this conception of Harlem: it is not (yet) the promised land, but one could nevertheless see in it the promise of greater community and opportunity for black Americans. Harlem, in short, was becoming the center of the long-held *aspiration* for a black home on the American continent.

This notion of an urban neighborhood as a potential homeland contrasts strikingly with earlier views of cities as iniquitous, corrosive of community, and essentially alienating. But, like the concept of Harlem-as-jungle, it had a rich intellectual pedigree. It draws, of course, on the Christian concept of a heavenly city, a utopian community of true believers.[35] But the city of God is an otherworldly ideal far removed from the concrete reality of actual urban life; black writers were also increasingly interested in the possibilities for community offered by the city of man. To explore those possibilities, they looked to a set of progressive ideas that were informing conversations about environmentalism and urban reform. Here, too, the Harlem Renaissance writers were part of a much broader early twentieth-century conversation about the consequences of modernization—and astute critics of the assumptions informing it.

One important strand of this conversation was the emerging discipline of urban sociology, which contributed substantially to black writers' conception of black urban neighborhoods. Sociological study of the urban black community matured in the early decades of the twentieth century, particularly at Atlanta University and the University of Chicago. W. E. B. Du Bois was largely responsible for Atlanta University's prominence in the field, coming to Atlanta after publishing his monumental study of *The Philadelphia Negro*, the first major empirical sociological study of an urban black community. He went on to take over the Atlanta University Study series on black urban immigrants. Under Du Bois's direction, the series' focus broadened considerably, producing studies on the class structure, economic condition, and religious and family organization of American blacks. However, Du Bois and his students paid close attention to the conditions of urban blacks, thus contributing to the evolving portrait of the black city.[36]

The other major contributor to this portrait was the University of Chicago, which took up the project under the guidance of Robert E. Park. Park arrived at Chicago in 1914 after a varied career that included working as a newspaper reporter, studying with John Dewey at the University of Michigan and William James, Josiah Royce, and George Santayana at Harvard, and doing doctoral study at various German universities. He also worked as a secretary and ghost writer for Booker T. Washington for several years, from which vantage he formulated his understanding of race relations. Park's approach to urban sociology—"the Chicago school"—had an important influence on the black intellectual tradition, due in part to Park's writings on the city and race relations but also to the work of his black students, including Franklin Frazier and Charles S. Johnson.[37]

Du Bois and Park differed in important respects in their understanding of the dynamics shaping the black city. However, they were both well-grounded in European sociology and American pragmatism, and both conceptualized the urban neighborhood as a community shaped by persons responding to a common social and natural environment, and sharing in a common consciousness. Du Bois and Park approached the neighborhood as the basic social unit of the city, suggesting that it could in theory be an organic community in which its inhabitants could experience solidarity and attachment to place.

Park's approach to urban sociology is particularly significant to our inquiry because it combines Deweyan pragmatism with the new discipline of ecology, constituting another connection between early twentieth-century race theory and environmentalism. In his pioneering essay "The City," Park essentially naturalizes the urban environment, bringing it within the ambit of ecological thought. The city, he explains, is the "natural habitat of civilized man." It thus shares some of the attributes of natural ecosystems and can be studied as a "human ecology." For Park, human ecology concerns the spatial distribution and organization of human populations, which are governed by various social forces—much like the distribution and organization of animal and plant populations.[38] But in contrast to European sociologists, who focused on abstractions like social structure and systems, Park's reliance on ecology gave his urban sociology a distinctly concrete, intensely visual and spatial quality. Much like the literary realism that was also influencing black environmental thought, Park's urban sociology was oriented toward description of the forms of life—their texture, look, and feel—that one found in the urban environment.[39]

These forms of life clustered in neighborhoods, which for Park are the basic urban social units: "organic," spontaneous communities that evolve because sheer proximity gives rise to communication, shared interests, and local sentiment.[40] Neighborhoods, ideally, should offer the chance to participate in a common cultural life—a concept derived from Dewey, described by one scholar as "a sense of solidarity based on membership in a 'we-group'" that provides "access to the range of experience offered within the society."[41] Indeed, Park considered the craving to participate in this common life fundamental to human nature. What the urban dweller needs is "an environment, a group in which he can live. . . . That means finding a place where he can have not only free expression of his energies and native impulses, but a place where he can find a vocation and be free to formulate a plan of life."[42]

There are several ways in which the common life—or common consciousness—of a community could be expressed, including newspapers and sociological studies. But one important vehicle for communal expression is the arts: as was discussed in Chapter 5, for pragmatists like Dewey, artistic expression was the chief means "of complete and unhindered communication between man and man that can occur in a world full of gulfs and walls that limit community of experience."[43] To the extent an urban community, with its dense economic, communication, and interpersonal networks, cultivated such expression, it served a vital human need to belong, to share in a common life.

But cities are not simply one big neighborhood. They are a "mosaic of little worlds," offering pockets of community (such as Harlem or Chicago's Black Belt)—but also the opportunity to cross borders from one community to another, to achieve cosmopolitanism through the aggregation of communities. The mosaic quality of city life, Park contends,

> makes it possible for individuals to pass quickly and easily from one moral milieu to another and encourages the fascinating but dangerous experiment of living at the same time in several different contiguous, perhaps, but widely separate worlds. All this tends to give to city life a superficial and adventitious character; it

tends to complicate social relationships and to produce new and divergent individual types.[44]

Park welcomed the increased mobility of city dwellers on the grounds that constant exposure to different "worlds" encouraged individuality and intcl lectual development. But he also worried about its impact on the cohesiveness of the community—the loss of the mechanisms of social control that order communal life in small towns, the resulting loss of a sense of solidarity, and a decrease in the participation in a common life that was essential to social integration. "The easy means of communication and of transportation," he worried, "tend to destroy the permanency and intimacy of the neighborhood."[45]

Park's arresting image of the city as a "mosaic of little worlds" and his worries about the conflicting tendencies in urban life to create and undermine community would resonate with black experience, resurfacing in literary and scholarly treatments of the black city. Black intellectuals were less happy, however, with his optimistic view of race relations—which he suggested inevitably improve through social interaction—as well as his natural history approach to urban neighborhoods. "The City" doesn't explore the forces that create neighborhoods, thus leaving the impression that they emerge out of the free choices of their inhabitants (usually responding to economic conditions). Moreover, Park implies that their inhabitants are—or become—fairly homogeneous in their values, outlook, and sentiments.[46] He thus ignores the segregation laws and mob violence that confined blacks involuntarily to certain neighborhoods, and he downplays the class conflicts that can divide racial communities.[47]

Parks's students, however, could look to Du Bois's earlier work, *The Philadelphia Negro*, for a corrective to Park's perspective on urban racial enclaves. Du Bois also takes the urban neighborhood as his basic social unit, and like Park he recognizes that there are forces cultivating in its residents a common consciousness.[48] But Du Bois's neighborhood is a much more complex entity than Park's. Indeed, his study of the Philadelphia Negro was groundbreaking in its fine-grained description of the class structure of Philadelphia's Seventh Ward. To outside observers, the Seventh Ward might look like a homogeneous mass of black folk, but Du Bois documented substantial differences in income, education, and values in this population.[49] He also discussed in detail how economic forces combined with racial prejudice to create segregated neighborhoods. Racial prejudice not only excluded wealthy blacks from the better neighborhoods, it limited their employment options and raised the price of black housing (by limiting its supply).[50] These factors in turn condemned most urban blacks to substandard housing and a dangerous, unhealthy physical environment. Indeed, Du Bois resisted the tendency to describe social conditions as the product of impersonal, universal laws of social development, emphasizing instead the role of racial prejudice. The foundation of blacks' social environment, he insisted, "is the widespread feeling all over the land, in Philadelphia as well as in Boston and New Orleans, that the Negro is something less than an American and ought not to be much more than what he is."[51] Du Bois in fact suggested that urban blacks suffer from much the same sort of alienation that southern rural blacks experienced, and for much the same reason: racial discrimination and lack of economic opportunity prevents them from securing control of the land and discourages them from making improvements to it.

Du Bois's analysis of the black urban neighborhood was echoed by Charles S. Johnson, who was both a student of Park and (as editor of *Opportunity*) a prominent voice in the Harlem Renaissance. In response to the Chicago race riot of 1919, Johnson was appointed director of research for the Chicago Commission on Race Relations. The result of his research was the 1922 report *The Negro in Chicago*. This study echoed Du Bois's understanding of "the Negro problem": that American blacks are isolated from the larger community. They may share to some extent in a common racial consciousness, but they do not share in the common life of the larger society.

Johnson's study confirms Du Bois's analysis of the influence of racial prejudice (and indeed racial violence) in creating segregated neighborhoods.[52] Following Park, the study acknowledges the challenges facing black immigrants from the South in adapting to city life and notes that race relations in some neighborhoods were better "adjusted" than in others. But, like Du Bois, the study also insists that "the 'Negro problem' is deeper and wider than the difficulties which center about the more specialized problems of Negro housing, Negro crime, and industrial relations involving Negroes." The commission's study of those problems "left a baffling residuum of causes of racial discord, deep rooted in the psychology of the white and Negro groups in contact."[53] Racial prejudice, for example, was central to blacks' housing problems; whites excluded blacks from their neighborhoods because they believed black neighbors depreciated property values. Indeed, this was "one of the strongest influences in creating and fostering race antagonism in Chicago."[54] Thus for Johnson, the division of the city into "little worlds" was problematic: instead of creating the opportunity to move among diverse organic neighborhoods, this segregation isolated communities from one another, trapping blacks into decaying neighborhoods and preventing their full participation in the common life of the city.

In sum, this sociological tradition develops, on one hand, a concept of the city as a mosaic of organic communities that could, through the symbolic expression of its inhabitants, offer its inhabitants participation in a common life. The urban neighborhood could thus carry the values that mainstream environmental thought associated with rural life—community, solidarity, and attachment to place—while the city itself could carry some of the features of natural ecosystems, such as variety and ordered complexity. But, on the other hand, this organic concept of neighborhood invited the same critique to which black theorists had subjected that other famously organic community, the plantation. Du Bois and Johnson recognized that urban black communities are created in part by racial intimidation and coercion, just as slave plantations were. Its inhabitants, like the slaves, may develop a racial group consciousness, but they are also divided among themselves and remain alienated from the common life shared by other city residents. And, as in the rural South, that alienation is both a cause and a result of the unhealthy, ugly, and decaying landscape.

THE BELOVED COMMUNITY

Nevertheless, black intellectuals in the 1920s remained fairly optimistic about the possibilities of the urban community. Much of this optimism derives from a more utopian theme in the black intellectual tradition: the idea of the "Beloved Community." The Beloved Community (a term coined by Josiah Royce) is, as historian Casey Blake explains, "a communitarian vision of self-realization through participation in a democratic culture." This vision inspired a range of progressive intellectuals, both black and white.[55] Indeed, the Beloved Community idea unites many of the intellectual trends we have been discussing; its advocates included urban reformers such as Lewis Mumford and Robert Park; the "Young Americans" of the lyrical left such as Waldo Frank, Van Wyck Brooks, and Randolph Bourne; and influential cultural pluralists such as Josiah Royce and John Dewey. It was also embraced by black theorists such as Alain Locke, Jean Toomer, Richard Wright, and, in later years, Martin Luther King Jr. It would eventually inform both the civil rights movement and the environmental movement.[56] And it united many of those responsible for fashioning the key terms of the Harlem Renaissance—especially those terms central to discourse about the urban community.

It is perhaps ironic, then, that the idea of the Beloved Community stems in large part from the anti-urban discourse of the nineteenth-century English social critics John Ruskin and William Morris. Ruskin and Morris helped to inspire the settlement movement, the "spearhead" of American urban reformers who (among other things) funded Du Bois's research on the Philadelphia Negro.[57] But Ruskin and Morris saw the city less as the site of a reconstituted modern community than as a symptom of a civilization in crisis: they worried about the effect of industrialization and urbanization on humans' relationship to the natural world and on the means of maintaining vital communal life. Importantly, they also thought art was central to their goal of vital, creative communities, which made their theories particularly interesting to the American pragmatists and cultural pluralists. But they were equally concerned with labor—with how the organization of labor affects humans' aesthetic and spiritual relationship to nature.

Ruskin and Morris responded to the rise of the industrial city by developing an ideal conception of community to be realized in a reformed version of English village life. They can be read as primitivists, seeking the regeneration of Western civilization through a return to a more simple life—but their social theories were considerably more sophisticated than those of most primitivists. Ruskin and Morris advocated a communal form of socialism, aimed at reforming society's values toward aesthetic and humanistic goals, which they considered inextricably linked. Good art, Ruskin maintained, "is the expression of national life and character. . . . [A] nation cannot be affected by any vice, or weakness, without expressing it, legibly, and for ever, either in bad art, or by want of art."[58] He reasoned that England's national character had been warped by the dominance of the profit motive in the economic and most other spheres of life; production of material goods, he argued, should be guided by higher motives, by aesthetic and humane considerations. Thus both Ruskin and Morris sought to reunite artistic and industrial production—to revive the artistry involved in making ordinary objects—in order to make manual labor more pleasurable and ennobling. That artistry in turn should be inspired by close attention to the beauty of nature, so that productive labor would be a means of communing with nature rather than a force alienating humans from the natural world. And socialism, they concluded, provided the best hope for creating the social conditions—equality, community, and a general orientation toward higher ends than profit—for accomplishing such a reform of industrial production.[59]

But Ruskin and Morris were equally interested, and for the same reasons, with preserving the beauty of the English countryside and country village. "How can I ask working-men passing up and down these hideous streets [of London] day by day to care about beauty?" wondered Morris. According to Ruskin, "Beautiful art can only be produced by people who have beautiful things around them." He reasoned, "It is impossible [for modern workmen] to have the right ideas about colour, unless they see the lovely colours of nature unspoiled; impossible for them to supply beautiful incident and action in their ornament, unless they see beautiful incident and action in the world about them."[60] Again, both Ruskin and Morris argued that socialist reform was critical to preserving natural beauty; only when the profit motive was no longer guiding economic life would the means of material production be arranged to be inspired by and to preserve the beauty of nature.

Ruskin and Morris had widespread influence in late nineteenth- and early twentieth-century England and America. Although they weren't themselves ecologists, their ideas about the simple life and preserving natural beauty were integral to the preservation and rural reform movements.[61] In particular, their focus on the relationships among labor, artistic production, and natural beauty addressed a fundamental concern of environmentalism: how industrial modes of production have affected individuals' and society's relationship to the natural world. Many early ecologists (such as Patrick Geddes and Elisée Reclus) drew from their writings a plan for social reform intended to lead to better stewardship and a closer harmony between man and nature.[62] Similarly, many American social theorists saw in their ideas a blueprint for more humane and vital urban communities.

American urban reformers, however, faced an additional challenge in the cultural diversity created by America's history of immigration and slavery. Accordingly, cultural pluralism was also integral to the idea of the Beloved Community. Josiah Royce, for example, envisioned national and ultimately international unity growing out of healthy, robust "provinces," defined as "any one part of a national domain, which is, geographically and socially, sufficiently unified to have a true consciousness of its own unity, to feel a pride in its own ideals and customs, and to possess a sense of its own distinction from other parts of the country."[63] Royce encouraged provincialism for its tendency to create cultural diversity, which supported individuality, and for its tendency to contribute to "well-knit [social] organization."

National unity, he argued, must grow together with local "independence of spirit."[64]

The "Young Americans"—including Waldo Frank, Lewis Mumford, Randolph Bourne, and Van Wyck Brooks—applied this set of ideas specifically to the urban environment, which in their eyes represented the dominant trends shaping modern communities in general. The United States in the twentieth century, they believed, would be an urban nation, so it is in the city that they hoped to find a viable model of community. Drawing on Ruskin's critique of the industrial separation of art and labor, Royce's cultural pluralism, and Dewey's pragmatic liberalism, they imagined a reformed democratic culture that would provide a common life for its inhabitants—a nation of small, tight-knit communities, like urban neighborhoods, that would provide a strong sense of place and social support for the expression of individuality, particularly through art.

Like Ruskin and Dewey, the Young Americans put special emphasis on the role of art in community-making. A healthy public culture, they argued, has as its end the flourishing of human personality, which ultimately takes the form of artistic expression.[65] But art not only expresses the individual's unique perspective on the common life of the group, it also serves as a way for humans to establish a meaningful connection to the external environment. Frank, for example, argued that modern Americans lived in a "jungle" of machines, a chaotic world "uncontrolled and unregenerate by man." They are essentially savages, lacking any higher concepts or ideals that would "assimilate their world together with their personal desire into some kind of Whole." Echoing Dewey, he insisted that humans needed to transform this chaos through "creative articulation" of its material. This would make the world into a medium for a sense of truth and beauty—or, as Dewey would put it, it would reconstitute on the plane of meaning the "union of sense, need, impulse and action characteristic of the live creature." Artistic production would thus turn the industrial jungle into a true homeland.[66] The city should become, in Bourne's words, "a communal house," well-ordered and beautiful—a fitting environment for "the good life of personality."[67] This line of thought would eventually inform Mumford's notion of regional citizenship, a notion that continues to inspire contemporary bioregionalists: full citizenship in one's culture by way of an education rooted in the lived experience of one particular region.[68]

The Beloved Community idea resonates with both the pragmatic influences in black thought and with the older theme of black agrarianism: the idea that it is man's calling to "finish Creation" by ordering the natural world to serve human economic, aesthetic, and spiritual needs. Thus it is not surprising that the ideal of the Beloved Community appealed to Alain Locke. As Charles Scruggs summarizes, Locke combined "Frederick Jackson Turner's thesis of the frontier, Josiah Royce's theory of the 'province,' and Robert Park's . . . investigations of city life" to create an image of Harlem as utopian home for a New Negro.[69] Specifically, Locke put forward an ideal vision of the city as a place that offered blacks a "life in common." Here in Harlem, he pointed out, was "the first concentration in history of so many diverse elements of Negro life." He continued, "It has attracted the African, the West Indian, the Negro American; has brought together the Negro of the North and the Negro of the South; the man from the city and the man from the town and village; the peasant, the student, the business man, the professional man, artist, poet, musician, adventurer and worker, preacher and criminal, exploiter and social outcast."[70] These diverse elements have been brought by "proscription and prejudice" into a "common area of contact and interaction." The result, Locke believed, was "a great race-welding. . . . Hitherto, it must be admitted that American Negroes have been a race more in name than in fact. . . . The chief bond between them has been that of a common condition rather than a common consciousness; a problem in common rather than a life in common. In Harlem, Negro life is seizing upon its first chances for group expression and self-determination."[71]

In other words, American blacks, like Waldo Franks's savages, confronted a chaotic external environment—a common condition—but had limited opportunity to give it meaning through "creative articulation" of its material.

This need to give meaning to the environment is precisely why Locke urged black artists to draw on the collective memory of slavery and the South—not to limit them to these primitivist themes but to begin the task of interpreting the black American experience, thus welding the black urban crowd into a community. Under this view, black art should arise out of, but also help to create, racial consciousness. Locke hoped that art would produce among blacks a "self-culture," which in turn would build community by orienting diverse individuals to a common life.[72] In theory, such expression would also create better mutual understanding between the races, leading to full participation by blacks in American political and economic institutions.[73] At the very least, however, it would bring black Americans into a more meaningful relationship with their environment.

For Locke, then, Harlem and other black urban neighborhoods seemed to

promise a chance for authentic cultural adaptation to the American landscape, through creative expression of the race's experience and through full
participation in the community that claims dominion over the land. The urban environment was particularly promising, he suggested, because its
"mosaic" quality helps to "enlarge personal experience," breaking down the
psychological barriers to self-expression.[74] And, although Locke didn't
highlight it, the black urban neighborhood also seemed to offer the means
for self-expression through independent black economic, social, and political institutions. At the very least, it should offer a paying audience for black
artists.

But that, of course, was a central problem with Locke's vision: the audience for black artists was in fact quite small—and mostly white. Harlem's
economic and political independence was largely illusory. As Ruskin and
Morris had argued, the kind of urban village Locke envisioned would require
a radical restructuring of the economic and political systems, which in turn
would require mass political mobilization and institutional reform—neither
of which was a major focus of the Harlem Renaissance artists and theorists.[75]
But if Locke avoided revolutionary politics, he did nevertheless emphasize
the political dimension of blacks' relationship to the environment: in order
to overcome their historic alienation from the land, he argued, blacks must
be free to interpret their experience with the external environment through
"creative articulation" of its material. The environment, under this view, is
not laden with inherent meaning waiting to be discovered; rather, we *give*
meaning to our environment. But this is a social process and therefore vulnerable to the forces—like racial oppression and inequality—that undermine
social functioning. If a community (through the denial of civil rights and
lack of economic opportunity) lacks the means of self-expression and the
ability to preserve and pass down its cultural traditions, its members won't
be able to make sense of their world. They will remain permanently alienated from their physical as well as their social environment.

Locke's theory thus echoes a theme we first encountered in the late nineteenth-century critique of black peonage: the claim that racial oppression
has alienated blacks from the land by interfering with their creative, responsible agency, thus impairing their ability to give meaning to the world.
A result of this oppression, then, is that the landscape carries only the
meaning given to it by white Americans—or, worse, it may carry no meaning
at all, like Waldo Franks's chaotic jungle. As was noted in Chapter 3, other
theorists (including Du Bois) had already explored the economic and politi-

cal conditions that undermined agency and creative stewardship in the rural South. Locke, however, was more interested in exploring the psychological barriers—the sense of inferiority and shame, the narrow experience and lack of intellectual stimulation—that inhibited black artistic expression. At least some of these problems, he hoped, could be addressed by creating black urban neighborhoods like Harlem. Because the city is culturally diverse, offers greater economic opportunity, and tends to concentrate races in certain neighborhoods while giving them (some) access to one another's worlds, it could support the sort of responsible agency—the creative interaction with the world—that would transform the jungle of white civilization into a black homeland.

HOME TO HARLEM?

The concept of the city as a mosaic of villages combined with the utopian appeal of the Beloved Community produced a vision of the urban neighborhood as a potential homeland for black Americans, where they could share in a common life and contribute to American civilization through their symbolic culture. That vision had obvious appeal to black activists: it recognized the value of a distinctively black culture and community, describing it as autonomous from white culture but still integral to American society. Moreover, the idea of the Beloved Community, which emphasized culturally authentic artistic production as a chief end of social life, provided to Harlem artists a potential explanation of the political and cultural significance of the Negro Arts movement—an explanation that goes beyond the simplistic assumptions of conventional primitivism.

Still, the tradition of urban sociology, along with its literary cousin, urban realism, persisted as a counterpoint to the utopian theme: Harlem might have the potential to be the promised land, but it had a long way to go before it realized that potential. Moreover, this pluralist vision of the city elided some difficult questions about class, race, and identity. The city may be a mosaic of villages, but black writers were deeply sensitive to the fact that those villages were not natural, organic communities; they were ghettoes defined by race and class. Park and Locke suggested that crossing into the city's other "little worlds" could lead to intellectual growth and interracial communication. But most blacks found the borders of those little worlds well defended; crossing them was difficult and dangerous. Moreover, those who could "pass" found the experience threatening to their identity.

Jessie Fauset's *Plum Bun* explores the lure and consequences of "passing" by following the heroine, Angela Murray, through the mosaic of social and geographic worlds that constitute New York. Angela moves from Greenwich Village, where she is white, to Harlem, where she sometimes becomes black, and through the social worlds of bohemian artists, black activists and intelligentsia, and liberal bourgeoisie, each requiring her to adopt a different persona. She is constantly reminded, however, that her mobility is a function of her fair skin; her dark-skinned friends keep encountering barriers—movie theaters, restaurants, and entire neighborhoods are off-limits to them. Like the narrative of Henry Bibb, Fauset's novel describes the landscape of racial barriers that continue to separate Parks's "little worlds."[76]

Moreover, although Angela's experiences do give her a greater sophistication—perhaps contributing in some respects to her intellectual development—it comes at a great price to her integrity. She longs for the community and sense of purpose and seriousness shared by the people of Harlem. Indeed, the most authoritative voice in the novel, a race leader reminiscent of W. E. B. Du Bois, lectures on the importance not of cosmopolitanism but of racial pride—even to the point of "an intense chauvinism that is content with its own types." Freedom from social conventions ultimately does little for Angela; she finds in the village of Harlem (in comparison to the life of the white bohemian artists) a life "fuller, richer, not finer but richer with the difference in quality that there is between velvet and silk."[77] The story uses primitivist tropes, but the richer, deeper life available in Harlem rests not on its inhabitants' connection to Africa but (following Locke) on their common struggles and sufferings, and the authenticity of their social relations—an authenticity that one must sacrifice if one is to "pass" among the different worlds of the city.

If crossing borders is problematic for blacks, so too is the more fundamental notion of Harlem as a village. To the extent that the concept of the Beloved Community rests on an organic concept of community—a concept that underlies Ruskin's and Morris's socialism, as well as Park's urban sociology—it tends to mask the social cleavages that can divide even a small village. Harlem itself was fractured by deep racial and class divisions, as Du Bois, Johnson, and the Harlem Renaissance writers made clear. Social striving is a central theme in Harlem Renaissance literature; Fauset's Angela, like Byron in Van Vechten's *Nigger Heaven*, must grapple with her racial and class identity precisely because she feels pressure to improve her social position. Cleavages of race and class do not disappear in the villages that make up the city; although Royce's provinces may achieve some cultural homogeneity, they cannot avoid grappling with these problems of difference.

Nor can they avoid the tensions between community and individualism that organic conceptions of community often elide. A number of the novels of the Harlem Renaissance explore that tension, frequently taking the form of a picaresque in which the hero or heroine attempts (usually unsuccessfully) to find a community that affirms his or her individuality.[78] In Nella Larsen's *Quicksand*, for example, the heroine Helga travels from a black college in the South to Chicago and New York in order to escape the stultifying, confining expectations of a rural black community. She eventually finds Harlem's expectations also too confining and flees to Denmark, where she enjoys "that blessed sense of belonging to herself alone and not to a race."[79] But the bohemian white community in Denmark can celebrate her difference only by forcing her into the role of the primitive; dissatisfied and lonely, she returns to New York, to her folk. "How absurd she had been to think that another country, other people could liberate her from the ties which bound her forever to these mysterious, these terrible, these fascinating, these lovable, dark hordes."[80] The novel ends in the rural South, where Helga is burdened by an unhappy marriage and the demands of motherhood, trapped once again in an oppressive set of social expectations. The novel highlights the restrictions on individual freedom that community solidarity requires. But it is not an unqualified endorsement of individual freedom, either. Helga lacks maturity and self-awareness, and much of her dissatisfaction stems from these character flaws. Like many of the novels of the Harlem Renaissance, *Quicksand* offers no neat resolutions to the apparently ineradicable tension between individualism and community.

Of course, advocates of the Beloved Community argued, cogently enough, that the development of individual personality requires the right kind of social support. Under their analysis, tensions between individualism and community are evidence that the community itself is defective; in Helga's case, it may be that racial oppression created too great a pressure toward racial solidarity, resulting in a stifling conformity that threatened individual personality. But advocates of the Beloved Community seldom considered the problem faced by the individual trying to decide to which community—particularly which racial community—he or she belonged. That question highlights the contingency and complexity of individual identity in a pluralist and racially oppressive society—a problem for any theory of urban reform that relies on an organic concept of community. The urban environment, in short, may exacerbate instead of resolve the tensions between individuality and community. The city may offer home and community, but it also offers the dangerous adventure of passing and the allure of escaping from oppressive social conventions.

THE WHITE CITY

By the 1940s, in the aftermath of the Great Depression and the resulting economic decline of urban black neighborhoods, the utopian theme in black literature was nearly submerged by the rise of a gritty, hard-headed urban realism. We see in this post-Renaissance literature a return to the nineteenth-century image of the city as dangerous, ugly, and corrupt. And, echoing another theme from nineteenth-century black literature, the physical degeneration of landscape is often explicitly connected to racial oppression. Still, the most famous work of urban realism of this period owes a substantial and well-recognized intellectual debt to the theorists of the Harlem Renaissance, to the Chicago school of urban sociology, and to the idea of the Beloved Community.[81]

Indeed, in Richard Wright's 1940 novel, *Native Son,* many now-familiar themes that animate black environmental thought culminate in a vivid portrait of the urban landscape. *Native Son* recounts the fate of Bigger Thomas, a young, angry black man struggling against poverty and racism in the Chicago ghetto, who ends up committing two murders and being condemned to death. Bigger's family immigrated from the rural South only to find themselves trapped, by poverty and lack of opportunity, in an urban ghetto. Wright describes the urban landscape as physically stimulating in its materiality and diversity: it is a "fabulous city," "huge, roaring, dirty, noisy, raw, stark, brutal."[82] It could be beautiful, as it is to Mary and Jan, the privileged whites that Bigger chauffeurs:

> "Isn't it glorious tonight?" [Mary] asked.
> "God, yes!" Jan said. . . .
> "That sky!"
> "And that water!"
> "It's so beautiful it makes you ache just to look at it," said Mary.[83]

Bigger, however, is oblivious to the beauty of the urban landscape. All he saw "stretching to one side of him was a vast sweep of tall buildings flecked with tiny squares of yellow light." The city to him is chaotic and brutal, a "dense jungle," a "wild forest" of "rank and choking vegetation."[84]

Bigger's reaction to the urban environment recalls the complaints of Henry Bibb and Hector St. John de Crèvecouer, that social injustice robs the landscape of its beauty: as stimulating as the city is, Bigger's aesthetic sense is virtually obliterated by the oppressive conditions he suffers. Wright, however, draws on the language of Locke and the Beloved Community to explain this obliteration: racial oppression has prevented the expression of blacks' common life, the creation of a symbolic culture in which Bigger could participate. Therefore the landscape has never been *interpreted* to Bigger by other blacks who share his experience. Because he doesn't understand it, he sees only chaos. At best, like Bibb and many other black protagonists, he can see only a landscape of racial barriers; indeed, in an echo of Harriet Jacobs's plight, he complains that blacks live in a prescribed area, a "cramped environment"—hemmed in (as Wright makes clear) by discriminatory housing and employment practices. As Bigger puts it, "They make us stay in one little spot."[85] His confinement is dramatically illustrated in his attempt to flee from the police, an incident reminiscent of the flight of fugitive slaves—but ultimately less successful. Like Henry Bibb, he seeks out abandoned buildings, alleys, and rooftops, spaces neglected by and therefore free of white control. But unlike the fugitive slaves, he is trying to flee from a neighborhood surrounded by white power. The urban environment is too densely packed to be a liberating space; he can't escape the confines of the White City.

This confinement is only one dimension of Bigger's sense of alienation from the city. Early on in the novel he contrasts himself with the native Africans he glimpses on a movie screen, "adjusted to their soil and at home in their world, secure from fear and hysteria."[86] Bigger, in comparison, is profoundly maladjusted. As his defense lawyer explains,

> Consider the mere physical aspect of our civilization. How alluring, how dazzling it is! How it excites the senses! How it seems to dangle within easy reach of everyone the fulfillment of happiness! . . . But in thinking of them remember that to many they are tokens of mockery. These bright colors may fill our hearts with elation, but to many they are daily taunts. Imagine a man walking amid such a scene, a part of it, and yet knowing that it is *not* for him![87]

The language recalls Dunbar's and Johnson's ambivalent descriptions of New York City, but it also echoes a familiar theme in black thought: to secure a proper aesthetic and spiritual relation to the physical landscape, Bigger must feel himself to be part of the community that claims dominion over that landscape. Tragically, the practices of racial segregation and exclusion separate him from the common life of the city. Thus, to him white society is merely "a sort of great natural force, like a stormy sky looking overhead, or like a deep swirling river stretching suddenly at one's feet in the dark."[88]

Indeed, the city is for Wright as it was for Park like a natural organism. But Wright emphasizes that its naturalistic quality is specifically the result of injustice: the city is a jungle *because racial oppression has made it so.* Oppression has robbed its black inhabitants of the capacity for creative action and expression, thus preventing them from becoming fully human. As a result, the relations between white and black inhabitants are purely animalistic; they do not interact as humans, communicating and entering into each other's subjective realities. Thus the White City, like Waldo Frank's jungle, is a landscape lacking human aesthetic or spiritual meaning—a chaotic, dangerous environment in which one can do no more than struggle to survive.

Perhaps even more troubling than this alienation from the White City, however, is Bigger's alienation from other blacks. He has fleeting moments when he senses the possibility of the urban racial community that Locke had imagined: "There were rare moments when a feeling and longing for solidarity with other black people would take hold of him." But "that dream would fade when he looked at the other black people near him. Even though black like them, he felt there was too much difference between him and them to allow for a common binding and a common life."[89] Wright doesn't consider the tensions between individuality and community that might trouble Bigger in such a Beloved Community; for him, the absence of community was a much greater disaster for individual development. What racial oppression had created in the black ghetto was not community but a more primitive kind of organic life—a life that grew "like a weed growing from under a stone," expressing itself primarily through crime and violence.[90]

Wright's vision of the city is uniquely powerful, but much of its power derives from its resonance with the long tradition of black environmental thought. Like Bibb and Du Bois before him, Wright juxtaposes blacks' actual condition—the black figure "veiled and bowed" in the King's Highway, the slaves "in the fields . . . still toiling under their task-masters without pay"— with the utopian image of the Beloved Community. Applying the lessons learned from a century of reflection on blacks' history with the American landscape, Wright suggests that one's relationship to the environment depends critically on freedom and social equality, which are essential to one's ability to participate in the common culture. Racial injustice, by excluding blacks from the community that claims dominion over the land, puts blacks in the same relation to the landscape that slaves suffered: unfree and homeless, incapable of creative action in response to the natural world.

CONCLUSION

Wright's vision of the city as an alienating, oppressive space constitutes one important dimension of black urban consciousness. But the other conceptions—the city as a liberating space, the locus of creative energy, a potential homeland—do not disappear from black literature. Indeed, it is significant that Langston Hughes chose the theme of montage for his 1951 collection of poems about Harlem. Many of the poems invoke the beauty and vitality of Harlem: the rhythms of jazz and blues, the "neon lights" and "Lenox Avenue busses/Taxis, subways," the wonder of the lights coming on in the early blue evening.[91] In "New Yorkers," we hear a faint echo of the Beloved Community from a girl escaping to Harlem from a place where "folks work hard / all their lives / until they die / and never own no parts / of earth nor sky."[92] Nevertheless, his collection is bracketed—confined, as it were—by the motif of a "dream deferred." His Harlem is seething with rebellious energy, punctuated by the rhythm of marching feet, beating out ("You think / It's a happy beat?")[93] Hughes's Harlem is richly textured, sensuous, and throbbing with energy, but it is also an environment under pressure, on the verge of exploding.

Still, Hughes's urban montage captures the sense of possibility black writers saw in the urban environment. Here was a place created by human hands, an environment that could be what humans made of it; its possibilities might not be unlimited, but they weren't fully determined by nature or history. Thus the city landscape, perhaps even more than the rural landscape, is a field for the play of human creativity: it is an opportunity for humans to fulfill their co-partnership with God in finishing Creation—not only by modifying the landscape itself to reflect human values but by interpreting it, giving meaning to it through creative articulation of its materials. To be sure, the city that appears in this tradition is, in some respects, an inherently dangerous environment for blacks. Its material attractions and freedom from social convention—in other words, its promise of freedom—pose moral and physical dangers to blacks as well as whites. But for black writers,

that danger is as much a result of racial oppression as it is an inevitable feature of city life. It is not just the lure of social status, wealth, and freedom
from social convention that threatens the black urban dweller. The practices
that exclude blacks from the larger community also create a dangerous
alienation that can degenerate into anarchy. Thus racial oppression turns
what should be a Beloved Community into a chaotic, violent jungle—the
decaying landscape of unsafe buildings, poisoned air, and toxic earth, de-
manding both political and environmental reform.

CONCLUSION

In a 1968 speech, Eldridge Cleaver declared that "from the very beginning, Afro-America has had a land hang-up." According to Cleaver, as slaves "black people learned to hate the land. From sunup to sundown, the slaves worked the land: plowing, sowing and reaping crops for somebody else, for profit they themselves would never see or taste." As a result, "blacks . . . have come to measure their own value according to the number of degrees they are away from the soil."[1] But Marsha Darling's research on black farmers tells a different story:

> In a number of the interviews where I asked black people what does your farm mean, they talked repeatedly about the value of being able to have a place where they could keep their family together—raise their family, nurture their family, take care of it—as well as a place where they could be producers instead of consumers and a place on which they could make major decisions. But I think for a whole other generation they very much talked of farming and one's ownership of a farm as having a home place where you could sink your roots and hold on.[2]

Black families that have left farming retain a strong connection to their families' homeplaces; those that have lost their land still cherish memories of it. Indeed, as Cleaver himself recognized, there has long been among blacks "a deep land hunger," an enduring desire to possess a land of their own.[3]

Darling's and Cleaver's insights capture the ambivalent legacy of slavery. According to its most influential critics, race slavery brought its victims into a problematic relationship to the American landscape—a relationship that only political activism aimed at rectifying race relations can correct. That analysis of the connection between racial oppression and blacks' relationship to the environment has had a persistent presence in black politics, manifesting itself most recently in the environmental justice movement. As Robert Bullard puts it, this movement is "an extension of the first protest against being uprooted from our homeland and brought to a strange land."

In order to dismantle contemporary systems of domination, he contends, "we have to understand the link, the correlation, the relationship between exploitation of the land and the exploitation of the people. The two are inseparable." Benjamin Chavis agrees: "Racism," he insists, "has always been used to justify the rape of the environment."[4] Environmental justice, thus understood, is part of black Americans' ongoing struggle to possess the land.

Such arguments, I contend, are part of a live tradition, linking stewardship and social justice in a way that continues to resonate with black Americans. Simply recovering that tradition—making visible an overlooked dimension of black experience, amplifying an unheard voice in our national conversation—is worthwhile in itself. But the ideas and arguments offered by black theorists can also enrich the study of black politics, black environmental history, and environmental theory generally. I want to conclude by drawing out some of the implications of this study for these other fields of investigation, beginning with black politics.

As I suggested in the introduction, conventional wisdom views black politics as distinct from and even opposed to environmental politics. But it should be clear by now that black politics has long had an environmental dimension. The antislavery movement drew support from early nineteenth-century efforts to reform southern agriculture to improve stewardship; activism aimed at securing civil rights for blacks and encouraging race consciousness was often explained by the activists as an effort to put black Americans into a more meaningful relationship to the American landscape. True, black environmental activism looks different from our usual picture of mainstream environmental politics; it has been aimed neither at preserving unique wilderness areas nor at resource conservation on a national scale. Instead, it has been local in scope and focused on access to open space and public services, pollution abatement, and local public health issues.

That focus has been evident from the earliest days of civil rights activism. One of the principles of the original Niagara Movement, for example, was a plea for "an opportunity to live in decent houses and localities, for a chance to rear our children in physical and moral cleanliness."[5] As was discussed in Chapter 3, that goal was embraced by the National Association of Colored Women and other black reform organizations, which sought not only to improve the quality of urban environments but to provide recreational opportunities for children and mothers in rural settings.[6]

Access to environmental amenities such as parks and beaches was of course a major source of racial conflict throughout the twentieth century,

and it accordingly remained an important focus of the civil rights movement. Historian Colin Fisher points out that the 1919 Chicago race riot, one
of the most violent in U.S. history, erupted over access to the city's water-
front; it was the culmination of a series of violent encounters between blacks
and whites at various parks and recreation facilities throughout the city.[7] By
the 1940s, the civil rights movement was aggressively seeking improved access to public parks and other green spaces. For example, in 1949 a multiracial group of about 100 residents and labor activists in Gary, Indiana, took
control of Marquette Beach, which had been the domain of white residents.
Although this "beachhead democracy" was short-lived, blacks in Gary and
other cities continued vigorous and sometimes militant campaigns for de-
segregation of green spaces. Historian Gregory Bush reports that memories
of those campaigns continue to inspire black activists today.[8]

A more recent manifestation of black environmental concern (and another source of friction between civil rights advocates and environmentalists) was a series of civil rights complaints lodged against the Environmental
Protection Agency (EPA) in the 1970s, protesting the exclusion of black
neighborhoods from environmental services. The United States Commission on Civil Rights concluded in its 1974 report that the agency was giving
grants to communities that practiced exclusionary zoning, that failed to provide equal levels of city services to minority neighborhoods, and that failed
to enact fair housing laws or to establish a fair housing agency. In one case,
for example, the EPA provided funds to Marshall, Texas, to construct a
sewage treatment plant that would serve 90 percent of the city's residents.
The 10 percent that would not be served were disproportionately black, and
they would be served only if they paid a special assessment. Only a few families were willing (or able) to pay the assessment, and most remained without
sewer services.[9] The commission's report documents several similar cases.

These complaints against the EPA laid the groundwork for Robert and
Linda Bullard's groundbreaking 1979 lawsuit, *Bean vs. Southwestern Waste
Management*, which was the first to charge a government body with "environmental discrimination": the racially discriminatory imposition of environmental harms. The suit charged that the siting of waste disposal facilities
in Houston, Texas, was racially biased, resulting in minority communities'
bearing a greater share of these locally undesirable land uses.[10] Subsequent
research has confirmed what casual observation suggests: in addition to
lacking environmental amenities, poor and minority communities have
borne a disproportionate share of environmental hazards.[11] To be sure,

scholars continue to debate the causes of this inequality, but few would argue with its deleterious effects—on the afflicted communities' health and sense of civic membership, as well as on their motivation to invest in their properties. Civil rights leaders like Whitney Young of the Urban League and George Wiley of the National Welfare Rights Organization had once urged progressives to focus on poverty and racial injustice rather than pollution,[12] but many civil rights activists have understood from the beginning that these problems are intertwined.

They are intertwined, as well, with the ongoing problem of black land loss, which occurred at a rate three times that of white farmers over the course of the twentieth century.[13] Land ownership accordingly remained a focus of black politics during the twentieth century, from the Southern Tenant Farmers' Union program of land reform and cooperative farming in the 1930s to the black nationalist program of land ownership in the 1960s. Even more recently, the National Black Farmers' Association and related organizations have defended black landowners by challenging discrimination in the administration of loan and subsidy programs by the U.S. Department of Agriculture.[14] These struggles to retain land ownership are conceptually linked to the environmental justice movement, just as W. E. B. Du Bois linked racial discrimination and lack of economic opportunity to low rates of property ownership and poor stewardship in both the rural South and in urban ghettoes. Indeed, environmental justice activist Sulaiman Madhi insists that land sovereignty is at the heart of the movement. Referencing the slogan "40 acres and a mule" and Malcolm X's dictum that "land is the basis of freedom," Madhi explains that fighting pollution is a question of "freeing the land, reclaiming the land," and having the land returned to the community "in a sustainable way."[15] Land loss and degraded environments, under this view, result from the same fundamental pattern of injustice toward black Americans.

That pattern of injustice and blacks' struggle against it lie at the center of the tradition of black environmental thought. The theoretical perspective offered by that tradition reveals that the contemporary environmental justice movement is continuous with earlier efforts by slaves and freedmen to possess the land: to secure the conditions for creative, responsible interaction with the natural environment on an economic, aesthetic, and spiritual level. As the 1991 People of Color Environmental Leadership Summit put it in "The Principles of Environmental Justice," environmental justice "affirms the sacredness of Mother Earth" and "mandates the right to ethical, balanced and responsible uses of land and renewable resources in the interest of a sustainable planet for humans and other living things."[16]

This tradition of black environmental thought also offers a useful theoretical approach to African American environmental history, providing a set of concepts, arguments, and questions that can guide research in this field. To map out that approach, however, we first have to extrapolate from the rich conversations explored in this study to develop a more systematic theory. This theory is necessarily a synthesis; it grows out of and is consistent with the tradition as a whole, although it may not be fully developed by any particular writer. We begin with the idea that it is the calling of human beings to "finish Creation"—a conception of humans' active, creative *telos* that seemed to inform even the secular twentieth-century expressions of this tradition. Under this view, humans are called to be stewards, co-partners with God (as George Washington Carver put it) in modifying the natural world to be more suitable to human needs—economic and social as well as (Du Bois would insist) aesthetic and spiritual needs. Such modification is not only legitimate, it is accorded special value as one of the chief sources of human dignity, an ennobling activity uniquely suited to confer economic, moral, and spiritual benefits. But it can confer these benefits only under the proper economic, political, and social conditions. The experiences of black Americans, as interpreted by black writers, teaches that in order for humans to realize the full benefits of their stewardship function, they must first realize social justice—particularly racial justice.

According to this theory, racial oppression has impaired effective stewardship in a number of ways. First, as the black agrarians argued eloquently, race slavery and peonage undermined the voluntariness of agricultural labor, which in turn transformed humans' common calling to finish Creation into a struggle for power between the master and the slave. This struggle for control of human labor (they claimed) took priority over the long-term health of the land, constituting one factor interfering with the adoption of better land management practices in the South during the nineteenth century. In addition, race slavery and peonage degraded the status of agricultural labor, depriving workers of the civil rights and social status they needed to exercise independent, responsible agency in their relationship to the land—and creating for both blacks and whites disincentives to stewardship. Even worse, racial oppression continued to alienate blacks from the land; denial of civil and political rights excluded blacks from the political community that claimed authority over the land, and (as Du Bois suggested)

the economic, social, and psychological effects of racism have made it difficult for blacks to express their collective ideals aesthetically and give meaning to the landscape. The result is a racially charged landscape—Richard
Wright's White City—which contributes to the sense of alienation that constitutes a central feature of racial oppression.

This theory thus suggests that social justice is connected to both stewardship and one's relationship to nature. That connection, however, is largely
speculative. It finds some support in what we know about the experiences of
black Americans, but it clearly needs further empirical investigation—beginning with a much richer and more detailed black environmental history.
I've provided merely a general overview of this history; what we need is a
fine-grained portrait of black Americans' experience with the American
landscape that would be attentive to both regional and social differences.
But the theory does suggest questions and hypotheses that could guide this
historical research.

Two claims in particular call for further empirical investigation. First,
were slaves good stewards? That is, how exactly did their productive activities—their hunting and gathering, coerced plantation agriculture, and labor
in craft and industrial occupations—relate them to and affect the material
world? Our theory suggests that slavery undermined incentives to stewardship, but slavery was a complex collection of practices, and slaves coped with
their situation in different ways. Did they find incentives to stewardship,
and if so, where?

Second, were (and are) black Americans alienated from the American
landscape? Our theory suggests that racism has this effect. But is this theory
too state-centered and too pessimistic about black Americans' capacity for
effective agency? Counterthemes in black environmental thought suggest
ways that blacks could use their connection to the natural world—through labor, art, and memory—as the basis of their sense of self in a culture of racial
oppression. We need further investigation of how such resistance to oppression, or simply the conduct of ordinary life in the interstices of an unjust social structure, could create a bond to the land. In general, we need to know
more about blacks' strategies for giving meaning to the world and for establishing an enduring sense of place and self—for making homes in the shadow
of oppression. How did such strategies evolve? What kind of bonds did they
create, and what kinds of meanings were given to the land? Further, how
were those meanings (and the land itself) passed on from one generation to

the next? That is, how did one generation put the land in the next generation's keeping?

Of course, we lack the answers to such questions not only for black Americans but for many other groups of Americans as well, including many white American communities. A better understanding of these communities' practices and experiences would help us better understand the specific effects of slavery, racism, and blacks' African heritage on their connection to the land. As was suggested in Chapter 1, that question demands a comparative approach that focuses not merely on the products of unrepresentative white elites but on the multicultural tapestry of the American folk.

Finally, we need to know whether the insights derived from the experiences of black Americans can be generalized. Can we draw any larger conclusions about how oppressing labor affects stewardship? Studies of the environmental effects of slave agriculture, in the United States and elsewhere, might give us more insight into that issue. For example, Richard Grove has opened up one route of investigation in his study of the development of eighteenth-century conservation ideology, which grew out of Europeans' experiences establishing agricultural colonies in fragile tropical ecosystems. He notes that these tropical colonies in Africa, the Caribbean, and the Americas typically relied on slave labor; some of their conservation-minded governors went so far as to link slave labor to the environmental degradation that accompanied this intensive form of commercial agricultural.[17] Further investigation of these early experiments with slave agriculture could offer insights into the connection between the oppression of labor and the abuse of the land.

But we could also examine more recent cases of American workers experiencing forms of oppression similar to slavery. Seasonal farm workers, for example, have often been members of racial minorities and recent immigrants, working under conditions close to peonage. Even today, they face poor working conditions, very low wages, and weak legal protections, creating the ideal conditions for exploitation.[18] Our theory suggests that such exploitation may make the workers less careful and create in them ambivalence toward the land: a sense of alienation from land and community coupled with a desire (and perhaps strategies) to come into a more meaningful and creative relationship with the natural world. We might find similar dynamics at work among small farmers in economically depressed regions, and even in fields other than agriculture. For example, Robert Gottlieb in

Environmentalism Unbound investigates the condition of industrial environmental workers such as janitors. He notes that janitors used to be considered skilled workers, but in the 1980s, many firms started using cheap immigrant labor to clean their facilities. Like seasonal farm workers, these workers are usually unskilled, uneducated, and racially marginalized, and they often lack basic legal protections.[19] They are therefore vulnerable to exploitation. Do their working conditions affect how they carry out their stewardship function? Do they affect these workers' moral and aesthetic relationship to the environment around them? This, too, is a promising field for study.

In sum, this tradition of black environmental thought suggests many avenues of research in black environmental and political history. But as a source of normative environmental theory, it may be more problematic. Specifically, we may worry that it fails to give us a sufficiently critical perspective on our relationship to the natural world. As I've argued, the black environmental tradition developed as a response to two major problems: the system of race slavery and oppression on one hand, and the claims of scientific racists on the other. The first severely restricted the ability of black Americans to own land, to move freely across the landscape, and to modify and interpret the landscape. The second legitimated racial oppression and promoted an environmental determinism that insisted blacks, as a race, had virtually no capacity for free, creative action. In response to these problems, black theorists have focused on the importance of creative agency in humans' relationship to nature. But that focus creates what appear to be three obstacles to developing a useful environmental ethic out of this tradition: anthropocentrism, resistance to any sort of environmental determinism, and a rejection of the individualistic perspective characteristic of American preservationism.

To take anthropocentrism first: the celebration of *mastery* in the black tradition can be read as idealizing a relationship of dominance toward nature. Ecocentric theorists have criticized that ideal as unjust because it doesn't give proper moral consideration to the interests of other members of the biotic community. Ecofeminists would further argue that the ideal of mastery is gendered, deriving from and reinforcing patriarchy. And even those theorists less sympathetic to these radical critiques would suggest that the notion of mastery vastly overestimates humans' ability to control the natural world, and that aiming for it does more harm than good.[20] For many environmentalists, a proper relationship to nature requires that we do as little damage to natural processes as possible, which usually means proceeding with humility, caution, and considerable restraint.

This ideal of restraint may also be problematic, however. Humans do after all have to modify the natural environment simply in order to survive. We inhabit a second nature, a landscape modified to human needs. Therefore, we need a workable concept of stewardship—that is, a concept that acknowledges our dependence on natural resources but also provides effective constraints on their use. The black tradition, I would suggest, offers such a concept. This tradition emphasizes that individuals are embedded in communities, so that individual action always takes place within a social context. Social traditions guide and contain individual efforts, giving them moral, aesthetic, and spiritual as well as economic and political meaning. One's proper relationship to the natural environment is therefore best understood as *response* rather than mastery: individual action is a response (emotionally and intellectually as well as physically) to a natural world that ongoing cultural practices have already funded with meaning. Moreover, the individual, as a member of this community, can be held responsible for his or her actions—unless, of course, social injustice has destroyed the conditions for such a responsive and responsible relationship to nature. In such cases, we do in fact end up with irresponsible, unconstrained exercises of power over nature (a de-cultured nature that now holds no meaning beyond its immediate material value to the individual). Such exercises of power, of course, typically involve similar exercises of power of other humans. It is in fact a key lesson of blacks' experience with the American landscape that mastering nature means mastering other humans. But by giving up some control over the labor of other humans, as respect for their status as co-equal stewards requires, we allow community to flourish and accept a less masterful—but more responsive—relationship to the natural world.

Still, some environmental ethicists might complain that even this qualified ethic of mastery remains too anthropocentric. Environmental ethics, some would argue, should be grounded on the recognition that natural entities can have intrinsic value; that means, at a minimum, that their moral value does not depend entirely on their use value to humans. Such a strong ecocentric position may be necessary to ensure that we preserve nonhumans even when it doesn't serve our immediate interests.[21] But the black tradition, I think, is not hostile to such nonanthropocentric perspectives. True black agrarianism derives from Christian agrarianism, which has been characterized as anthropocentric. But Christian agrarianism is better conceived as theocentric: it asserts that the natural world is God's creation, and its moral value derives not from its usefulness to man but from its source and its purpose—which is not merely to serve humans but to witness God's glory and power. This Christian worldview came under attack in the late nineteenth century (by, among others, the scientific racists), and it is at this point, I would suggest, that American public discourse became filled with claims that nature has no purpose or value except to serve man—or, more precisely, to serve those humans who win the struggle for survival.[22] But this is precisely the intellectual moment in which progressive theorists like Du Bois and Locke turned to pragmatism in order to develop an alternative language for moral argument—to argue *against* that impoverished view of our relationship to nature. In other words, the black pragmatists and environmentalists can be seen as allies combating the Social Darwinist ethic of unlimited exploitation of people and of nature.

That historical point notwithstanding, however, we might still worry that black progressives' turn to pragmatism leads away from ecocentrism. Pragmatists, after all, contend that value derives from human experience; it is human action that funds the natural world with meaning and value. That position seems to make the value of nonhuman entities a function of their value to humans.[23] I think that conclusion is misguided, however. Pragmatists can in fact talk about nature's intrinsic value, as long as we understand that concept as articulating an aspect of humans' *experience* with nature. That is, we do experience natural entities as having a value independent of our own use of it. As Anthony Weston suggests, "A day's hike in the woods is worthwhile even if it does not contribute to peace of mind or animal-watching ability or job performance: the experience, as well as the woods itself considered even apart from my experience, is simply good 'for what it is in itself.'"[24] As long as we are able to describe such experiences, they can be preserved in the community's collective memory, thus becoming part of the meaning that we (as members of that community) find in nature. Black progressives simply direct our attention to the social conditions necessary for such concepts to make sense. In the absence of a functioning community and a coherent tradition, we are unlikely to find any meaning in nature, intrinsic or otherwise.

In short, neither the ideal of mastery nor the pragmatic influences in the black tradition necessarily lead us to the view that nonhuman entities aren't worthy of moral consideration in themselves. There is, however, a second concern with this tradition: that its rejection of environmental determinism and insistence on human creativity poses too great a divide between nature and culture. After all, one aim of the environmental movement is to bring our industrial culture into "harmony" with nature. What exactly that means is often obscure, but it seems to require that the natural environment should determine the shape of or at least inspire human cultural production. Wes Jackson, for example, encourages us to "become native" to a place by building an agriculture and a culture that connects us to the local landscape. Peter Berg advises us to "live in place": to follow the necessities and pleasures of life as they are uniquely presented by a particular site, and to evolve ways to ensure the long-term occupancy of that site. Bioregionalists call for human society "to be more conscious of its locale, or region, or life-place . . . ; to get to know one's place intimately in order to fit human communities to the Earth."[25] Clearly, achieving a sustainable lifestyle is only part of their goal; advocates of a "sense of place" hope that a sensitivity to the dynamics and beauty of the local landscape will result in a more meaningful relationship with nature, a better sense of community, and a richer cultural life.

As I have noted, this notion of a "sense of place" has its roots in the literary realism that also had a strong influence on black progressivism. Accordingly, both black progressives and bioregionalists emphasize the realist principle that cultural vitality rests on maintaining a close connection of some sort between nature and art. Nevertheless, the black tradition poses a challenge to the advocates of a "sense of place." First, in rejecting scientific racism, the black cultural relativists (such as Du Bois and Locke) also rejected the environmental determinism that made culture an automatic expression of a group's biological heritage, as well as the Romantic concept of nature as a vital spiritual force inspiring human creativity. That left an apparent chasm between nature and culture. For Boas, for example, nature was merely scenery, without any determinative relation to culture at all. Under his view, the natural environment can shape human culture only very loosely; all the important and interesting cultural differences must be explained by history. This Boasian divide makes it difficult to make sense of the project of "getting back to nature." Everything of value in human culture is a product of social traditions, many of which may preserve recollections of other places and may even be maladaptive in the community's current place.

This theoretical perspective thus fits uncomfortably with place-based ethics. Alain Locke, for example, makes it clear that natural environment does influence the shape of a culture; it is recorded and preserved in collective memory. But for Locke, this means that black culture should reflect not a sense of place but a sense of *places:* the places that both shaped and scarred the black American community. For a black artist with a strong racial consciousness, the forests and fields of the North should call to mind the forests and fields of the South; a New York market becomes a tropical oasis; the rivers of America will (as in Langston Hughes's poem) call to mind the Euphrates, the Congo, and the Nile.[26] The meaning of the landscape may be tied to the race's experience in a different place. Thus a vital, meaningful culture might in some ways *distance* us from local nature rather than simply connecting us to it. It will constantly remind us of the other places that shaped our group's consciousness; it will remind us that we are still, to some extent, strangers in a strange land.

Nevertheless, this tradition does offer a way to bridge the Boasian divide between nature and culture. As I've argued, Locke expressed concern about the effects on human culture of our increasing distance from nature. Following Dewey, he used the concept of *experience* to bridge the divide, arguing that a vital culture is one that expresses intense experience with the external environment. Thus his critique of industrial civilization rests not on romantic environmental determinism but on the continuing need for intense experience in our increasingly routinized and mechanized lives. This focus on experience instead of nature's vital force is not entirely unproblematic, of course. In the first place, by rejecting the vitalist concept of nature, it tends to diminish the spiritual dimension of humans' relationship to nature—a dimension that was important to the Romantics and is still important to many in the environmental movement. But more troublesome, I think, is that Locke's view does not necessarily privilege experience with nature over experience with the built environment. Under Locke's theory, one's "sense of place" need not derive from one's experience with plants, soils, and animals (the kind of experience bioregionalists emphasize) but could evolve from one's experience with billboards, pavement, and hot dog vendors. From Locke's perspective, the problem is not that we lack experience with local nature; rather, it is that oppressive, deadening, and routinized environments diminish our capacity to experience and find meaning in the world in general (both natural and man-made).

In spite of that refusal to privilege experience with nature, however, Locke's pragmatism may still be a good foundation for modern preservationism and urban reform. Under Locke's reasoning, the point of cultivating a sense of place is to enrich the group's culture by expressing one's direct, firsthand experience with the world, interacting with it as a social being carrying a live tradition (a tradition, to be sure, that might have been forged elsewhere). A group maintains cultural vitality by continuing to record its members' actual experience with their changing environment. Wilderness, healthy rural communities, and green, livable cities arguably offer the kind of rich, intense experience that funds the world with meaning and contributes to cultural vitality. Moreover, under Locke's view, preserving at least some ecologically distinctive places is one way to maintain a collective memory of those places, which is critical to preserving the traditions that guide our use of the natural world. Wilderness preservation, from this perspective, may be an important part of identity politics and critical to creating a culture that supports sensitive use of the natural world.

This point brings us to the final potential conflict between black environmental thought and the mainstream tradition of American preservationism. One important theme in American preservationism is the claim that wilderness is valuable because it allows individuals to escape from social conventions, demands, and oppressions. The natural world as experienced by Henry David Thoreau and John Muir had an independent reality and meaning that could challenge the social conventions constraining individual freedom.[27] Thus Thoreau claimed to find a freedom not merely civil but natural in the wilderness. But in the black tradition, civil freedom is a *precondition* for natural freedom. *Freedom* means primarily the freedom to make a home and community, and to participate in a vital culture that gives meaning to the landscape. It also, of course, means the freedom to leave home, to start over somewhere else. But these are all the actions of citizens—not disembodied, presocial selves—seeking a more meaningful relationship to a land over which they already have collective dominion.

More specifically, writers in the black tradition generally treat individuals as embedded in a social context; they come to the natural world as members of a group, drawing on their group's collective memory to interpret it. By emphasizing the social dimension of individual experience, black theorists are able to give a nuanced account of how racial and class identities are implicated in the individual's relationship to nature. However, this approach offers little insight into how an individual's contact with the natural world can *liberate* one from those very social structures that make it available. As Du Bois pointed out in his reflections on Bar Harbor, communing with nature didn't give him relief from social oppression; it instead led him to reflect on the oppressive social structures he had to negotiate in order to achieve contact with the natural world.

Of course, Du Bois didn't deny that wilderness can carry the value Thoreau and Muir claimed for it. But he would probably explain that experience of natural freedom using Lockean terms: the meaning that Thoreau and Muir found in nature—its freedom and independence from human society— was imposed on the landscape by the community of which they were very much integrated members. Thoreau, in contrast, might criticize that view as giving too little credit to nature's "givenness"—its resistance to human modification and control—and to the possibility of individual acts of liberation and self-creation. Perhaps the natural world does, in some sense, come to us preinterpreted, suggesting certain meanings and possibilities simply by virtue of how we and the natural world have evolved together.

Indeed, even in the black tradition we find a persistent hope that nature's "givenness" could serve as the foundation for a secure sense of self in a racially oppressive society. "The grand old earth," as Frederick Douglass put it, "has no prejudice against race, color, or previous condition of servitude, but flings open her ample breast to all who will come to her for succor and relief."[28] Booker T. Washington and George Washington Carver thought that gardening provided an opportunity for creative action unavailable in most other domains of work. More recently, Carl Anthony has echoed this theme, suggesting that "the knowledge of the earth, and of our place in its long evolution, can give us a sense of identity and belonging that can act as a corrective to the hubris and pride that have been weapons of our oppressors."[29] That hope, however, has often been denied; instead of natural freedom, black Americans have too commonly found a landscape of racial barriers inscribed by white power. To fully realize the possibilities of creative interaction with nature, they argue, the land itself must be liberated from racial injustice. That perspective remains an important counterpoint to the individualism of the American wilderness tradition.

In sum, black environmental thought offers a critical normative perspective not only on our environmental practices but on the mainstream tradition of environmental thought itself. Its central message is this: we have inherited a world scarred by history. Slavery and racism have shaped the meaning of the American landscape, its physical features, its patterns of possession and dispossession. To make sense of this landscape, we need to draw on the conceptual resources embedded in the black political tradition: ideas about stewardship, the social foundations of environmental virtue, and the role of memory and tradition in relating humans to the natural world. Black Americans have seen the strange rendings of nature wrought by racial oppression. Listening to their voices leads to a deeper understanding of our common task: to redeem and to possess a land cursed by injustice—to make of our shared world "a more fitting home" for human lives.[30]

NOTES

INTRODUCTION

1. W. E. B. Du Bois, *The Souls of Black Folk* [1903] (New York: Penguin Books, 1989), 90.

2. W. E. B. Du Bois, *Darkwater: Voices from within the Veil* [1920] (New York: Humanity Books, 2003), 227–228; Stephen Fox, *The American Conservation Movement* (Madison: University of Wisconsin Press, 1981), 136.

3. Du Bois, *Darkwater*, 229.

4. Fox, *American Conservation Movement*, 345–351; see also Chapter 5.

5. On immigration control, see Edward Abbey, "Down the River with Henry Thoreau" [1981] in *Down the River* (New York: Plume, 1991), 17; Murray Bookchin and Dave Foreman, *Defending the Earth* (Cambridge, Mass.: South End Press, 1991), 41–42. On tensions between social justice advocates and environmentalists, see Robert Gottlieb, *Forcing the Spring* (Washington, D.C.: Island Press, 1993), 254; Robert Gottlieb, *Environmentalism Unbound* (Cambridge, Mass.: MIT Press, 2001), 52–53.

6. Dorceta Taylor, "Blacks and the Environment: Toward an Explanation of the Concern and Action Gap between Blacks and Whites," *Environment & Behavior* 21 (March 1989): 175–205. See 176–178 for summary of the literature.

7. Ibid.; Paul Mohai, "Public Concern and Elite Involvement in Environmental-Conservation Issues," *Social Science Quarterly* 66 (December 1985): 820–838; Paul Mohai, "Black Environmentalism," *Social Science Quarterly* 71 (December 1990): 744–765; Robert Jones, "Blacks Just Don't Care: Unmasking Popular Stereotypes about Concern for the Environment among African-Americans," *International Journal of Public Administration* 25 (2002): 221–251.

8. Colin Fisher, "African Americans, Outdoor Recreation, and the 1919 Chicago Riot," and Elizabeth Blum, "Women, Environmental Rationale, and Activism during the Progressive Era," in *"To Love the Wind and the Rain": African Americans and Environmental History*, ed. Dianne Glave and Mark Stoll (Pittsburgh: University of Pittsburgh Press, 2006), 63–76, 77–92.

9. Robert Bullard, *Dumping in Dixie*, 3rd ed. (Boulder, Colo.: Westview Press, 2000); Luke Cole and Sheila Foster, *From the Ground Up* (New York: New York University Press, 2001).

10. The central text defining the canon of American environmentalism is Roderick Nash's *Wilderness and the American Mind* (New Haven, Conn.: Yale University

Press, 1967). Standard histories of environmental politics also define environmentalism as aimed at protecting the environment or human health. Samuel Hays, *Beauty, Health, and Permanence* (Cambridge: Cambridge University Press, 1987); Gottlieb, *Forcing the Spring.*

11. George Hutchinson, *The Harlem Renaissance in Black and White* (Cambridge, Mass.: Harvard University Press, 1996), 24. Cf. Adolph Reed, *W. E. B. Du Bois and American Political Thought* (New York: Oxford University Press, 1997), 11–12. Reed argues that we should treat black thought as relatively autonomous from white discourses; Du Bois and Hegel, he points out, were not working on the same problematique. Reed's point is well taken, but I believe we can identify continuities between black and white conversations without losing sight of the different problems that black writers had in mind.

12. I am indebted to Melvin Rogers for this point.

13. Social ecologists and ecofeminists have begun to address these issues in recent decades, but not with the depth of insight that comes from black theorists speaking from their own experiences and in their own voices. For a discussion of the lack of attention to racial issues in conventional environmentalism and a social ecologist perspective on such issues, see Bookchin and Foreman, *Defending the Earth.*

14. Hutchinson, *The Harlem Renaissance in Black and White.*

15. William Cronon, "The Trouble with Wilderness," in *Uncommon Ground,* ed. William Cronon (New York: W. W. Norton, 1996), 73.

16. On this theme, see Peter Harrison, "Subduing the Earth: Genesis 1, Early Modern Science, and the Exploitation of Nature," *Journal of Religion* 79 (January 1999): 86–109; Carolyn Merchant, "Reinventing Eden: Western Culture as a Recovery Narrative," in Cronon, *Uncommon Ground.*

CHAPTER ONE. STRANGE RENDINGS OF NATURE

1. "William Bradford Faces a 'Hideous and Desolate Wilderness,' 1620–1635," in *Major Problems in American Environmental History,* ed. Carolyn Merchant (Lexington, Mass.: D. C. Heath, 1993), 68; "Thomas Morton Praises the New English Canaan," in ibid., 72.

2. Roderick Nash, *Wilderness and the American Mind,* 3rd ed. (New Haven, Conn.: Yale University Press, 1982); Leo Marx, *The Machine in the Garden* (Oxford: Oxford University Press, 1964); Henry Nash Smith, *Virgin Land* (Cambridge, Mass.: Harvard University Press, 1950); Simon Schama, *Landscape and Memory* (New York: Vintage Books, 1995); Carolyn Merchant, *Ecological Revolutions* (Chapel Hill: University of North Carolina Press, 1989).

3. "The Interesting Narrative of the Life of Olaudah Equiano, or Gustavus Vassa, the African" [1789], in *I Was Born a Slave,* ed. Yuval Taylor (Chicago: Lawrence Hill Books, 1999), 1: 64, 60.

4. Joseph Holloway, "The Origins of African-American Culture," in *Africanisms in American Culture,* ed. Joseph Holloway (Bloomington: Indiana University Press,

1990); John Blassingame, *The Slave Community*, 2nd ed. (Oxford: Oxford University Press, 1979), 72–75; Margaret Creel, *"A Peculiar People": Slave Religion and Community-Culture among the Gullahs* (New York: New York University Press, 1988), 52–63. Many West Africans were exposed to Islam, as well.

5. John Hudson, *Across This Land: A Regional Geography of the United States* (Baltimore: Johns Hopkins University Press, 2002), 141, 101, 118, 173, 178, 184.

6. Albert Cowdry, *This Land, This South* (Lexington: University Press of Kentucky, 1983), 5–6, 37.

7. Mart Stewart, "'Let Us Begin with the Weather?': Climate, Race, and Cultural Distinctiveness in the American South," in *Nature and Society in Historical Context*, ed. Mikulás Teich, Roy Porter, and Bo Gustafsson (Cambridge: Cambridge University Press, 1997), 248–250; John Thornton, *Africa and Africans in the Making of the Atlantic World, 1400–1680* (Cambridge: Cambridge University Press, 1992), 142–143.

8. Mart Stewart, *"What Nature Suffers to Groe"* (Athens: University of Georgia Press, 1996), 54.

9. Thomas D. Clark, *The Greening of the South* (Lexington: University Press of Kentucky, 1984), 2–3, 15.

10. Cowdry, *This Land, This South*, 75–76.

11. Hudson, *Across This Land*, 175.

12. Carville Earle, *The Evolution of a Tidewater Settlement System* (Chicago: Department of Geography, 1975), 18; Steven Stoll, *Larding the Lean Earth* (New York: Hill and Wang, 2002), 129–130.

13. Cowdry, *This Land, This South*, 34–35.

14. Stewart, *"What Nature Suffers to Groe,"* 87.

15. Cowdry, *This Land, This South*, 66–67.

16. Ibid., 73–74.

17. Ibid., 75.

18. Robert Fogel, *Without Consent or Contract* (New York: W. W. Norton, 1989), 22, 29–30.

19. Peter Kolchin, *American Slavery*, 3rd ed. (New York: Hill and Wang, 2003), 101.

20. Fogel, *Without Consent or Contract*, 31–32.

21. Blassingame, *The Slave Community*, xii, 105–106; Holloway, "The Origins of African-American Culture," 16–17; Ira Berlin, *Generations of Captivity* (Cambridge, Mass.: Belknap Press, 2003), 70, 74–76. An Africanized slave culture also developed in the southwest in the early nineteenth century, with the rise of the Cotton Kingdom. Berlin, *Generations of Captivity*, 148–149.

22. Ira Berlin, *Many Thousands Gone* (Cambridge, Mass.: Belknap Press, 1998), 12, 29–46, 105–108.

23. Stewart, *"What Nature Suffers to Groe,"* 90.

24. J. Hector St. John de Crèvecoeur, *Letters from an American Farmer* [1781] (New York: Penguin Classic, 1963), 54. For further discussion, see Chapter 2.

25. Stewart, *"What Nature Suffers to Groe,"* 98, 103–104, 133–134, 138. See also Judith Carney, *Black Rice* (Cambridge, Mass.: Harvard University Press, 2001), 78–98.

26. Stewart, *"What Nature Suffers to Groe,"* 130; Carney, *Black Rice*, 98–101; Philip D. Morgan, "Work and Culture: The Task System and the World of Lowcountry Blacks, 1700–1880," in *Material Life in America*, ed. Robert St. George (Boston: Northeastern University Press, 1988), 205, 207; Berlin, *Generations of Captivity*, 64; Dylan Penningroth, *The Claims of Kinfolk* (Chapel Hill: University of North Carolina Press, 2003), 46–49.

27. Charles Joyner, *Shared Traditions* (Urbana: University of Illinois Press, 1999), 9.

28. See, e.g., Elizabeth Blum, "Power, Danger, and Control: Slave Women's Perceptions of Wilderness in the Nineteenth Century," *Women's Studies* 31 (March–April 2002): 248 (comparing white elite views with those of slaves and Native Americans).

29. Joyner, *Shared Traditions*, 9; Blassingame, *The Slave Community*, 101; David Hackett Fischer, *Albion's Seed* (New York: Oxford University Press, 1989), 340–344.

30. Joel Chandler Harris, *Uncle Remus and his Friends* (London: Osgood, McIvaine, 1896), 62–68.

31. Lawrence Levine, *Black Culture and Black Consciousness* (New York: Oxford University Press, 1977), 103–104.

32. Ibid., 133.

33. Joyner, *Shared Traditions*, 98–99; see Stewart, *"What Nature Suffers to Groe,"* 179, for a similar interpretation.

34. See Lawrence Levine, "Some Go Up and Some Go Down: The Meaning of the Slave Trickster," in *The Hofstadter Aegis: A Memorial*, ed. Stanley Elkins and Eric McKitrick (New York: Alfred A. Knopf, 1974).

35. Mechal Sobel, *Trabelin' On* (Westport, Conn.: Greenwood Press, 1979), 40, 72.

36. Levine, *Black Culture and Black Consciousness*, 86–87; Blassingame, *The Slave Community*, 30–31, 181–182.

37. Sobel, *Trabelin' On*, 227; Levine, *Black Culture and Black Consciousness*, 539–545.

38. Fischer, *Albion's Seed*, 278 n17.

39. Dell Upton, "White and Black Landscapes in Eighteenth-Century Virginia," in *Material Life*, 361–363; John Vlach, *Back of the Big House* (Chapel Hill: University of North Carolina Press, 1993), 3–5, 35–37.

40. Upton, "White and Black Landscapes," 364.

41. Ibid., 366; Roger Abrahams, *Singing the Master* (New York: Pantheon Books, 1992), 37, 41; Stewart, *"What Nature Suffers to Groe,"* 133; Berlin, *Generations of Captivity*, 58.

42. "Narrative of the Life and Adventures of Henry Bibb, an American Slave" [1849], in Taylor, *I Was Born a Slave*, 2: 41–42.

43. Vlach, *Back of the Big House*, 12–17; Berlin, *Generations of Captivity*, 134; Morgan, "Work and Culture."

44. Blassingame, *The Slave Community*, 179; Genovese, *Roll, Jordan, Roll*, 537–538; John Boles, *Black Southerners, 1619–1869* (Lexington: University Press of Kentucky, 1983), 89; Stewart, *"What Nature Suffers to Groe,"* 129.

45. Frances Anne Kemble, *Journal of a Residence on a Georgian Plantation in 1838–1839* (Athens: University of Georgia Press, 1984), 58, 68.

46. Morgan, "Work and Culture," 207; Genovese, *Roll, Jordan, Roll*, 30; Joyner, *Shared Traditions*, 96–97; Penningroth, *Claims of Kinfolk*, 46–60.

47. *Alabama Narratives*, ed. Jan Hillegas and Ken Lawrence, from *The American Slave: A Composite Autobiography*, Supp. Series 1, ed. George Rawick (Westport, Conn.: Greenwood Press, 1977), 1: 21.

48. Edward Magdol, *A Right to the Land* (Westport, Conn.: Greenwood Press, 1977), 12–13, 131–132.

49. Sharla Fett, *Working Cures* (Chapel Hill: University of North Carolina Press, 2002), 39.

50. Stewart, "What Nature Suffers to Groe," 136; Fett, *Working Cures*, 71–74; Blum, "Power, Danger, and Control," 257–259.

51. Fett, *Working Cures*, 36–37, 81, 85.

52. Stewart, "What Nature Suffers to Groe," 144–145.

53. Ibid., 145.

54. Kemble, *Journal of a Residence on a Georgian Plantation*, 98; Fett, *Working Cures*, 50.

55. *Alabama Narratives*, 1: 20, 42; *South Carolina Narratives*, from *An American Slave*, Supp. Series, 2: 2.

56. William Mathew, *Edmund Ruffin and the Crisis of Slavery in the Old South* (Athens: University of Georgia Press, 1988), 57.

57. Fett, *Working Cures*, 43–45, 76–82.

58. The seminal work in this tradition is Lucien Lévy-Bruhl, *How Natives Think* [1910], trans. Lilian Clare (Princeton, N.J.: Princeton University Press, 1985).

59. See, e.g., E. E. Evans-Pritchard, *Witchcraft, Oracles, and Magic among the Azande* (Oxford: Clarendon Press, 1968). See also the discussion of George Washington Carver's philosophy in Chapter 3.

60. Fett, *Working Cures*, 44–45.

61. Frederick Douglass, *The Narrative and Selected Writings* (New York: Modern Library, 1984), 79.

62. E. Franklin Frazier, *The Negro Church in America* (New York: Schocken Books, 1963), 13.

63. Blassingame, *The Slave Community*, 74, citing Henry Ravenal, "Recollections of Plantation Life," *Yale Review* 25 (June 1936): 776. See generally Holloway, *Africanisms in American Culture*.

64. Melville Herskovits, *The Myth of the Negro Past* (New York: Harper, 1941), 232–233.

65. Creel, "A Peculiar People," 47–48, 231, 260, 287.

66. Ibid., 251.

67. Levine, *Black Culture and Black Consciousness*, 59–60.

68. Genovese, *Roll, Jordan, Roll*, 247–249.

69. Levine, *Black Culture and Black Consciousness*, 23, 39, 51, 53.

70. Albert Raboteau, "African Americans, Exodus, and the American Israel," in

Down by the Riverside, ed. Larry Murphy (New York: New York University Press, 2000), 23.

71. Levine, *Black Culture and Black Consciousness,* 51.

72. Genovese, *Roll, Jordan, Roll,* 252.

73. Quoted in Levine, *Black Culture and Black Consciousness,* 50.

74. "My Bondage and Freedom" [1855], in *Frederick Douglass: Autobiographies* (New York: Literary Classics of the United States, 1994), 308.

75. Melvin Dixon, *Ride Out the Wilderness: Geography and Identity in Afro-American Literature* (Urbana: University of Illinois Press, 1987), 18–19, 23–24.

76. Martin Delany, *Blake, or the Huts of America* [1861–1863] (Boston: Beacon Press, 1970), 69–70.

77. Nell Painter, *Exodusters* (New York: W. W. Norton, 1976), 191, 195. I've modernized the spelling in these passages.

78. *Alabama Narratives,* 1: 73. I've adjusted the spelling used by the interviewer.

CHAPTER TWO. A LAND CURSED BY INJUSTICE

1. William Pease and Jane Pease, *Black Utopia* (Madison: Historical Society of Wisconsin, 1963), 16 (italics in original).

2. Ibid.

3. Albert Cowdry, *This Land, This South: An Environmental History* (Lexington: University Press of Kentucky, 1983), 79, 88, 96; William Mathew, *Edmund Ruffin and the Crisis of Slavery in the Old South* (Athens: University of Georgia Press, 1988), 153.

4. Ira Berlin, *Many Thousand Gone* (Cambridge, Mass.: Belknap Press, 1998), 268–271.

5. Steven Stoll, *Larding the Lean Earth* (New York: Hill and Wang, 2002), 19–20, 124–128; Margaret Rossiter, *The Emergence of Agricultural Science* (New Haven, Conn.: Yale University Press, 1975).

6. Ira Berlin, *Generations of Captivity* (Cambridge, Mass.: Belknap Press, 2003), 161–163, 168; Cowdry, *This Land, This South,* 72.

7. Berlin, *Generations of Captivity,* 175, 176.

8. Benjamin Quarles, *Black Abolitionists* (Oxford: Oxford University Press, 1969), 17.

9. Ibid., 200–215; Eric Foner, *Politics and Ideology in the Age of the Civil War* (New York: Oxford University Press, 1980), 43–44.

10. Ibid., 16–17; R. J. M. Blackett, *Building an Antislavery Wall* (Baton Rouge: Louisiana State University Press, 1983), 48–49.

11. Quarles, *Black Abolitionists,* 19; Blackett, *Building an Antislavery Wall,* 51.

12. Herbert Aptheker, *Abolitionism* (Boston: Twayne Publishers, 1989), xiii.

13. "Criticism in the Jungle," in *Black Literature and Literary Theory,* ed. Henry Louis Gates (New York: Methuen, 1984), 4.

14. James Montmarquet, *The Idea of Agrarianism* (Moscow: University of Idaho Press, 1989); Victor Davis Hanson, *Fields without Dreams* (New York: Free Press,

1996); Clarence Glacken, *Traces on the Rhodian Shore* (Berkeley: University of California Press, 1967), 116–117, 144–145, 175.

15. Roderick Nash, *Wilderness and the American Mind*, 3rd ed. (New Haven, Conn.: Yale University Press, 1967), 31, 34–35.

16. On American agrarianism, see Drew McCoy, *The Elusive Republic* (Chapel Hill: University of North Carolina Press, 1980); Jean Yarbrough, *American Virtues* (Lawrence: University Press of Kansas, 1998); Kimberly Smith, *Wendell Berry and the Agrarian Tradition* (Lawrence: University Press of Kansas, 2003).

17. On civic republicanism, see J. G. A. Pocock, *The Machiavellian Moment* (Princeton, N.J.: Princeton University Press, 1975); Gordon Wood, *The Creation of the American Republic, 1776–1787* (New York: W. W. Norton, 1969); Bernard Bailyn, *The Ideological Origins of the American Revolution*, 2nd ed. (Cambridge, Mass.: Belknap University Press, 1992), 34–54.

18. John Locke, *Second Treatise of Civil Government* [1690] (New York: Hafner Press, 1947), para. 25–51. This reading of Locke follows the interpretation of Richard Ashcraft, in *Revolutionary Politics and Locke's Two Treatises* (Princeton, N.J.: Princeton University Press, 1986), 261–274. See also Jeremy Waldron, *God, Locke, and Equality* (Cambridge: Cambridge University Press, 2002), 163–165, 170–177.

19. Thomas Jefferson, "Notes on Virginia," in *The Life and Selected Writings of Thomas Jefferson*, ed. Adrienne Koch and William Peden (New York: Random House, 1993), 259.

20. Smith, *Wendell Berry and the Agrarian Tradition*, 17–20; George Fredrickson, *The Black Image in the White Mind* (Hanover, N.H.: Wesleyan University Press, 1971), 58–61, 65–67. Fredrickson points out that this aristocratic ideology was probably confined to the upper class.

21. J. Hector St. John de Crèvecoeur, *Letters from an American Farmer* [1781] (New York: Penguin Classic, 1963), 168–170, 178.

22. Ibid., 166, 168, 71–72, 78.

23. McCoy, *Elusive Republic*, 13–47.

24. Ibid., 60–63.

25. Crèvecoeur, *Letters from an American Farmer*, 80.

26. Ibid., 69.

27. Ibid., 67, 51–52, 58–59.

28. Arthur Young, *A Six Months Tour through the North of England* [1771], 4 vols. (New York: Augustus M. Kelley, 1967); *American Husbandry* [1775], ed. Henry Carman (New York: Columbia University Press, 1939); Adam Smith, *An Inquiry into the Nature and Causes of the Wealth of Nations*, 2 vols. (Indianapolis: Liberty Fund, 1981); Elizabeth Fox-Genovese, *The Origins of Physiocracy* (Ithaca, N.Y.: Cornell University Press, 1976). The first American agricultural associations were founded in 1781 (New Jersey) and 1785 (Philadelphia), and the first American journal devoted to agriculture, *The Agricultural Museum*, began publication in 1810, followed by the more successful *The American Farmer* in 1819. Percy Wells Bidwell and John Falconer, *History of Agriculture in the Northern United States* (Washington, D.C.: Carnegie Institute, 1925), 184–191; Wayne Rasmussen, *Readings in the History of American*

Agriculture (Urbana: University of Illinois Press, 1960), 41–42, 51–52; Stoll, *Larding the Lean Earth*, passim.

29. Glacken, *Traces on the Rhodian Shore*, 131–134, 175. Classical and medieval farmers did of course understand the benefits of letting fields lie fallow but believed that fields under cultivation could be made more productive through tillage and manuring.

30. James Madison, "Address Delivered before the Agricultural Society of Albemarle," *American Farmer* 1 (Aug. 20, 1819): 161–163; 1 (Aug. 27, 1819): 169–171; 1 (September 3, 1819): 177–179; Stoll, *Larding the Lean Earth*, 36–40, 49–54, 55–56.

31. Leon Litwack, *North of Slavery* (Chicago: University of Chicago Press, 1961), 4.

32. Dorse Hagler, "The Agrarian Theme in Southern History to 1860" (PhD dissertation, University of Missouri, 1968), 193–203; Stoll, *Larding the Lean Earth*, 133–134.

33. Adam Smith, *An Inquiry into the Nature and Causes of the Wealth of Nations*, 2 vols. (Indianapolis: Liberty Fund, 1981), 1: 98–99, 385–392; 2: 684. Modern economists would point out that even with a free market in labor and commodities, stewardship does not always pay. However, Smith's critique of slavery suggests that the disincentives to stewardship will typically be stronger under a slave system.

34. Judith Carney, *Black Rice* (Cambridge, Mass.: Harvard University Press, 2001), 78–98.

35. On the difficulties of controlling slave labor in a mixed farming regime, see Berlin, *Many Thousand Gone*, 268–269.

36. The French Physiocrats favored large landholdings for this reason, although they did not typically endorse slave agriculture. Vaggi Gianni, *The Economics of Francois Quesnay* (Durham, N.C.: Duke University Press, 1987), 98–101; James McLain, *The Economic Writings of Du Pont de Nemours* (Newark: University of Delaware Press, 1977), 120–122; Richard Grove, *Green Imperialism* (Cambridge: Cambridge University Press, 1995), 190–199, 205–206.

37. Smith, *Wealth of Nations*, 1: 385–386, 2: 832.

38. Anna Bramwell, *Ecology in the 20th Century* (New Haven, Conn.: Yale University Press, 1989), 66–71. On the influence of liberal economic theory in general on environmental thought, see Grove, *Green Imperialism*, 168–263.

39. Linda Kerber, *Federalists in Dissent* (Ithaca, N.Y.: Cornell University Press, 1970), 23–66. The quote, from a letter from Robert Griswold to Fanny Griswold, December 10, 1800, is on 24.

40. "Henry Clay's Speech," *African Repository* 6 (March 1831): 9–10.

41. Ruffin, "Slavery and Free Labor Described and Compared" [1859], quoted in Mathews, *Edmund Ruffin and the Crisis of Slavery*, 59. See also Dorse Hagler, "The Agrarian Theme in Southern History to 1860," 194–197.

42. Eric Foner, *Free Soil, Free Labor, Free Men* (Oxford: Oxford University Press, 1995), ix–xxxix.

43. "Narrative of Williams Wells Brown, A Fugitive Slave" [1847], in *I Was Born A Slave*, ed. Yuval Taylor, 2 vols. (Chicago: Lawrence Hill Books, 1999), 1: 703.

44. "Twelve Years a Slave: Narrative of Solomon Northrup" [1853], in ibid., 2: 174.

45. "The Life of Josiah Henson" [1849], in ibid., 1: 751.

46. Ibid., 1: 752. See also Ball, "Slavery in the United States" [1836], in ibid., 1: 468.

47. Litwack, *North of Slavery*, 175–177.

48. Letter to the Editor, Colored American, February 7, 1838, in *Black Abolitionist Papers*, 5 vols., ed. C. Peter Ripley (Chapel Hill: University of North Carolina Press, 1991), 3: 257, 258.

49. Douglass, "An Address to the Colored People of the United States" [1848], in *African-American Social and Political Thought, 1850–1920*, ed. Howard Brotz (New Brunswick, N.J.: Transaction, 1992), 212. But see "Letter to Harriet Beecher Stowe" [1853], in ibid., 222–223 (arguing that blacks are reluctant to go into farming, and so should have the opportunity for industrial education).

50. Edward Magdol, *A Right to the Land* (Westport, Conn.: Greenwood Press, 1977), 12–13, 17–18.

51. Ball, "Slavery in the United States," in *I Was Born a Slave*, 1: 265, 266, 276, 279, 280.

52. Ibid., 1: 282–284 (italics in original).

53. "Narrative of the Life of Frederick Douglass, an American Slave" [1845], in *I Was Born a Slave*, 1: 589; "The Fugitive Blacksmith; or, Events in the History of James W. L. Pennington" [1849], 2: 114, 147; "Narrative of the Sufferings of Lewis and Milton Clarke" [1846], in ibid., 1: 634; "The Life of John Thompson, a Fugitive Slave" [1861], in ibid., 2: 431.

54. "Narrative of the Life and Adventures of Henry Bibb" [1849], in ibid., 2: 36.

55. Ibid., 2: 83; see also "Narrative of the Life of Frederick Douglass," in ibid., 1: 589.

56. Jean-Jacques Rousseau, *A Discourse on Inequality* [1755] (London: Penguin Classics, 1984), 116.

57. *Letters from an American Farmer*, 174–175.

58. Harriet Jacobs, "Incidents in the Life of a Slave Girl" [1861], in *Slave Narratives* (New York: Library of America, 2000), 763, 803.

59. "Narrative of the Life and Adventures of Henry Bibb," in *I Was Born a Slave*, 2: 19. See also "Narrative of Williams Wells Brown, A Fugitive Slave," in ibid., 1: 752.

60. On the relationship between religion and politics in the slave narratives, see Kimberly Smith, *The Dominion of Voice* (Lawrence: University Press of Kansas, 1999), 221–223.

61. The abolitionist text that best achieves this fusion is Harriet Beecher Stowe's *Uncle Tom's Cabin*. However, Stowe's use of religious imagery probably had more to do with the conventions of sentimental novels than with the influence of slave culture. Jane Tompkins, *Sensational Designs* (Oxford: Oxford University Press, 1985), 122–146.

62. "Slave Life in Georgia" [1855], in *I Was Born a Slave*, 2: 392.

63. "Slavery in the United States," in ibid., 1: 378. See also "Narratives of the Sufferings of Lewis and Milton Clarke," in ibid., 1: 633.

64. "Narratives of the Sufferings of Lewis and Milton Clarke," in ibid., 1: 627.

65. "Slavery in the United States," in ibid., 1: 384.

66. "Running a Thousand Miles for Freedom; or, The Escape of William and Ellen Craft" [1860], in ibid., 2: 487. See also "Narrative of the Life and Adventures of Henry Bibb," in ibid., 2: 17.

67. Charles Nichols, "The Slave Narrators and the Picaresque," in Charles Davis and Henry Louis Gates, *The Slave's Narrative* (Oxford: Oxford University Press, 1985), 283–298; Robert Bone, *Down Home* (New York: G. P. Putnam's Sons, 1975), xix.

68. Magdol, *A Right to the Land*, 26–27.

69. "Slave Life in Georgia," in *I Was Born a Slave*, 2: 347; "The Life of John Thompson," in ibid., 2: 439.

70. "The Life of Josiah Henson," in ibid., 1: 727, 728.

71. In Brotz, *African-American Social and Political Thought, 1850–1920*, 56.

72. Ibid., 57, 58.

73. Ibid.

74. Ibid., 62, 63.

75. Ibid., 63, 64. Delany made a similar argument in *Blake, or Huts of America* [1861–1863] (Boston: Beacon Press, 1970), 261, 287. See also Alexander Crummell, "The Relations and Duties of Free Colored Men in America to Africa" [1860], in Brotz, *African-American Social and Political Thought*, 172; Douglass, "Prejudice not Natural" [1849], in ibid., 214. Later black writers would pick up this theme. Booker T. Washington, "Our New Citizen" [1896], in ibid., 359; "The American Negro and His Economic Value" [1907], in ibid., 417–419; Frances E. W. Harper, "Iola LeRoy, or Shadows Uplifted" [1893], in *Three Classic African American Novels*, ed. Henry Louis Gates (New York: Vintage Classics, 1990), 431; Charles Chesnutt, "An Inside View of the Negro Question" [1889], in *Charles W. Chesnutt: Essays and Speeches*, ed. Josephy McElrath Jr., Robert Leitz III, and Jesse Crisler (Stanford, Calif.: Stanford University Press, 1999), 62.

76. "Twelve Years a Slave," in *I Was Born a Slave*, 2: 230, 229.

77. "Narrative of the Life of Frederick Douglass, an American Slave," in ibid., 1: 540, 543; J. Lee Greene, *Blacks in Eden* (Charlottesville: University Press of Virginia, 1996), 20.

78. "Address before the Tennessee Colored Agricultural and Mechanical Association," in Brotz, *African-American Social and Political Thought*, 286–287.

79. Ibid., 288–289.

80. Ibid., 290.

81. Ibid., 291.

82. Ibid.

83. Ibid., 296–297.

84. *Without Consent or Contract* (New York: W. W. Norton, 1989), 72–80; Allan Bogue, "Fogel's Journey through the Slave States," *Journal of Economic History* 50, 3 (September 1990): 699–710; Mathews, *Edmund Ruffin and the Crisis of Slavery in the Old South*, 15–16, 153.

85. David Hackett Fischer, *Albion's Seed* (New York: Oxford University Press, 1989), 244, 252.

86. Eugene Genovese, *Roll, Jordan, Roll* (New York: Vintage Books, 1972), 285–324.

87. The ASPCA was founded by Henry Bergh in 1866; the animal welfare movement resulted in most states adopting protective legislation by 1877. Emily Leavitt et al., *Animals and Their Legal Rights* (Washington, D.C.: Animal Welfare Institute, 1968).

88. Fischer, *Albion's Seed*, 364.

89. *Alabama Narratives*, ed. Jan Hillegas and Ken Lawrence, from *The American Slave: A Composite Autobiography*, Supp. Series 1, ed. George Rawick (Westport, Conn.: Greenwood Press, 1977), 1: 35.

90. Leon Litwack, *Been in the Storm So Long* (New York: Vintage Books, 1979), 199.

91. "The Nature of Slavery" [1850], in Brotz, *African-American Social and Political Thought*, 216–217.

CHAPTER THREE. POSSESSING THE LAND

1. George Perkins Marsh, *Man and Nature* [1864] (Cambridge, Mass.: Belknap Press, 1965), 11–12.

2. Willard Cochrane, *Development of American Agriculture* (Minneapolis: University of Minnesota Press, 1979), 93. Cochrane points out that the prices of nonfarm goods were falling as well, but farmers usually held their purchase of nonfarm-produced consumer goods to a minimum.

3. Theodore Saloutos, *Farmer Movements in the South* (Berkeley: University of California Press, 1960), 28, 29.

4. Edward Magdol, *A Right to the Land* (Westport, Conn.: Greenwood Press, 1977), 3–4, 55–56; Eric Foner, *Reconstruction* (New York: Harper and Row, 1988), 104–106; Laura Edwards, *Gendered Strife and Confusion* (Urbana: University of Illinois Press, 1991), 66–67; Nell Painter, *Exodusters* (New York: W. W. Norton, 1976), 67–68; August Meier, *Negro Thought in America, 1880–1915* (Ann Arbor: University of Michigan Press, 1963), 10–11.

5. Foner, *Reconstruction*, 69–70, 235; 159, 161, 245–246; Magdol, *A Right to the Land*, 188.

6. Thomas D. Clark, *The Greening of the South* (Lexington: University Press of Kentucky, 1984), 16; Gilbert Fite, *Cotton Fields No More* (Lexington: University Press of Kentucky, 1984), 2.

7. Pete Daniels, *Breaking the Land* (Urbana: University of Illinois Press, 1985), 4, 162–163; Fite, *Cotton Fields No More*, 5.

8. William Cohen, "Negro Involuntary Servitude in the South, 1865–1940: A Preliminary Analysis," *Journal of Southern History* 42 (Feb. 1976): 33–34; Steven Hahn, *A Nation under Our Feet* (Cambridge, Mass.: Harvard University Press, 2003), 441–451.

9. Foner, *Reconstruction*, 135.

10. Ibid., 138–139.

11. Albert Cowdry, *This Land, This South* (Lexington: University Press of Kentucky, 1983), 107.

12. Fite, *Cotton Fields No More*, 10, 22–29, 84–85.

13. Foner, *Reconstruction*, 81; Leon Litwack, *Been in the Storm So Long* (New York: Vintage Books, 1979), 311–314.

14. Painter, *Exodusters*, 184; August Meier, *Negro Thought in America, 1880–1915* (Ann Arbor: University of Michigan Press, 1963), 59.

15. Fite, *Cotton Fields No More*, 21; Thomas Mitchell, "From Reconstruction to Deconstruction," *Northwestern University Law Review* 95 (Winter 2001): 526; Magdol, *A Right to the Land*, 211.

16. Steven Stoll, *Larding the Lean Earth* (New York: Hill and Wang, 2002), 173–213.

17. We might add the animal welfare movement to this list, but animal welfare was motivated less by a vision of environmental stewardship than by humanitarian concerns; its relationship to the environmental movement was and remains complex. See Emily Leavitt et al., *Animals and Their Legal Rights* (Washington, D.C.: Animal Welfare Institute, 1968), 1–47.

18. Samuel Hays, *Beauty, Health, and Permanence* (Cambridge: Cambridge University Press, 1993); Robert Gottlieb, *Forcing the Spring* (Washington, D.C.: Island Press, 1993).

19. Cassandra Johnson and J. M. Bowker, "African-American Wildland Memories," *Environmental Ethics* 26 (Spring 2004): 57–75; Cowdry, *This Land, This South*, 113–114; Clark, *The Greening of the South*, 24, 29, 30–31.

20. Cowdry, *This Land, This South*, 104, 106.

21. E.g., W. E. B. Du Bois, "Declaration of Principles of the Niagara Movement," in *African-American Social and Political Thought, 1850–1920*, ed. Howard Brotz (New Brunswick: Transaction, 1992), 534.

22. Cowdry, *This Land, This South*, 114–118; Stuart Marks, *Southern Hunting in Black and White* (Princeton, N.J.: Princeton University Press, 1991), 48.

23. Cowdry, *This Land, This South*, 120; Clark, *The Greening of the South*, 26–31.

24. Marks, *Southern Hunting*, 68; Edwards, *Gendered Strife and Confusion*, 124; Dylan Pennington, *The Claims of Kinfolk* (Chapel Hill: University of North Carolina Press, 2003), 143.

25. Marks, *Southern Hunting*, 40, 56; Edwards, *Gendered Strife and Confusion*, 225–226; Fite, *Cotton Fields No More*, 8–9. T. Thomas Fortune may also have captured some of the popular view of conservation when he complained that aristocrats in Europe had turned arable land into parks and game preserves; such land, he argued, should be confiscated and given to the poor to farm. *Black and White: Land, Labor and Politics in the South* [1884] (New York: Arno Press, 1968), 222.

26. Alan Marcus, *Agricultural Science and the Quest for Legitimacy* (Ames: Iowa State University Press, 1985); Lester Stephens, "Farish Furman's Formula: Scientific Farming and the 'New South,'" *Agricultural History* 50 (April 1976): 377–390; Fite, *Cotton Fields No More*, 68–90.

27. Cochrane, *The Development of American Agriculture*, 240.

28. Cowdry, *This Land, This South*, 108.

29. Marcus, *Agricultural Science and the Quest for Legitimacy*, 6.

30. Saloutos, *Farmer Movements in the South*, 57–58; Marcus, *Agricultural Science and the Quest for Legitimacy*, 9–11; Fite, *Cotton Fields No More*, 68–76; Daniels, *Breaking the Land*, 6, 10, 16.

31. Gottlieb, *Forcing the Spring*, 47–80; Kimberly Smith, *Wendell Berry and the Agrarian Tradition* (Lawrence: University Press of Kansas, 2003), 11–62.

32. James D. Anderson, *The Education of Blacks in the South, 1860–1935* (Chapel Hill: University of North Carolina Press, 1986), 73–77; Dianne Glave, "'A Garden So Brilliant with Colors, So Original in Its Design,'" *Environmental History* 8 (July 2003): 399–404.

33. Elizabeth Sanders, *Roots of Reform* (Chicago: University of Chicago Press, 1999), 179–339; Lawrence Goodwyn, *The Populist Moment* (Oxford: Oxford University Press, 1978).

34. R. Douglas Hurt, *American Agriculture* (Ames: Iowa State University Press, 1994), 189–194; Wayne Rasmussen, *Readings in the History of American Agriculture* (Urbana: University of Illinois Press, 1960), 114; Saloutos, *Farmer Movements in the South*, 40–41; Sanders, *Roots of Reform*, 314–324; James Ferguson, "The Grange and Farmer Education in Mississippi," *Journal of Southern History* 8 (Feb.–Nov. 1942): 497–512.

35. Theodore Mitchell, *Political Education in the Southern Farmers' Alliance, 1887–1900* (Madison: University of Wisconsin Press, 1987), 134–135; Saloutos, *Farmer Movements in the South*, 63.

36. Meier, *Negro Thought in America*, 46; Hahn, *A Nation under Our Feet*, 376–384, 396–397, 412–425, 431–440.

37. Meier, *Negro Thought in America*, 42, 31.

38. For one of the earliest accounts of this unfulfilled promise, see W. E. B. Du Bois, *The Souls of Black Folk* [1903] (New York: Penguin Classics, 1989), 13–35. See also Fortune, *Black and White*, 238.

39. Litwack, *Been in the Storm So Long*, 316–317; Magdol, *A Right to the Land*, 138.

40. "Address before the Tennessee Colored Agricultural and Mechanical Association," in Brotz, *African-American Social and Political Thought*, 290, 297. See also Kelly Miller, "Race Adjustment" [1908], 131, in *Race Adjustment and the Everlasting Stain* (New York: Arno Press, 1968), 131.

41. "The Call of Providence to the Descendants of Africa in America" [1862], in ibid., 126. Delany used the same language in "The Condition, Elevation, Emigration, and Destiny of the Colored People of the United States" [1852], in Brotz, *African-American Social and Political Thought*, 97.

42. Wilson Moses, *The Golden Age of Black Nationalism, 1850–1925* (Hamden, Conn.: Archon Books, 1978), 157.

43. "The Condition, Elevation, Emigration, and Destiny of the Colored People of the United States" [1852], in Brotz, *African-American Social and Political Thought*, 111, 101, 103.

44. "The African Problem and Its Method of Solution" [1890], in Brotz, *African-*

American Social and Political Thought, 136. See also Alexander Crummell, "African Civilization Society Constitution" [1858], in ibid., 192.

45. Painter, *Exodusters,* 103, 130.

46. W. E. B. Du Bois, *The Philadelphia Negro* [1899] (New York: Benjamin Blom, 1967), 354. See also W. E. B. Du Bois, "The Immediate Program of the American Negro" [1915], in *Negro Protest Thought in the Twentieth Century,* ed. Francis Broderick and August Meier (Indianapolis: Bobbs-Merrill, 1965), 55–60.

47. Charles W. Chesnutt, "The Future of the Negro" [1882], in *Charles W. Chesnutt: Essays and Speeches,* ed. Josephy McElrath Jr., Robert Leitz III, and Jesse Crisler (Stanford, Calif.: Stanford University Press, 1999), 31; "Why I Am a Republican" [1892], in ibid., 95. See also Archibald Grimke, "Modern Industrialism and the Negroes of the United States" [1907], in Brotz, *African-American Social and Political Thought,* 464–480.

48. Booker T. Washington, *Working with the Hands* (New York: Doubleday, Page, 1904), 9.

49. Ibid., 10.

50. Ibid., 64, 157.

51. Ibid., 116.

52. Ibid., 15–16.

53. Ibid., 34, 48.

54. Saloutos, *Farmer Movements in the South,* 61; Daniels, *Breaking the Land,* 162–163; Fite, *Cotton Fields No More,* 87.

55. Fite, *Cotton Fields No More,* 84–85.

56. Booker T. Washington, "The Negro and the Labor Problem of the South" [1907], in Brotz, *African-American Social and Political Thought,* 402–404.

57. Sanders, *Roots of Reform.*

58. W. E. B. Du Bois, *The Souls of Black Folk* [1905] (New York: Penguin Books, 1989), 102–103, 113.

59. Ibid., 127, 129.

60. W. E. B. Du Bois, *The Quest of the Silver Fleece* [1911] (New York: Negro Universities Press, 1969), 404.

61. Fortune, *Black and White,* 35, 39, 197, 219, 220, 238, 207.

62. But see ibid., 198.

63. Charles W. Chesnutt, "The Marrow of Tradition" [1905], in *Three Classic African-American Novels,* ed. Henry Louis Gates (New York: Vintage Classics, 1990), 684–685.

64. Du Bois, *Souls of Black Folk,* 108, 110.

65. Du Bois, *Quest of the Silver Fleece,* 410–413.

66. In McElrath, Leitz, and Crisler, *Charles W. Chesnutt: Essays and Speeches,* 146.

67. "Narrative of the Life of Frederick Douglass, an American Slave," in *I Was Born a Slave,* ed. Yuval Taylor (Chicago: Lawrence Hill Books, 1999), 549.

68. "The Folly of Colonization" [1894], in Brotz, *African-American Social and Political Thought,* 330; "African Civilization Society" [1859], in ibid., 266. A similar ar-

gument is made by Grimke, "Modern Industrialism and the Negroes of the United States," 475.

69. Ibid. Henry Highland Garnet agreed on the need for a strong home feeling. "The Past, the Present, and the Destiny of the Colored Race" [1848], in Brotz, *African-American Social and Political Thought*, 201–202. See also Fortune, *Black and White*, 124–125.

70. Delany, "The Condition, Elevation, Emigration, and Destiny of the Colored People of the United States" [1852], in Brotz, *African-American Social and Political Thought*, 79.

71. Alexander Crummell, "The Relations and Duties of Free Colored Men in America to Africa" [1860], in ibid., 172. See also Fortune, *Black and White*, 213, 217.

72. Magdol, *A Right to the Land*, 169–173, 175–199, 200–210; Hahn, *A Nation under Our Feet*, 135–140.

73. Hahn, *A Nation under Our Feet*, 317–363.

74. Nancy Cott, *The Bonds of Womanhood* (New Haven, Conn.: Yale University Press, 1977); Barbara Welter, "The Cult of True Womanhood: 1820–1860," in *The American Family in Social-Historical Perspective*, 3rd ed., ed. Michael Gordon (New York: St. Martin's Press, 1983); Ruth Bloch, "American Feminine Ideals in Transition," *Feminist Studies* 4 (June 1978): 101–126; Deborah White, *Ar'n't I a Woman*, rev. ed. (New York: W. W. Norton, 1999), 56–58; Edwards, *Gendered Strife and Confusion*, 129–144; Sieglinde Lemke, "Introduction," in Elizabeth Davis, *Lifting as They Climb* (New York: G. K. Hall, 1996), xx–xxi.

75. On natural beauty as a policy goal, see Martin Melosi, *Garbage in the Cities* (College Station: Texas A&M University Press, 1981), 105–133; Kimberly Smith, "Mere Taste: Democracy and the Politics of Beauty," *Wisconsin Environmental Law Review* 7 (Summer 2000): 151–195.

76. Carolyn Merchant, "Women of the Progressive Conservation Movement, 1900–1916," *Environmental Review* 8 (Spring 1984): 57–85; Edwards, *Gendered Strife and Confusion*, 134, 139.

77. Andrew Jackson Downing, *Victorian Cottage Residences* [1842] (New York: Dover, 1981), viii–ix.

78. Ibid., ix.

79. Crummell, "The Black Women of the South" [1891], in *Destiny and Race: Selected Writings, 1840–1898*, ed. Wilson J. Moses (Amherst: University of Massachusetts Press, 1992), 215.

80. "The Problem of Housing the Negro, Pt. I" [1901], in *Writings by W. E. B. Du Bois in Periodicals Edited by Others, 1891–1909*, 4 vols., ed. Herbert Aptheker (Millwood, N.Y.: Kraus-Thomson, 1982), 1: 93.

81. Ibid.

82. Du Bois, *The Philadelphia Negro*, 5. See also W. E. B. Du Bois, "The Negro in the Large Cities" [1907], in Du Bois, *Writings by W. E. B. Du Bois in Periodicals Edited by Others*, 1: 382.

83. "The Problem of Housing the Negro, Pt. III" [1901], in ibid., 1: 120.

84. "Sociology and Industry in Southern Education" [1907], in ibid., 1: 370.

85. Washington, *Working with the Hands*, 98, 94.

86. Elizabeth Blum, "Women, Environmental Rationale, and Activism during the Progressive Era," in *"To Love the Wind and the Rain": African Americans and Environmental History*, ed. Dianne Glave and Mark Stoll (Pittsburgh: University of Pittsburgh Press, 2006), 82–85; Wilson Moses, *The Golden Age of Black Nationalism, 1850–1925* (Hamden, Conn.: Archon Books, 1978), 103–104, 118.

87. Washington, *Working with the Hands*, 153.

88. Booker T. Washington, *The Story of My Life and Work* [1900] (New York: Negro Universities Press, 1969), 281–282.

89. "Nature Study and Gardening for Rural Schools" [1910], in *George Washington Carver: In His Own Words*, ed. Gary Kremer (Columbia: University of Missouri Press, 1987), 101.

90. Carver to Judge Leon McCord, Dec. 13, 1927, in ibid., 137.

91. Carver to Mr. Woods, Sept. 7, 1940, in ibid., 141. The idea of man as a co-creator, finishing and perfecting God's work, has a long history in classical and Christian thought. Clarence Glacken, *Traces on the Rhodian Shore* (Berkeley: University of California, 1967), 116–117, 144–145, 175.

92. W. E. B. Du Bois, "The Work of Negro Women in Society" [1902], in Du Bois, *Writings by W.E.B. Du Bois in Periodicals Edited by Others*, 1: 141.

93. W. E. B. Du Bois, "The Development of a People" [1904], in ibid., 1: 212. He returns to this theme in his 1920 work, *Darkwater: Voices from within the Veil* (New York: Humanity Books, 2003), 185.

94. E.g., W. E. B. Du Bois, "Criteria of Negro Art" [1926], in *The Oxford W. E. B. Du Bois Reader*, ed. Eric Sundquist (Oxford: Oxford University Press, 1996), 324.

95. Edwards, *Gendered Strife and Confusion*, 145–161.

96. Ibid., 148, 157, 158; Richard Westmacott, *African-American Gardens and Yards in the Rural South* (Knoxville: University of Tennessee Press, 1992), 25, 31.

97. Glave, "'A Garden So Brilliant with Colors, So Original in Its Design,'" 399–402.

98. Westmacott, *African-American Gardens and Yards*, 104–106.

99. Du Bois, *Souls of Black Folk*, 35.

100. Val Plumwood, *Feminism and the Mastery of Nature* (London: Routledge, 1993); David Ehrenfeld, *The Arrogance of Humanism* (New York: Oxford University Press, 1978); Eric Katz, "The Big Lie: Human Restoration of Nature," in *Environmental Ethics*, ed. Andrew Light and Holmes Rolston III (Oxford: Blackwell, 2003), 390–397.

CHAPTER FOUR. RACE NATURES

1. Anna Bramwell, *Ecology in the 20th Century* (New Haven: Yale University Press, 1989), 104–132, 177–194; Simon Schama, *Landscape and Memory* (New York: Random House, 1995), 75–184.

2. Arnold Rampersad, *The Art and Imagination of W. E. B. Du Bois* (Cambridge, Mass.: Harvard University Press, 1976), 68–70, 74–75.

3. Pete Daniels, *Breaking the Land* (Urbana: University of Illinois Press, 1985), 3–16; Albert Cowdry, *This Land, This South* (Lexington: University Press of Kentucky, 1983), 127–131.

4. Matthew Pratt Guterl, *The Color of Race in America, 1900–1940* (Cambridge, Mass.: Harvard University Press, 2001), 14–67; Joel Williamson, *The Crucible of Race* (Oxford: Oxford University Press, 1984), 119–139; George Fredrickson, *The Black Image in the White Mind* (Hanover, N.H.: Wesleyan University Press, 1971), 256–257.

5. Williamson, *The Crucible of Race*, 224–247; John Hope Franklin, *From Slavery to Freedom*, 6th ed. (New York: Alfred A. Knopf, 1988), 235–237, 282.

6. Williamson, *The Crucible of Race*, 249–253.

7. Ibid., 249–252; C. Vann Woodward, "*Strange Career* Critics," *Journal of American History* 75 (December 1988): 858–860; Leon Litwack, *Been in the Storm So Long* (New York: Vintage Books, 1979), 262–263.

8. Schama, *Landscape and Memory*, 135–184. For an interesting literary exploration of the complex meanings of trees in black culture, see Alice Walker, *Meridian* (New York: Pocket Books, 1976), 38–48.

9. W. E. B. Du Bois, *Darkwater* [1920] (New York: Humanity Books, 2003), 227–231.

10. Milton Sernett, *Bound for the Promised Land* (Durham, N.C.: Duke University Press, 1997), 3–12, 17; Steven Hahn, *A Nation under Our Feet* (Cambridge, Mass.: Harvard University Press, 2003), 465–466; Carole Marks, "The Social and Economic Life of Southern Blacks during the Migration," in *Black Exodus*, ed. Alferdteen Harrison (Jackson: University Press of Mississippi, 1991), 36.

11. Sernett, *Bound for the Promised Land*, 58–60.

12. T. Lynn Smith, "The Redistribution of the Negro Population of the United States, 1910–1960," *Journal of Negro History* 51 (July 1966): 159; *Statistical Abstract of the United States, 1930*, No. 52 (Washington, D.C.: Government Printing Office, 1930), 45; *Statistical Abstract of the United States, 1940*, No. 62 (Washington, D.C.: Government Printing Office, 1941), 20.

13. August Meier, *Negro Thought in America, 1880–1915* (Ann Arbor: University of Michigan Press, 1963), 178–182.

14. Ibid., 264.

15. Franklin, *From Slavery to Freedom*, 265–268; Guterl, *The Color of Race*, 55–57.

16. Franklin, *From Slavery to Freedom*, 268–273.

17. Nathan Huggins, *Harlem Renaissance* (Oxford: Oxford University Press, 1971), 41–43.

18. Clarence Glacken, *Traces on the Rhodian Shore* (Berkeley: University of California Press, 1967), 108–110.

19. Ibid., 80–115; Ronald Meek, *Social Science and the Ignoble Savage* (Cambridge: Cambridge University Press, 1976), 163; Ivan Hannaford, *Race: The History of an Idea in the West* (Washington, D.C.: Woodrow Wilson Center Press, 1996), 168; William Stanton, *The Leopard's Spots* (Chicago: University of Chicago Press, 1960), 7–9.

20. Johann G. von Herder, *Reflections on the Philosophy of the History of Mankind*, abridged [1784–1791] (Chicago: University of Chicago Press, 1968), 5, 10, 20; Georg

W. F. Hegel, *Lectures on the Philosophy of World History* [1830], trans. H. B. Nisbet (Cambridge: Cambridge University Press, 1975), 152–196.

21. Heinrich von Treitschke, *Politics* [1892], 2 vols., trans. Blanche Dugdale and Torben de Bille (New York: Macmillan, 1916), I: 272–283.

22. On the rise and fall of polygenism, see Stanton, *The Leopard's Spots.*

23. Johann Friedrich Blumenbach, *On the Natural Varieties of Mankind* [1775], trans. Thomas Bendyshe (New York: Bergman, 1969), 194–196; J. B. Lamarck, *Zoological Philosophy* [1809], trans. Hugh Elliot (Chicago: University of Chicago Press, 1984), 2–6.

24. Charles Darwin, *The Descent of Man,* 2nd ed. [1877], vol. 21 of *The Works of Charles Darwin,* ed. Paul Barrett and R. B. Freeman (New York: New York University Press, 1989), 30–68; Paul Boller, *American Thought in Transition* (Lanham, Md.: University Press of America, 1981), 1–3.

25. Madison Grant, *The Passing of the Great Race,* 4th rev. ed. (New York: Charles Scribner's Sons, 1924), 37–44. The first edition was published in 1916.

26. Darwin, *The Descent of Man,* 31–32, 81, 97, 127–128.

27. Indeed, even some scientific racists were troubled by the materialist model; Joseph Le Conte, for example, tried to counter it by arguing that reason rather than natural selection was now the dominant force driving racial development, and that the endpoint of evolution was the development of a free (undetermined) human spirit. Joseph Le Conte, *Evolution,* 2nd rev. ed. (New York: D. Appleton, 1902), 86, 329.

28. William James, *The Principles of Psychology* [1890], 2 vols. (Cambridge, Mass.: Harvard University Press, 1981), I:133–137, 142–143; II:1215–1234; Daniel Bjork, *The Compromised Scientist: William James and the Development of American Psychology* (New York: Columbia University Press, 1983), 7–9.

29. On James's influence on Du Bois, see Shamoon Zamir, *Dark Voices: W. E. B. Du Bois and American Thought, 1888–1903* (Chicago: University of Chicago Press, 1995), 11–25. Zamir argues that Du Bois was skeptical of James's voluntarism, but he does not examine Du Bois's post-1903 writings, which show a stronger Jamesian (and Boasian) influence.

30. William McDougall, *The Group Mind,* 2nd rev. ed. (New York: G. P. Putnam's Sons, 1920), 293. See also Herbert Spencer, "Social Statics" [1851], in *On Social Evolution,* ed. J. D. Y. Peel (Chicago: University of Chicago Press, 1972), 8–9, 33; Frederick Hoffman, "Race Traits and Tendencies of the American Negro," *Publications of the American Economic Association* 11, Nos. 1–3 (1896): 1–329; Nathaniel Shaler, *The Neighbor* (Boston: Houghton Mifflin, 1904); Henry F. Osborn, *Men of the Old Stone Age,* 3rd ed. (New York: Charles Scribner's Sons, 1918); McDougall, *The Group Mind,* 156, 163; Grant, *The Passing of the Great Race,* xix–xxi, 13–16.

31. McDougall, *The Group Mind,* 287–290.

32. Donald Worster, *Nature's Economy,* 2nd ed. (Cambridge: Cambridge University Press, 1994), 39–44.

33. H. G. Schenck, *The Mind of the European Romantics* (London: Constable, 1966), 169; Joseph Beach, *The Concept of Nature in Nineteenth-Century English Poetry*

(New York: Macmillan, 1939), 45–109; Worster, *Nature's Economy*, 17–18; Erich Heller, *The Disinherited Mind* (Philadelphia: Dufur and Saifer, 1952), 5–17.

34. Le Conte, *Evolution*, 8, 28, 3.

35. McDougall, *The Group Mind*, 287; Grant, *The Passing of the Great Race*, 97, 99, 169–170, 215. See also Lothrop Stoddard, *The Rising Tide of Color against White World-Supremacy* (New York: Charles Scribner's Sons, 1920), 168.

36. Le Conte, *Evolution*, 97.

37. Hannaford, *Race*, 190.

38. Nathaniel Shaler, "Nature and Man in America," *Scribner's Magazine* 8 (1890): 360.

39. Ibid., 361–363, 365. See also McDougall, *The Group Mind*, 303; Grant, *The Passing of the Great Race*, 169–171.

40. Émile Boutmy, *The English People*, trans. E. English (New York: G. P. Putnam's Sons, 1904), 13.

41. Henry Thomas Buckle, *History of Civilization in England*, 2 vols. (New York: D. Appleton, 1880), 1: 85–86.

42. McDougall, *The Group Mind*, 298.

43. Ibid., 300–301.

44. John Haller, *Outcasts from Evolution* (Urbana: University of Illinois Press, 1971), 36, 51–52. These theorists tended to think of evolution as the unfolding of "latent potential."

45. Shaler, *The Neighbor*, 135; Grant, *The Passing of the Great Race*, 77. See also Stoddard, *The Rising Tide of Color*, xiii, 100–102.

46. Haller, *Outcasts from Evolution*, 80, quoting Nott, *Instincts of Races* [1866], 4–5.

47. Grant, *The Passing of the Great Race*, 209.

48. Stephen Fox, *The American Conservation Movement* (Madison: University of Wisconsin Press, 1981), 345–351. See also Guterl, *The Color of Race*, 27, 30.

49. Theodore Roosevelt, *Citizenship, Politics, and the Elemental Virtues* (New York: Charles Scribner's Sons, 1925), 468–475; "The Strenuous Life" in *Theodore Roosevelt: An American Mind*, ed. Mario DiNunzio (New York: Penguin Books, 1994), 184–189.

50. Robert Marshall, "The Problem of the Wilderness," *Scientific Monthly* 30 (February 1930): 142, 148. See also Roderick Nash, "The American Cult of the Primitive," *American Quarterly* 18 (Fall 1966): 517–537; Denis Cosgrove, "Habitable Earth: Wilderness, Empire, and Race in America," in *Wild Ideas*, ed. David Rothenberg (Minneapolis: University of Minnesota Press, 1995), 34–36.

51. Fredrickson, *Black Image in the White Mind*, 254.

52. Joseph Tillinghast, *The Negro in Africa and America* (New York: Macmillan, 1902), 125.

53. Frederickson, *Black Image in the White Mind*, 314–315. It was, however, shared by T. Thomas Fortune, *Black and White: Land, Labor, and Politics in the South* [1884] (New York: Arno Press, 1968), 194.

54. Fredrickson, *Black Image in the White Mind*, 234–255.

55. Grant, *The Passing of the Great Race*, 87–88; Stoddard, *Rising Tide of Color*, 87–103.

56. Alexander Crummell, "The Destined Superiority of the Negro" [1877], in *Destiny and Race*, ed. Wilson Moses (Amherst: University of Massachusetts Press, 1992), 198, 201–203; Wilson Moses, *The Golden Age of Black Nationalism, 1850–1925* (Hamden, Conn.: Archon Books, 1978), 75–78; Fredrickson, *Black Image in the White Mind*, 97–129.

57. Edward Blyden, "The Call of Providence to the Descendants of Africa in America" [1862], in *African-American Social and Political Thought, 1850–1920*, ed. Howard Brotz (New Brunswick, N.J.: Transaction, 1992), 137–138.

58. "The Condition, Elevation, Emigration, and Destiny of the Colored People of the United States" [1852], in ibid., 103.

59. Ibid., 125; "The African Problem and Its Method of Solution" [1890], in ibid., 136.

60. W. E. B. Du Bois, *The Negro* [1915] (Oxford: Oxford University Press, 1970), 62–85, 93–94.

61. "The Call of Providence," in Brotz, *African-American Social and Political Thought*, 114, 137–138.

62. "An Appeal to the Soul of White America" [1923], in ibid., 556.

63. "The True Solution of the Negro Problem" [1922], in ibid., 554–555; "An Appeal to the Soul of White America," in ibid., 555–559; "The Negro's Place in World Reorganization"[1923], in ibid., 566–568. See also Blyden, "The African Problem and Its Method of Solution," in ibid., 138; Alexander Crummell, "The Relations and Duties of Free Colored Men in America to Africa" [1860], in ibid., 172–173; "The Race Problem in America" [1888], in ibid., 185.

64. "African Fundamentalism" [1925], in *Marcus Garvey: Life and Lessons*, ed. Robert Hill and Barbara Bair (Berkeley: University of California Press, 1987), 6 (italics added).

65. David Levering Lewis, *W. E. B. Du Bois: Biography of a Race* (New York: Henry Holt, 1993), 1: 131; Williamson, *The Crucible of Race*, 406.

66. In *The Oxford W. E. B. Du Bois Reader*, ed. Eric Sundquist (Oxford: Oxford University Press, 1996), 39–40.

67. Ibid., 40. For an insightful discussion of this passage, see Adolph Reed, *W. E. B. Du Bois and American Political Thought* (New York: Oxford University Press, 1997), 120–122.

68. W. E. B. Du Bois, "Conservation of Races," in Sundquist, *The Oxford W. E. B. Du Bois Reader*, 41, 44

69. Ibid., 42–43.

70. "The Work of Negro Women in Society," [1902], in *Writings by W. E. B. Du Bois in Periodicals Edited by Others*, ed. Herbert Aptheker (Millwood, N.Y.: Kraus-Thomson, 1982), 1: 139; "The Development of a People" [1904], in ibid., 1: 210.

71. Kelly Miller, "Race Adjustment" [1908], in *Race Adjustment and the Everlasting Stain* (New York: Arno Press, 1968), 92, 161.

72. Ibid., 237, 234–236.

73. Ibid., 34, 37, 28.

74. Vernon Williams, *Rethinking Race* (Lexington: University Press of Kentucky, 1996), 4–36.

75. Lewis, *W. E. B. Du Bois*, 351–352, 414. Boas did not attend the conference, but he submitted a paper, "The Instability of Human Types." See *Papers on Inter-Racial Problems Communicated to the First Universal Races Congress*, ed. G. Spiller (London: P. S. King and Sons, 1911), 99–103.

76. Jeffrey Stewart, "Introduction," in Alain Locke, *Race Contacts and Interracial Relations* [1915], ed. Jeffrey Stewart (Washington, D.C.: Howard University Press, 1992), xxiv.

77. Williams, *Rethinking Race*, 18–25.

78. Franz Boas, *The Mind of Primitive Man*, rev. ed. (New York: Macmillan, 1938), 35–115. Boas does, nevertheless, identify the three major modern "races" as Negro, Mongolid, and European. Ibid., 106.

79. Ibid., 178–181, 197–198.

80. Ibid., 190–191.

81. Ibid., 200.

82. Franz Boas, *Primitive Art* [1927] (Irvington-on-Hudson, N.Y.: Capitol, 1951), 11–12. William James offers an account of creativity that fits Boas's model, arguing that the basic structure of the brain may be shaped by the race's experience with the natural environment, but this "fashioning from without brings the elements into collocations which set new internal forces free to exert their effects, in turn." These internal, spontaneously generated effects constitute our "free mental play" and can vary enormously even among persons subjected to the same environment. James, *Principles of Psychology*, 2: 1234.

83. Boas, *The Mind of Primitive Man*, 268–271.

84. W. E. B. Du Bois, "The First Universal Races Congress" [1911], in *The Oxford W. E. B. Du Bois Reader*, 54–59.

85. W. E. B. Du Bois, *The Negro* [1915] (Oxford: Oxford University Press, 1970), 9, 63.

86. Ibid., 85, 89–90, 96.

87. Locke, *Race Contacts and Interracial Relations*, 11, 22, 25.

88. Ibid., 96–97; Alain Locke, "The Contribution of Race to Culture" [1930], in *The Philosophy of Alain Locke*, ed. Leonard Harris (Philadelphia: Temple University Press, 1989), 203.

89. Locke, *Race Contacts and Interracial Relations*, 99–100; Locke, "The Contribution of Race to Culture," 205.

90. Marcus Garvey, "Racial Ideals" [1924], in Brotz, *African-American Social and Political Thought*, 575.

CHAPTER FIVE. BLACK FOLK

1. Albert Barnes, "Negro Art and America," in *The New Negro*, ed. Alain Locke [1925] (New York: Atheneum, 1983), 24.

2. "Negro Art: Past and Present" [1936], in *The American Negro: His History and Literature* (New York: Arno Press/New York Times, 1969), 51.

3. Alain Locke, "The New Negro," in *The New Negro*, 3.

4. James De Jongh, *Vicious Modernism* (Cambridge: Cambridge University Press, 1990), 5–6; David Levering Lewis, *When Harlem Was in Vogue* (New York: Alfred A. Knopf, 1981), 25.

5. James Weldon Johnson, *Black Manhattan* (New York: Alfred A. Knopf, 1930), 3.

6. George Hutchinson, *The Harlem Renaissance in Black and White* (Cambridge, Mass.: Harvard University Press, 1995), 125–126.

7. Lewis, *When Harlem Was in Vogue*, 25–30.

8. De Jongh, *Vicious Modernism*, 8.

9. Lewis, *When Harlem Was in Vogue*, 3–5.

10. David Levering Lewis, Introduction to *The Portable Harlem Renaissance Reader*, ed. David Levering Lewis (New York: Penguin, 1994), xviii–xix.

11. Nathan Huggins, *The Harlem Renaissance* (Oxford: Oxford University Press, 1971), 7; Robert Bone, *Down Home* (New York: G. P. Putnam's Sons, 1975), 128–29; De Jongh, *Vicious Modernism*, 10–11; Hutchinson, *Harlem Renaissance in Black and White*, 20.

12. Hutchinson, *Harlem Renaissance in Black and White*, 33–124.

13. Casey Blake, *Beloved Community* (Chapel Hill: University of North Carolina Press, 1990), 5; Charles Scruggs, *Sweet Home* (Baltimore: Johns Hopkins University Press, 1993), 3.

14. Colin Rhodes, *Primitivism and Modern Art* (London: Thames and Hudson, 1994), 7, 29.

15. Arthur O. Lovejoy, *A Documentary History of Primitivism and Related Ideas*, 2 vols. (Baltimore: Johns Hopkins University Press, 1935), 1: 1–15; Hoxie N. Fairchild, *The Noble Savage* (New York: Columbia University Press, 1928), 25–28.

16. E. B. Tylor, *Primitive Culture*, 2 vols. [1871] (New York: Harper and Brothers, 1958), 2: 270.

17. Rhodes, *Primitivism and Modern Art*, 16–17.

18. Ibid., 152–153.

19. Ibid., 23–24, 158.

20. August Mack, "Masks," in *Blau Reiter Almanac* [1912], ed. Wassily Kandinsky and Franz Marc (Munich: R. Piper, 1965), 85.

21. Wassily Kandinsky, *Concerning the Spiritual in Art and Painting in Particular* [1912], trans. Michael Sadleir (New York: Wittenborn Art Books, 1947), 23.

22. Robert Goldwater, *Primitivism in Modern Art*, enlarged ed. (Cambridge, Mass.: Belknap Press, 1986), 7–8.

23. Ibid., 29–30, quoting *Das Unbekannte Afrika* (Munich: C. H. Beck, 1923), 4.

24. Rhodes, *Primitivism and Modern Art*, 111, 114.

25. Barnes, "Negro Art and America," in Locke, *The New Negro*, 19–20.

26. Quoted in Gelett Burgess, "The Wild Men of Paris" [1910], in *Primitivism and Twentieth-Century Art*, ed. Jack Flam and Miriam Deutch (Berkeley: University of California Press, 2003), 39.

27. Marius de Zayas, "African Negro Art" [1916], quoted in ibid., 93–94.

28. Elie Faure, "L'Histoire de l'art," in ibid., 55–56.

29. David Jordan, Introduction to *Regionalism Reconsidered*, ed. David Jordan (New York: Garland, 1994), ix–x; Bone, *Down Home*, 7–10.

30. Michael Kowalewski, "Bioregional Perspectives in American Literature," in Jordan, *Regionalism Reconsidered*, 29–46; Kirkpatrick Sale, *Dwellers in the Land* (San Francisco: Sierra Club Books, 1985); Peter Berg, *Reinhabiting a Separate Country* (San Francisco: Planet Drum Foundation, 1978); *Home! A Bioregional Reader*, ed. Van Andruss, Christopher Plant, Judith Plant, and Eleanor Wright (Philadelphia: New Society, 1990).

31. William Dean Howells, *Criticism and Fiction* (New York: Harper and Brothers, 1891), 16, 30.

32. Ibid., 61. See also Hamlin Garland, *Crumbling Idols* [1894], ed. Jane Johnson (Cambridge, Mass.: Harvard University Press, 1960), 3–4, 37.

33. On organic ideas of nationality in environmental thought, see Anna Bramwell, *Ecology in the 20th Century* (New Haven, Conn.: Yale University Press, 1989); Denis Cosgrove, "Habitable Earth: Wilderness, Empire, and Race in America," in David Rothenberg, ed., *Wild Ideas* (Minneapolis: University of Minnesota Press, 1995).

34. Howells, *Criticism and Fiction*, 55.

35. Garland, *Crumbling Idols*, 59.

36. Lewis, *The Portable Harlem Renaissance Reader*, xviii–xix; Hutchinson, *Harlem Renaissance in Black and White*, 94–105.

37. Chesnutt, *The Conjure Woman and Other Tales* [1899], ed. Richard Brodhead (Durham, N.C.: Duke University Press, 1993), 6, 7.

38. Bone, *Down Home*, 80.

39. Chesnutt, *The Conjure Woman*, 34, 55.

40. Bone, *Down Home*, 86–88; Cary Wintz, *Black Culture and the Harlem Renaissance* (Houston: Rice University Press, 1988), 56; Richard E. Baldwin, "The Art of *The Conjure Woman*," in *Critical Essays on Charles W. Chesnutt*, ed. Joseph McElrath (New York: G. K. Hall, 1999), 170–180.

41. Chesnutt, *The Conjure Woman*, 79.

42. See Houston Baker Jr., *Modernism and the Harlem Renaissance* (Chicago: University of Chicago Press, 1987), on masking as a central theme in black literature.

43. Howells, *Criticism and Fiction*, 144; Du Bois, "On the Souls of Black Folk" [1904], in *The Oxford W. E. B. Du Bois Reader*, ed. Eric Sundquist (Oxford: Oxford University Press, 1996), 305. See also Baker, *Modernism and the Harlem Renaissance*, 62.

44. W. E. B. Du Bois, *The Souls of Black Folk* [1903] (New York: Penguin Books, 1989), 155–156.

45. Ibid., 161, 210, 214. The third gift is his labor.

46. Du Bois, *Souls of Black Folk*, 51–62, 186–203.

47. Baker, *Modernism and the Harlem Renaissance*, 64. See also Adolph Reed, *W. E. B. Du Bois and American Political Thought* (New York: Oxford University Press,

1997), 25, 58, 110–118 (on the primitivist and antiprimitivist elements in Du Bois's thought).

48. W. E. B. Du Bois, *The Quest of the Silver Fleece* [1911] (New York: Negro Universities Press, 1969), 13, 16, 44, 46.

49. Ibid., 125, 127–128.

50. Ibid., 400.

51. Ibid., 433.

52. Arnold Rampersad, *The Art and Imagination of W. E. B. Du Bois* (Cambridge, Mass.: Harvard University Press, 1976), 74, 87; Keith Byerman, *Seizing the Word* (Athens: University of Georgia Press, 1994), 34; Scruggs, *Sweet Home*, 32–34. My interpretation is closer to that of Adoph Reed, although he emphasizes Du Bois's elitism more than I do. See Reed, *W. E. B. Du Bois and American Political Thought*, 58.

53. Du Bois, *The Quest of the Silver Fleece*, 256–257.

54. David Nicholls, *Conjuring the Folk* (Ann Arbor: University of Michigan Press, 2000), 132 (arguing similarly that the "folk" concept was used by black writers as a vehicle for exploring the meaning of modernity).

55. James Weldon Johnson, *The Autobiography of an Ex-Coloured Man* [1912] (New York: Hill and Wang, 1960).

56. Ibid., 87, 100, 142.

57. Ibid., 52, 169–170.

58. Ibid., 181, 191, 211.

59. Locke, "The Negro Youth Speaks," in Locke, *The New Negro*, 47, 51–52.

60. Ibid., 52.

61. Locke, "The Legacy of the Ancestral Arts," in Locke, *The New Negro*, 254–255.

62. John Dewey, *The Influence of Darwin on Philosophy and Other Essays* [1910] (Amherst, N.Y.: Prometheus Books, 1997), 85–86, 145.

63. John Dewey, *Art as Experience* (New York: Perigree Books, 1934); Hutchinson, *Harlem Renaissance in Black and White*, 44–48.

64. Dewey, *Art as Experience*, 17–19, 25, 26.

65. Ibid., 105.

66. Ibid., 19; Hutchinson, *The Harlem Renaissance in Black and White*, 44–48.

67. Dewey, *Art as Experience*, 21, 27.

68. Locke, "Ethics of Culture" [1923], in *The Philosophy of Alain Locke*, ed. Leonard Harris (Philadelphia: Temple University Press, 1989), 180–181; Locke, "The Negro and His Music" [1936], in Locke, *The American Negro*, 82–83, 87, 94 (criticizing commercialization of jazz).

69. Hutchinson, *The Harlem Renaissance in Black and White*, 58–59.

70. Locke, "The Negro Youth Speaks," in Locke, *The New Negro*, 47.

71. Locke develops his argument that race is the product of European exploitation of the colored peoples of the world in *Race Contacts and Interracial Relations* [1915], ed. Jeffrey Stewart (Washington, D.C.: Howard University Press, 1992).

72. Locke, "The New Negro," in Locke, *The New Negro*, 4.

73. Ibid.

74. Ibid., 15.

75. Waldo Frank, "Foreword to the 1923 Edition," in Jean Toomer, *Cane*, ed. Darwin Turner (New York: W. W. Norton, 1988), 138, 140; Montgomery Gregory, "Self-Expression in *Cane*" [1923], in ibid., 166.

76. Darwin Turner, "Introduction to the 1975 Edition," in Toomer, *Cane*, 128.

77. "Song of the Son," in Toomer, *Cane*, 14.

78. Quoted in Locke, "The Negro Youth Speaks," in Locke, *The New Negro*, 51.

79. Frank, "Foreword," in Toomer, *Cane*, 139.

80. "Blood-Burning Moon," in Toomer, *Cane*, 35–37.

81. Locke, *Race Contacts and Interracial Relations*, 96–100; Locke, "The Contribution of Race to Culture" [1930], in *The Philosophy of Alain Locke*, 205–206; Locke, "The Negro and His Music," in *The American Negro*, 8.

82. Locke, *Race Contacts and Interracial Relations*, 98.

83. Locke, "Negro Art: Past and Present," in *The American Negro*, 61.

84. Wintz, *Black Culture*, 80; Arna Bontemps, "The Negro Renaissance: Jean Toomer and the Harlem of the 1920s," in *Anger and Beyond: The Negro Writer in the United States*, ed. Herbert Hill (New York: Harper and Row, 1966), 22–23; Mabel Dillard, "The Veil Replaced," in *Jean Toomer: A Critical Evaluation*, ed. Therman O'-Daniel (Washington, D.C.: Howard University Press, 1988), 80; Darwin Turner, "Another Passing," in ibid., 82.

85. George Schuyler, "The Negro-Art Hokum" [1926], in Lewis, *The Portable Harlem Renaissance Reader*, 97.

86. Bone, *Down Home*, 115–119, 249, 286.

87. Zora Neale Hurston, "Drenched in Light" [1924], in *The Complete Stories of Zora Neale Hurston* (New York: Harper Perennial, 1995), 17–25.

88. Langston Hughes, "The Ways of White Folks" [1934], in *The Collected Works of Langston Hughes*, 15 vols., ed. R. Baxter Miller (Columbia: University of Missouri Press, 2002), XV:30.

89. Nicholls, *Conjuring the Folk*, 14–17, 43–62.

90. W. E. B. Du Bois, "Criteria of Negro Art" [1926], in *Writings of W. E. B. Du Bois*, ed. Nathan Huggins (New York: Library of America, 1986), 994.

91. Ibid., 1001.

92. Aaron Wildavsky, "Aesthetic Power or the Triumph of the Sensitive Minority over the Vulgar Mass," *Daedalus* 96 (Fall 1967): 1115–1128; Roderick Nash, "The American Cult of the Primitive," *American Quarterly* 18 (Fall 1966): 517–537.

93. Du Bois, "Criteria of Negro Art," 995–996, 1000.

94. The most well-known version of this judgment is Huggins, *Harlem Renaissance*; Houston Baker reviews its influence in *Modernism and the Harlem Renaissance*, 9–10.

95. Du Bois, "Criteria of Negro Art," 994–995.

CHAPTER SIX. URBAN MONTAGE

1. "A Place at the Table," *Sierra* (May/June 1993), 57–58.

2. James De Jongh, *Vicious Modernism* (Cambridge: Cambridge University

Press, 1990), 25; Yoshinobu Hakutani and Robert Butler, "Introduction," in *The City in African-American Literature*, ed. Yoshinobu Hakutani and Robert Butler (London: Associated University Press, 1995), 9; Charles Scruggs, *Sweet Home* (Baltimore: Johns Hopkins University Press, 1993), 1–4; but see Toni Morrison, "City Limits, Village Values: Concepts of the Neighborhood in Black Fiction," in *Literature and the Urban Experience*, ed. Michael Joyce and Ann Watts (New Brunswick, N.J.: Rutgers University Press, 1981), 35–44 (arguing that black writers have been hostile to the city but favorable to the urban neighborhood).

3. Scruggs, *Sweet Home*, 50; Robert Bone, *Down Home* (New York: G. P. Putnam's Sons, 1975), 112.

4. In *Great Short Stories by American Women*, ed. Candace Ward (Toronto: Dover Publishing, 1996), 1–2.

5. Rogers Smith, *Civic Ideals* (New Haven, Conn.: Yale University Press, 1997), 349–357, 358–365; Stephen Fox, *The American Conservation Movement* (Madison: University of Wisconsin Press, 1981), 345–350.

6. "The Condition, Elevation, Emigration, and Destiny of the Colored People of the United States" [1852], in *African-American Social and Political Thought, 1850–1920*, ed. Howard Brotz (New Brunswick, N.J.: Transaction, 1992), 92.

7. "An Address to the Colored People of the United States" [1848], in Brotz, *African-American Social and Political Thought*, 212; see also T. Thomas Fortune, *Black and White: Land, Labor, and Politics in the South* [1884] (New York: Arno Press, 1968), 35.

8. "Twelve Years a Slave" [1853], in *I Was Born a Slave*, 2 vols., ed. Yuval Taylor (Chicago: Lawrence Hill Books, 1999), 2: 173.

9. Ibid., 2: 174.

10. Robert Butler, "The City as Liberating Space in *Life and Times of Frederick Douglass*," in Hakutani and Butler, *The City in African-American Literature*, 21.

11. Ibid., 23–25.

12. "Incidents in the Life of a Slave Girl" [1861], in *Slave Narratives*, ed. William Andrews and Henry Louis Gates (New York: Library of America, 2000), 775, 780.

13. "Narrative of the Life of Frederick Douglass, an American Slave," in Taylor, *I Was Born a Slave*, 1: 540, 543; "An Address to the Colored People of the United States" [1848] in Brotz, *African-American Social and Political Thought*, 212; "Address before the Tennessee Colored Agricultural and Mechanical Association," in ibid., 286–297; Butler, "The City as Liberating Space," 32–33.

14. Paul Laurence Dunbar, *The Sport of the Gods* [1902] (Miami: Mnemosyne, 1969), 81.

15. Ibid., 82.

16. Ibid., 89, 113–114.

17. Cary Wintz, *Black Culture and the Harlem Renaissance* (Houston: Rice University Press, 1988), 94; Charles Scruggs, "Crab Antics and Jacob's Ladder: Aaron Douglas's Two Views of Nigger Heaven," in *Harlem Renaissance Re-Examined: A Revised and Expanded Edition*, ed. Victor Kramer and Robert Russ (Troy, N.J.: Whitston, 1997), 185–189.

18. Carl Van Vechten, *Nigger Heaven* [1926] (Urbana: University of Illinois Press, 2000), 171.

19. Ibid., 107.

20. Ibid., 161–164, 279–281.

21. Ibid., 89.

22. "Jazz at Home," in *The New Negro*, ed. Alain Locke [1925] (New York: Touchstone, 1992), 218, 217, 224.

23. Claude McKay, *Home to Harlem* [1928] (Boston: Northeastern University Press, 1987), 30.

24. Claude McKay, "The Tropics in New York," in Locke, *The New Negro*, 135.

25. But see Scruggs, "Crab Antics and Jacob's Ladder," arguing that focusing on Van Vechten's primitivism distracts from the moral and intellectual argument of the novel.

26. "Van Vechten's Nigger Heaven" (review) in *W. E. B. Du Bois: Writings*, ed. Nathan Huggins (New York: Library of America, 1986), 1216–1218; Wintz, *Black Culture and the Harlem Renaissance*, 130–139, 144–146.

27. "The Younger Literary Movement" [1924], in *W. E. B. Du Bois: Writings*, 1208–1210; "'Porgy,' by DuBose Heyward" (review) [1926], in ibid., 1215.

28. Wintz, *Black Culture and the Harlem Renaissance*, 144, 183–184.

29. McKay, *Home to Harlem*, 264–266, 287.

30. James Weldon Johnson, *The Autobiography of an Ex-Coloured Man* [1912] (New York: Hill and Wang, 1960), 90.

31. James Weldon Johnson, *Black Manhattan* (New York: Alfred A. Knopf, 1930), 3.

32. Ibid., 159.

33. Fisher, "City of Refuge," in Locke, *The New Negro*, 57–58.

34. Locke, "The New Negro," in *The New Negro*, 14.

35. On the heavenly city motif in black literature, see Scruggs, *Sweet Home*, 24–28.

36. David Levering Lewis, *W. E. B. Du Bois: Biography of a Race* (New York: Henry Holt, 1993), 218–223.

37. Barbara Lal, *The Romance of Culture in an Urban Civilization* (New York: Routledge, 1990), 18–22; George Hutchinson, *The Harlem Renaissance in Black and White* (Cambridge, Mass.: Harvard University Press, 1995), 50–58.

38. Robert Park, "The City," in Robert Park, Ernest Burgess, and Roderick McKenzie, *The City* (Chicago: University of Chicago Press, 1925), 1–2.

39. Fred Matthews, *Quest for an American Sociology* (Montreal: McGill-Queen's University Press, 1977), 128.

40. Park, "The City," 7.

41. Lal, *The Romance of Culture in an Urban Civilization*, 44.

42. Park, "Community Organization and Juvenile Delinquency," in Park, Burgess, and McKenzie, *The City*, 111.

43. Ibid., 105.

44. Park, "The City," 41–42.

45. Ibid., 41–42, 9.

46. Ibid., 6, 8. Park does mention racial prejudice briefly on p. 9.

47. Lal, *The Romance of Culture in an Urban Civilization*, 59, 62. Lal points out that Park addresses these issues in later works.

48. W. E. B. Du Bois, *The Philadelphia Negro* (New York: Benjamin Bloom, 1899), 8.

49. Ibid., 73–82.

50. Ibid., 295–296.

51. Ibid., 284.

52. Chicago Commission on Race Relations, *The Negro in Chicago* (Chicago: University of Chicago Press, 1922), 475, 436–519, 605–612.

53. Ibid., 604, 608, 629–630.

54. Ibid., 608.

55. Casey Blake, *Beloved Community* (Chapel Hill: University of North Carolina Press, 1990), 3, 107–109, 124.

56. Scruggs, *Sweet Home*, 3.

57. Allen Davis, *Spearheads for Reform* (New York: Oxford University Press, 1967), 4–8.

58. Ruskin, "Traffic," in *The Crown of Wild Olive* (New York: John Wiley and Sons, 1874), 52.

59. Ruskin, "Work," in *The Crown of Wild Olive*, 3–43; William Morris, "Innate Socialism" [1878], in *News from Nowhere and Selected Writings and Designs* (New York: Penguin Books, 1962), 84–105.

60. Morris, "Innate Socialism," 95; Ruskin, "Modern Manufacturing and Design" [1859], in *The Genius of John Ruskin* (New York: George Braziller, 1963), 223–224, 226.

61. Whether we should consider Ruskin "green" is hotly debated, but his influence on English preservationism is unquestioned, as is his influence on American back-to-the-land movements. See *Ruskin and the Environment*, ed. Michael Wheeler (Manchester, UK: Manchester University Press, 1995), 2–3; Fox, *The American Conservation Movement*, 85, 353; Anna Bramwell, *Ecology in the Twentieth Century* (New Haven, Conn.: Yale University Press, 1989), 75, 78, 81, 96–98.

62. Bramwell, *Ecology in the Twentieth Century*, 75, 78; Blake, *Beloved Community*, 194–199.

63. "Provincialism" [1908], in *The Basic Writings of Josiah Royce*, 2 vols., ed. John McDermott (Chicago: University of Chicago Press, 1969), 2: 1069.

64. Ibid., 2: 1072, 1074, 1070.

65. Blake, *Beloved Community*, 5–6, 124.

66. Waldo Frank, *The Re-Discovery of America* (New York: Charles Scribner's Sons, 1929), 70.

67. Randolph Bourne, *The Radical Will: Selected Writings, 1911–1918*, ed. Olaf Hansen (New York: Urizen Books, 1977), 278, 264.

68. Blake, *Beloved Community*, 293; Peter Berg and Raymond Dasmann, "Reinhabiting California," in *Reinhabiting a Separate Country*, ed. Peter Berg (San Francisco: Planet Drum Foundation, 1978), 217; *Home! A Bioregional Reader*, ed. Van Andruss, Christopher Plant, Judith Plant, and Eleanor Wright (Philadelphia: New Society, 1990), 2.

69. Scruggs, *Sweet Home*, 1–2.

70. Locke, "The New Negro," in *The New Negro*, 6.

71. Ibid., 7.

72. Hutchinson, *The Harlem Renaissance in Black and White*, 48, 58, 91.

73. Locke, "The New Negro," in *The New Negro*, 12.

74. Ibid., 10.

75. Wintz, *Black Culture and the Harlem Renaissance*, 24–28; Nathan Huggins, *Harlem Renaissance* (Oxford: Oxford University Press, 1971), 30, 48.

76. Jessie Redmon Fauset, *Plum Bun* [1928] (London: Pandora Press, 1985), 108, 74.

77. Ibid., 219, 98.

78. Bone, *Down Home*, 115, 118.

79. Nella Larsen, *Quicksand* [1929] (New Brunswick, N.J.: Rutgers University Press, 1986), 64.

80. Ibid., 95.

81. Richard Wright, "Introduction," in St. Clair Drake and Horace Cayton, *Black Metropolis* (New York: Harcourt, Brace, 1945), xviii.

82. Richard Wright, *Native Son and How "Bigger" Was Born* (Cutchogee, N.Y.: Buccaneer Books, 1940), 529; Scruggs, *Sweet Home*, 79–80.

83. Wright, *Native Son*, 77.

84. Ibid., 78, 169, 456.

85. Ibid., 169, 263, 378–379, 410.

86. Ibid., 38.

87. Ibid., 459. See also 279.

88. Ibid., 129.

89. Ibid.

90. Ibid., 455, 463.

91. Langston Hughes, "Montage of a Dream Deferred" [1951], in *Collected Works of Langston Hughes*, 15 vols., ed. Arnold Rampersad (Columbia: University of Missouri Press, 2001), 3: 33, 34.

92. Ibid., 34.

93. Ibid., 27.

CONCLUSION

1. *Eldridge Cleaver: Post-Prison Writings and Speeches*, ed. Robert Scherer (New York: Random House, 1967), 57–58.

2. *Homecoming: Sometimes I Am Haunted by Memories of Red Dirt and Clay*, produced and directed by Charlene Gilbert, in association with Independent Television Service, 1998. Distributed by California Newsreel, San Francisco. Videocassette.

3. Scherer, *Eldridge Cleaver: Post-Prison Writings and Speeches*, 63; Michael Dawson, *Black Visions* (Chicago: University of Chicago Press, 2001), 96, 99.

4. *Proceedings: The First National People of Color Environmental Leadership Summit* (New York: United Church of Christ Commission for Racial Justice, 1991), 29; "A

Place at the Table," *Sierra* (May/June 1993), 60. See also Robert Bullard, *Dumping in Dixie*, 3rd ed. (Boulder, Colo.: Westview Press: 2000), 28; Andrew Szasz, *Ecopopulism* (Minneapolis: University of Minnesota Press, 1994), 6, 82; David Schlosberg, "Environmental and Ecological Justice: Theory and Practice in the United States," in *The State and the Global Ecological Crisis*, ed. John Barry and Robyn Eckersley (Cambridge, Mass.: MIT Press, 2005), 97–116 (on how the environmental justice movement links racial oppression to abuse of the earth).

5. "Declaration of Principles of the Niagara Movement" [1905], in *African-American Social and Political Thought, 1850–1920*, ed. Howard Brotz (New Brunswick: Transaction, 1992), 534; Andrew Hurley, *Environmental Inequalities* (Chapel Hill: University of North Carolina Press, 1995), 120–123; Robert Gottlieb, *Environmentalism Unbound* (Cambridge, Mass.: MIT Press, 2001), 52–53.

6. Elizabeth Blum, "Women, Environmental Rationale, and Activism during the Progressive Era," in *"To Love the Wind and the Rain": African Americans and Environmental History*, ed. Dianne Glave and Mark Stoll (Pittsburgh: University of Pittsburgh Press, 2006), 77–92.

7. Colin Fisher, "African Americans, Outdoor Recreation, and the 1919 Chicago Race Riot," in Glave and Stoll, *"To Love the Wind and the Rain,"* 63–76.

8. Dorceta Taylor, *Race, Class, Gender, and American Environmentalism* (U.S. Department of Agriculture, Forest Service, 2002), 27–28; Gregory Bush, "Politicized Memories in the Struggle for Miami's Virginia Key Beach," in Glave and Stoll, *"To Love the Wind and the Rain,"* 164–188.

9. U.S. Commission on Civil Rights, *The Federal Civil Rights Enforcement Effort*, vol. 6 (1975), 596–601, 633.

10. *Bean v. Southwestern Waste Management Corp.*, 482 F. Supp. 673 (S.D. Tex, 1979); Bullard, *Dumping in Dixie*, xiv.

11. Luke Cole and Sheila Foster, *From the Ground Up* (New York: New York University Press, 2001), 54–79.

12. Gottlieb, *Environmentalism Unbound*, 52.

13. Environmental Working Group, *Obstruction of Justice*, Part I (2005), available at www.ewg.org/reports/blackfarmers.

14. Dawson, *Black Visions*, 93–97; Environmental Working Group, *Obstruction of Justice*, Part I; *Pigford v. Glickman*, 185 F.R.D. 82 (D.D.C. 1999); Thomas Mitchell, "From Reconstruction to Deconstruction: Undermining Black Landownership, Political Independence, and Community through Partition Sales of Tenancies in Common," *Northwestern Law Review* 95 (Winter 2001): 505–507.

15. Remarks of Sulaiman Madhi, in *Proceedings: The First National People of Color Environmental Leadership Summit* (New York: United Church of Christ Commission for Racial Justice, 1991), 43.

16. The principles can be accessed through the Environmental Justice Resource Center website, http://www.ejrc.cau.edu/princej.html.

17. Richard Grove, *Green Imperialism* (Cambridge: Cambridge University Press, 1995), 206.

18. *Hidden Slaves: Forced Labor in the United States* (report published by Free the Slaves, Washington, D.C., and Human Rights Center, University of California at Berkeley, September 2004), 1, 16–17.

19. Gottlieb, *Environmentalism Unbound*, 145–180.

20. Val Plumwood, *Feminism and the Mastery of Nature* (London: Routledge, 1993); David Ehrenfeld, *The Arrogance of Humanism* (New York: Oxford University Press, 1978); Eric Katz, "The Big Lie: Human Restoration of Nature," in *Environmental Ethics*, ed. Andrew Light and Holmes Rolston III (Oxford: Blackwell, 2003), 390–397.

21. Anthony Weston provides a brief overview of these arguments in "Beyond Intrinsic Value: Pragmatism in Environmental Ethics," in *Environmental Pragmatism*, ed. Andrew Light and Eric Katz (London: Routledge, 1996), 285–287.

22. Donald Worster develops this argument in *Nature's Economy*, 2nd ed. (Cambridge: Cambridge University Press, 1994), 173–179.

23. Eric Katz, "Searching for Intrinsic Value," in Light and Katz, *Environmental Pragmatism*, 307–318.

24. Weston, "Beyond Intrinsic Value," 295.

25. Wes Jackson, *Becoming Native to This Place* (Washington, D.C.: Counterpoint, 1994), 103; Peter Berg and Raymond Dasmann, "Reinhabiting California," in *Reinhabiting a Separate Country*, ed. Peter Berg (San Francisco: Planet Drum Foundation, 1978), 217; *Home! A Bioregional Reader*, ed. Van Andruss, Christopher Plant, Judith Plant, and Eleanor Wright (Philadelphia: New Society, 1990), 2.

26. Langston Hughes, "The Negro Speaks of Rivers," in *The New Negro*, ed. Alain Locke [1925] (New York: Atheneum, 1983), 141.

27. Kimberly Smith, *Wendell Berry and the Agrarian Tradition* (Lawrence: University Press of Kansas, 2003), 39–45.

28. "Address before the Tennessee Colored Agricultural and Mechanical Association," in *African-American Social and Political Thought, 1850–1920*, ed. Howard Brotz (New Brunswick: Transaction, 1992), 290.

29. Carl Anthony, "Reflections on African American Environmental History," in Glave and Stoll, *"To Love the Wind and the Rain,"* 203.

30. Ibid., 209.

BIBLIOGRAPHY

Abbey, Edward. *Down the River.* New York: Plume, 1991.

Abrahams, Roger. *Singing the Master.* New York: Pantheon Books, 1992.

American Husbandry [1775]. Edited by Henry Carman. New York: Columbia University Press, 1939.

Anderson, James D. *The Education of Blacks in the South, 1860–1935.* Chapel Hill: University of North Carolina Press, 1986.

Andrews, William, and Henry Louis Gates, eds. *Slave Narratives.* New York: Library of America, 2000.

Andruss, Van, Christopher Plant, Judith Plant, and Eleanor Wright. *Home! A Bioregional Reader.* Philadelphia: New Society, 1990.

Anthony, Carl. "A Place at the Table." *Sierra* (May/June 1993): 57–58.

Aptheker, Herbert. *Abolitionism.* Boston: Twayne Publishers, 1989.

Ashcraft, Richard. *Revolutionary Politics and Locke's Two Treatises.* Princeton, N.J.: Princeton University Press, 1986.

Bailyn, Bernard. *The Ideological Origins of the American Revolution,* 2nd ed. Cambridge, Mass.: Belknap Press, 1992.

Baker, Houston, Jr. *Modernism and the Harlem Renaissance.* Chicago: University of Chicago Press, 1987.

Baldwin, Richard E. "The Art of *The Conjure Woman.*" In *Critical Essays on Charles W. Chesnutt,* edited by Joseph McElrath. New York: G. K. Hall, 1999.

Barry, John, and Robyn Eckersley, ed. *The State and the Global Ecological Crisis.* Cambridge, Mass.: MIT Press, 2005.

Beach, Joseph. *The Concept of Nature in Nineteenth-Century English Poetry.* New York: Macmillan., 1939.

Bean v. Southwestern Waste Management Corp., 482 F. Supp. 673 (S.D. Tex, 1979).

Berg, Peter, ed. *Reinhabiting a Separate Country.* San Francisco: Planet Drum Foundation, 1978.

Berlin, Ira. *Generations of Captivity.* Cambridge, Mass.: Belknap Press, 2003.

———. *Many Thousands Gone.* Cambridge, Mass.: Belknap Press, 1998.

Bidwell, Percy Wells, and John Falconer. *History of Agriculture in the Northern United States.* Washington, D.C.: Carnegie Institute, 1925.

Bjork, Daniel. *The Compromised Scientist: William James and the Development of American Psychology.* New York: Columbia University Press, 1983.

Blackett, R. J. M. *Building an Antislavery Wall.* Baton Rouge: Louisiana State University Press, 1983.

Blake, Casey. *Beloved Community*. Chapel Hill: University of North Carolina Press, 1990.

Blassingame, John. *The Slave Community*, 2nd ed. Oxford: Oxford University Press, 1979.

Bloch, Ruth. "American Feminine Ideals in Transition." *Feminist Studies* 4 (June 1978): 101–126.

Blum, Elizabeth. "Power, Danger, and Control: Slave Women's Perceptions of Wilderness in the Nineteenth Century." *Women's Studies* 31 (March–April 2002): 247–266.

Blumenbach, Johann Friedrich. *On the Natural Varieties of Mankind* [1775]. Translated by Thomas Bendyshe. New York: Bergman, 1969.

Boas, Franz. *The Mind of Primitive Man*, rev. ed. New York: Macmillan., 1938.

———. *Primitive Art* [1927]. Irvington-on-Hudson, N.Y.: Capitol, 1951.

Bogue, Allan. "Fogel's Journey through the Slave States." *Journal of Economic History* 50 (September 1990): 699–710.

Boles, John. *Black Southerners, 1619–1869*. Lexington: University Press of Kentucky, 1983.

Boller, Paul. *American Thought in Transition*. Lanham, Md.: University Press of America, 1981.

Bone, Robert. *Down Home*. New York: G. P. Putnam's Sons, 1975.

Bontemps, Arna. "The Negro Renaissance: Jean Toomer and the Harlem of the 1920's." In *Anger and Beyond: The Negro Writer in the United States*, edited by Herbert Hill. New York: Harper and Row, 1966.

Bookchin, Murray, and Dave Foreman. *Defending the Earth*. Cambridge, Mass.: South End Press, 1991.

Bourne, Randolph. *The Radical Will: Selected Writings, 1911–1918*. Edited by Olaf Hansen. New York: Urizen Books, 1977.

Boutmy, Émile. *The English People*. Translated by E. English. New York: G. P. Putnam's Sons, 1904.

Bramwell, Anna. *Ecology in the 20th Century*. New Haven, Conn.: Yale University Press, 1989.

Broderick, Francis, and August Meier, eds. *Negro Protest Thought in the Twentieth Century*. Indianapolis: Bobbs-Merrill, 1965.

Brotz, Howard, ed. *African-American Social and Political Thought, 1850–1920*. New Brunswick, N.J.: Transaction, 1992.

Buckle, Henry Thomas. *History of Civilization in England*. 2 vols. New York: D. Appleton, 1880.

Bullard, Robert. *Dumping in Dixie*, 3rd ed. Boulder, Colo.: Westview Press, 2000.

Butler, Robert. "The City as Liberating Space in *Life and Times of Frederick Douglass*," in *The City in African-American Literature*, edited by Yoshinobu Hakutani and Robert Butler. London: Associated University Press, 1995.

Byerman, Keith. *Seizing the Word*. Athens: University of Georgia Press, 1994.

Carney, Judith. *Black Rice*. Cambridge, Mass.: Harvard University Press, 2001.

Carver, George Washington. *George Washington Carver: In His Own Words.* Edited by Gary Kremer. Columbia: University of Missouri Press, 1987.

Chesnutt, Charles W. *Charles W. Chesnutt: Essays and Speeches.* Edited by Josephy McElrath Jr., Robert Leitz III, and Jesse Crisler. Stanford, Calif.: Stanford University Press, 1999.

———. *The Conjure Woman and Other Tales* [1899]. Edited by Richard Brodhead. Durham, N.C.: Duke University Press, 1993.

Chicago Commission on Race Relations. *The Negro in Chicago.* Chicago: University of Chicago Press, 1922.

Clark, Thomas. *The Greening of the South.* Lexington: University Press of Kentucky, 1984.

Clay, Henry. "Henry Clay's Speech," *African Repository* 6 (March 1831): 9–10.

Cleaver, Eldridge. *Eldridge Cleaver: Post-Prison Writings and Speeches.* Edited by Robert Scherer. New York: Random House, 1967.

Cochrane, Willard. *Development of American Agriculture.* Minneapolis: University of Minnesota Press, 1979.

Cohen, William. "Negro Involuntary Servitude in the South, 1865–1940: A Preliminary Analysis." *Journal of Southern History* 42 (February 1976): 31–60.

Cole, Luke, and Sheila Foster. *From the Ground Up.* New York: New York University Press, 2001.

Cosgrove, Denis. "Habitable Earth: Wilderness, Empire, and Race in America." In *Wild Ideas,* edited by David Rothenberg. Minneapolis: University of Minnesota Press, 1995.

Cott, Nancy. *The Bonds of Womanhood.* New Haven, Conn.: Yale University Press, 1977.

Cowdry, Albert. *This Land, This South.* Lexington: University Press of Kentucky, 1983.

Creel, Margaret. *"A Peculiar People": Slave Religion and Community-Culture among the Gullahs.* New York: New York University Press, 1988.

Crèvecoeur, J. Hector St. John de. *Letters from an American Farmer* [1781]. New York: Penguin Classic, 1963.

Cronon, William, ed. *Uncommon Ground.* New York: W. W. Norton, 1996.

Crummell, Alexander. *Destiny and Race.* Edited by Wilson Moses. Amherst: University of Massachusetts Press, 1992.

Daniels, Pete. *Breaking the Land.* Urbana: University of Illinois Press, 1985.

Darwin, Charles. *The Descent of Man,* 2nd ed. [1877]. Vol. 21 of *The Works of Charles Darwin,* edited by Paul Barrett and R. B. Freeman. New York: New York University Press, 1989.

Davis, Allen. *Spearheads for Reform.* New York: Oxford University Press, 1967.

Davis, Elizabeth. *Lifting as They Climb.* New York: G. K. Hall, 1996.

Davis, Rebecca Harding. "Life in the Iron-Mills." In *Great Short Stories by American Women,* edited by Candace Ward. Toronto: Dover, 1996.

Dawson, Michael. *Black Visions.* Chicago: University of Chicago Press, 2001.

De Jongh, James. *Vicious Modernism.* Cambridge: Cambridge University Press, 1990.

Delany, Martin. *Blake, or the Huts of America* [1861–1863]. Boston: Beacon Press, 1970.

Dewey, John. *Art as Experience.* New York: Perigree Books, 1934.

———. *The Influence of Darwin on Philosophy and Other Essays* [1910]. Amherst, N.Y.: Prometheus Books, 1997.

Dillard, Mabel. "The Veil Replaced." In *Jean Toomer: A Critical Evaluation,* edited by Therman O'Daniel. Washington, D.C.: Howard University Press, 1988.

Dixon, Melvin. *Ride out the Wilderness: Geography and Identity in Afro-American Literature.* Urbana: University of Illinois Press, 1987.

Douglass, Frederick. *The Narrative and Selected Writings.* New York: Modern Library, 1984.

———. *Frederick Douglass: Autobiographies.* New York: Literary Classics of the United States, 1994.

Downing, Andrew Jackson. *Victorian Cottage Residences* [1842]. New York: Dover, 1981.

Drake, St. Clair, and Horace Cayton. *Black Metropolis.* New York: Harcourt, Brace, 1945.

Du Bois, W. E. B. *Darkwater: Voices from within the Veil* [1920]. New York: Humanity Books, 2003.

———. *The Negro* [1915]. Oxford: Oxford University Press, 1970.

———. *The Philadelphia Negro* [1899]. New York: Benjamin Blom, 1967.

———. *The Quest of the Silver Fleece* [1911]. New York: Negro Universities Press, 1969.

———. *The Souls of Black Folk* [1903]. New York: Penguin Books, 1989.

———. *The Oxford W. E. B. Du Bois Reader.* Edited by Eric Sundquist. Oxford: Oxford University Press, 1996.

———. *Writings.* Edited by Nathan Huggins. New York: Library of America, 1986.

———. *Writings by W. E. B. Du Bois in Periodicals Edited by Others, 1891–1909.* 4 vols. Edited by Herbert Aptheker. Millwood, N.Y.: Kraus-Thomson, 1982.

Dunbar, Paul Laurence. *The Sport of the Gods* [1902]. Miami: Mnemosyne, 1969.

Earle, Carville. *The Evolution of a Tidewater Settlement System.* Chicago: Department of Geography, 1975.

Edwards, Laura. *Gendered Strife and Confusion.* Urbana: University of Illinois Press, 1991.

Ehrenfeld, David. *The Arrogance of Humanism.* New York: Oxford University Press, 1978.

Environmental Working Group. *Obstruction of Justice,* Part I, 2005. Available at www.ewg.org/reports/blackfarmers.

Evans-Pritchard, E. E. *Witchcraft, Oracles, and Magic among the Azande.* Oxford: Clarendon Press, 1968.

Fairchild, Hoxie N. *The Noble Savage.* New York: Columbia University Press, 1928.

Fauset, Jessie Redmon. *Plum Bun* [1928]. London: Pandora Press, 1985.

Ferguson, James. "The Grange and Farmer Education in Mississippi." *Journal of Southern History* 8 (February–November 1942): 497–512.

Fett, Sharla. *Working Cures*. Chapel Hill: University of North Carolina Press, 2002.

Fischer, David Hackett. *Albion's Seed*. New York: Oxford University Press, 1989.

Fite, Gilbert. *Cotton Fields No More*. Lexington: University Press of Kentucky, 1984.

Flam, Jack, and Miriam Deutch, eds. *Primitivism and Twentieth-Century Art*. Berkeley: University of California Press, 2003.

Fogel, Robert. *Without Consent or Contract*. New York: W. W. Norton, 1989.

Foner, Eric. *Free Soil, Free Labor, Free Men*. Oxford: Oxford University Press, 1995.

———. *Politics and Ideology in the Age of the Civil War*. New York: Oxford University Press, 1980.

———. *Reconstruction*. New York: Harper and Row, 1988.

Fortune, T. Thomas. *Black and White: Land, Labor, and Politics in the South* [1884]. New York: Arno Press, 1968.

Fox, Stephen. *The American Conservation Movement*. Madison: University of Wisconsin Press, 1981.

Fox-Genovese, Elizabeth. *The Origins of Physiocracy*. Ithaca, N.Y.: Cornell University Press, 1976.

Frank, Waldo. *The Re-Discovery of America*. New York: Charles Scribner's Sons, 1929.

Franklin, John Hope. *From Slavery to Freedom*, 6th ed. New York: Alfred A. Knopf, 1988.

Frazier, E. Franklin. *The Negro Church in America*. New York: Schocken Books, 1963.

Fredrickson, George. *The Black Image in the White Mind*. Hanover, N.H.: Wesleyan University Press, 1971.

Garland, Hamlin. *Crumbling Idols* [1894]. Edited by Jane Johnson. Cambridge, Mass.: Harvard University Press, 1960.

Garvey, Marcus. *Marcus Garvey: Life and Lessons*. Edited by Robert Hill and Barbara Bair. Berkeley: University of California Press, 1987.

Gates, Henry Louis, ed. *Black Literature and Literary Theory*. New York: Methuen, 1984.

———. *Three Classic African-American Novels*. New York: Vintage Classics, 1990.

Genovese, Eugene. *Roll, Jordan, Roll*. New York: Vintage Books, 1972.

Gianni, Vaggi. *The Economics of Francois Quesnay*. Durham, N.C.: Duke University Press, 1987.

Glacken, Clarence. *Traces on the Rhodian Shore*. Berkeley: University of California Press, 1967.

Glave, Dianne. "'A Garden So Brilliant with Colors, So Original in Its Design.'" *Environmental History* 8 (July 2003): 399–404.

Glave, Dianne, and Mark Stoll, ed. *"To Love the Wind and the Rain": African Americans and Environmental History*. Pittsburgh: University of Pittsburgh Press, 2006.

Goldwater, Robert. *Primitivism in Modern Art*, enlarged ed. Cambridge, Mass.: Belknap Press, 1986.

Goodwyn, Lawrence. *The Populist Moment*. Oxford: Oxford University Press, 1978.

Gordon, Michael. *The American Family in Social-Historical Perspective*, 3rd ed. New York: St. Martin's Press, 1983.

Gottlieb, Robert. *Environmentalism Unbound*. Cambridge, Mass.: MIT Press, 2001.

———. *Forcing the Spring*. Washington, D.C.: Island Press, 1993.

Grant, Madison. *The Passing of the Great Race*, 4th rev. ed. New York: Charles Scribner's Sons, 1924.

Greene, J. Lee. *Blacks in Eden*. Charlottesville: University Press of Virginia, 1996.

Grove, Richard. *Green Imperialism*. Cambridge: Cambridge University Press, 1995.

Guterl, Matthew Pratt. *The Color of Race in America, 1900–1940*. Cambridge, Mass.: Harvard University Press, 2001.

Hagler, Dorse. "The Agrarian Theme in Southern History to 1860." PhD diss., University of Missouri, 1968.

Hahn, Steve. *A Nation under Our Feet*. Cambridge, Mass.: Harvard University Press, 2003.

Hakutani, Yoshinobu, and Robert Butler, eds. *The City in African-American Literature*. London: Associated University Press, 1995.

Haller, John. *Outcasts from Evolution*. Urbana: University of Illinois Press, 1971.

Hannaford, Ivan. *Race: The History of an Idea in the West*. Washington, D.C.: Woodrow Wilson Center Press, 1996.

Hanson, Victor Davis. *Fields without Dreams*. New York: Free Press, 1996.

Harris, Joel Chandler. *Uncle Remus and His Friends*. London: Osgood, McIvaine, 1896.

Harrison, Peter. "Subduing the Earth: Genesis 1, Early Modern Science, and the Exploitation of Nature." *Journal of Religion* 79 (January 1999): 86–109.

Hays, Samuel. *Beauty, Health, and Permanence*. Cambridge: Cambridge University Press, 1987.

Hegel, Georg. *Lectures on the Philosophy of World History* [1830]. Translated by H. B. Nisbet. Cambridge: Cambridge University Press, 1975.

Heller, Erich. *The Disinherited Mind*. Philadelphia: Dufur and Saifer, 1952.

Herder, Johann G. von. *Reflections on the Philosophy of the History of Mankind*, abridged [1784–1791]. Chicago: University of Chicago Press, 1968.

Herskovits, Melville. *The Myth of the Negro Past*. New York: Harper and Brothers, 1941.

Hidden Slaves: Forced Labor in the United States. Report published by Free the Slaves, Washington, D.C., and Human Rights Center, University of California at Berkeley, September 2004.

Hillegas, Jan, and Ken Lawrence, eds. *Alabama Narratives*. In *The American Slave: A Composite Autobiography*, Supp. Series 1, ed. George Rawick. Westport, Conn.: Greenwood Press, 1977.

Hoffman, Frederick. "Race Traits and Tendencies of the American Negro." *Publications of the American Economic Association* 11, 1–3 (1896):1–329.

Holloway, Joseph, ed. *Africanisms in American Culture*. Bloomington: Indiana University Press, 1990.

Homecoming: Sometimes I Am Haunted by Memories of Red Dirt and Clay. Produced and directed by Charlene Gilbert, in association with Independent Television Service, 1998. Distributed by California Newsreel, San Francisco. Videocassette.

Howells, William Dean. *Criticism and Fiction*. New York: Harper and Brothers, 1891.

Hudson, John. *Across This Land: A Regional Geography of the United States.* Baltimore: Johns Hopkins University Press, 2002.

Huggins, Nathan. *Harlem Renaissance.* Oxford: Oxford University Press, 1971.

Hughes, Langston. *The Collected Works of Langston Hughes.* Edited by R. Baxter Miller. Columbia: University of Missouri Press, 2002.

Hurley, Andrew. *Environmental Inequalities.* Chapel Hill: University of North Carolina Press, 1995.

Hurston, Zora Neale. *The Complete Stories of Zora Neale Hurston.* New York: Harper Perennial, 1995.

Hurt, R. Douglas. *American Agriculture.* Ames: Iowa State University Press, 1994.

Hutchinson, George. *The Harlem Renaissance in Black and White.* Cambridge, Mass.: Harvard University Press, 1996.

Jackson, Wes. *Becoming Native to This Place.* Washington, D.C.: Counterpoint, 1994.

James, William. *The Principles of Psychology* [1890]. Cambridge, Mass.: Harvard University Press, 1981.

Jefferson, Thomas. *The Life and Selected Writings of Thomas Jefferson.* Edited by Adrienne Koch and William Peden. New York: Random House, 1993.

Johnson, Cassandra, and J. M. Bowker. "African-American Wildland Memories." *Environmental Ethics* 26 (Spring 2004): 57–75.

Johnson, James Weldon. *The Autobiography of an Ex-Coloured Man* [1912]. New York: Hill and Wang, 1960.

———. *Black Manhattan.* New York: Alfred A. Knopf, 1930.

Jones, Robert. "Blacks Just Don't Care: Unmasking Popular Stereotypes about Concern for the Environment among African-Americans." *International Journal of Public Administration* 25 (2002): 221–251.

Jordan, David. Introduction to *Regionalism Reconsidered,* edited by David Jordan. New York: Garland, 1994.

Joyner, Charles. *Shared Traditions.* Urbana: University of Illinois Press, 1999.

Kandinsky, Wassily. *Concerning the Spiritual in Art and Painting in Particular* [1912]. Translated by Michael Sadleir. New York: Wittenborn Art Books, 1947.

Kandinsky, Wassily, and Franz Marc. *Blau Reiter Almanac* [1912]. Munich: R. Piper, 1965.

Katz, Eric. "The Big Lie: Human Restoration of Nature." In *Environmental Ethics,* edited by Andrew Light and Holmes Rolston III. Oxford: Blackwell, 2003.

———. "Searching for Intrinsic Value." In *Environmental Pragmatism,* ed. Andrew Light and Eric Katz. London: Routledge, 1996.

Kemble, Frances Anne. *Journal of a Residence on a Georgian Plantation in 1838–1839.* Athens: University of Georgia Press, 1984.

Kerber, Linda. *Federalists in Dissent.* Ithaca, N.Y.: Cornell University Press, 1970.

Kolchin, Peter. *American Slavery,* 2nd ed. New York: Hill and Wang, 2003.

Kowalewski, Michael. "Bioregional Perspectives in American Literature." In *Regionalism Reconsidered,* edited by David Jordan. New York: Garland, 1994.

Lal, Barbara. *The Romance of Culture in an Urban Civilization.* New York: Routledge, 1990.

Lamarck, J. B. *Zoological Philosophy* [1809]. Translated by Hugh Elliot. Chicago: University of Chicago Press, 1984.

Larsen, Nella. *Quicksand* [1929]. New Brunswick, N.J.: Rutgers University Press, 1986.

Leavitt, Emily, et al. *Animals and Their Legal Rights.* Washington, D.C.: Animal Welfare Institute, 1968.

Le Conte, Joseph. *Evolution,* 2nd rev. ed. New York: D. Appleton, 1902.

Levine, Lawrence. *Black Culture and Black Consciousness.* New York: Oxford University Press, 1977.

———. "Some Go Up and Some Go Down: The Meaning of the Slave Trickster." In *The Hofstadter Aegis: A Memorial,* edited by Stanley Elkins and Eric McKitrick. New York: Alfred A. Knopf, 1974.

Lévy-Bruhl, Lucien. *How Natives Think* [1910]. Translated by Lilian Clare. Princeton, N.J.: Princeton University Press, 1985.

Lewis, David Levering, ed. *The Portable Harlem Renaissance Reader.* New York: Penguin, 1994.

———. *W. E. B. Du Bois: Biography of a Race.* New York: Henry Holt, 1993.

———. *When Harlem Was in Vogue.* New York: Alfred A. Knopf, 1981.

Litwack, Leon. *Been in the Storm So Long.* New York: Vintage Books, 1979.

———. *North of Slavery.* Chicago: University of Chicago Press, 1961.

Locke, Alain. *The American Negro: His History and Literature.* New York: Arno Press New York Times, 1969.

———. *The Philosophy of Alain Locke.* Edited by Leonard Harris. Philadelphia: Temple University Press, 1989.

———. *Race Contacts and Interracial Relations* [1915]. Edited by Jeffrey Stewart. Washington, D.C.: Howard University Press, 1992.

———, ed. *The New Negro* [1925]. New York: Atheneum, 1983.

Locke, John. *Second Treatise of Civil Government* [1690]. New York: Hafner Press, 1947.

Lovejoy, Arthur O. *A Documentary History of Primitivism and Related Ideas.* 2 vols. Baltimore: Johns Hopkins Press, 1935.

Madison, James. "Address Delivered before the Agricultural Society of Albemarle," *American Farmer* 1 (August 20, 1819): 161–163; 1 (August 27, 1819): 169–171; 1 (September 3, 1819): 177–179.

Magdol, Edward. *A Right to the Land.* Westport, Conn.: Greenwood Press, 1977.

Marcus, Alan. *Agricultural Science and the Quest for Legitimacy.* Ames: Iowa State University Press, 1985.

Marks, Carole. "The Social and Economic Life of Southern Blacks during the Migration." In *Black Exodus,* edited by Alferdteen Harrison. Jackson: University Press of Mississippi, 1991.

Marks, Stuart. *Southern Hunting in Black and White.* Princeton, N.J.: Princeton University Press, 1991.

Marsh, George Perkins. *Man and Nature* [1864]. Cambridge, Mass.: Belknap Press, 1965.

Marshall, Robert. "The Problem of the Wilderness." *Scientific Monthly* 30 (February 1930): 141–148.

Marx, Leo. *The Machine in the Garden*. Oxford: Oxford University Press, 1964.

Mathew, William. *Edmund Ruffin and the Crisis of Slavery in the Old South*. Athens: University of Georgia Press, 1988.

Matthews, Fred. *Quest for an American Sociology*. Montreal: McGill-Queen's University Press, 1977.

McCoy, Drew. *The Elusive Republic*. Chapel Hill: University of North Carolina Press, 1980.

McDougall, William. *The Group Mind*, 2nd rev. ed. New York: G. P. Putnam's Sons, 1920.

McKay, Claude. *Home to Harlem* [1928]. Boston: Northeastern University Press, 1987.

McLain, James. *The Economic Writings of Du Pont de Nemours*. Newark: University of Delaware Press, 1977.

Meek, Ronald. *Social Science and the Ignoble Savage*. Cambridge: Cambridge University Press, 1976.

Meier, August. *Negro Thought in America, 1880–1915*. Ann Arbor: University of Michigan Press, 1963.

Melosi, Martin. *Garbage in the Cities*. College Station: Texas A&M University Press, 1981.

Merchant, Carolyn. *Ecological Revolutions*. Chapel Hill: University of North Carolina Press, 1989.

———. "Women of the Progressive Conservation Movement, 1900–1916." *Environmental Review* 8 (Spring 1984): 57–85.

———, ed. *Major Problems in American Environmental History*. Lexington, Mass.: D. C. Heath, 1993.

Miller, Kelly. *Race Adjustment and the Everlasting Stain*. New York: Arno Press, 1968.

Mitchell, Theodore. *Political Education in the Southern Farmers' Alliance, 1887–1900*. Madison: University of Wisconsin Press, 1987.

Mitchell, Thomas. "From Reconstruction to Deconstruction: Undermining Black Landownership, Political Independence, and Community through Partition Sales of Tenancies in Common." *Northwestern Law Review* 95 (Winter 2001): 505–507.

Mohai, Paul. "Black Environmentalism," *Social Science Quarterly* 71 (December 1990): 744–765.

———. "Public Concern and Elite Involvement in Environmental-Conservation Issues." *Social Science Quarterly* 66 (December 1985): 820–838.

Montmarquet, James. *The Idea of Agrarianism*. Moscow: University of Idaho Press, 1989.

Morgan, Philip D. "Work and Culture: The Task System and the World of Lowcountry Blacks, 1700–1880." In *Material Life in America*, edited by Robert St. George. Boston: Northeastern University Press, 1988.

Morris, William. *News from Nowhere and Selected Writings and Designs*. New York: Penguin Books, 1962.

Morrison, Toni. "City Limits, Village Values: Concepts of the Neighborhood in Black Fiction." In *Literature and the Urban Experience*, edited by Michael Joyce and Ann Watts. New Brunswick, N.J.: Rutgers University Press, 1981.

Moses, Wilson. *The Golden Age of Black Nationalism, 1850–1925*. Hamden, Conn.: Archon Books, 1978.

Nash, Roderick. "The American Cult of the Primitive." *American Quarterly* 18 (Fall 1966): 517–537.

———. *Wilderness and the American Mind*. New Haven, Conn.: Yale University Press, 1967.

Nicholls, David. *Conjuring the Folk*. Ann Arbor: University of Michigan Press, 2000.

Nichols, Charles. "The Slave Narrators and the Picaresque." In *The Slave's Narrative*, edited by Charles Davis and Henry Louis Gates. Oxford: Oxford University Press, 1985.

Osborn, Henry F. *Men of the Old Stone Age*, 3rd ed. New York: Charles Scribner's Sons, 1918.

Painter, Nell. *Exodusters*. New York: W. W. Norton, 1976.

Park, Robert, Ernest Burgess, and Roderick McKenzie. *The City*. Chicago: University of Chicago Press, 1925.

Pease, William, and Jane Pease. *Black Utopia*. Madison: Historical Society of Wisconsin, 1963.

Penningroth, Dylan. *The Claims of Kinfolk*. Chapel Hill: University of North Carolina Press, 2003.

Pigford v. Glickman, 185 F.R.D. 82 (D.D.C. 1999).

Plumwood, Val. *Feminism and the Mastery of Nature*. London: Routledge, 1993.

Pocock, J. G. A. *The Machiavellian Moment*. Princeton, N.J.: Princeton University Press, 1975.

Proceedings: The First National People of Color Environmental Leadership Summit. New York: United Church of Christ Commission for Racial Justice, 1991.

Quarles, Benjamin. *Black Abolitionists*. Oxford: Oxford University Press, 1969.

Raboteau, Albert. "African Americans, Exodus, and the American Israel." In *Down by the Riverside*, edited by Larry Murphy. New York: New York University Press, 2000.

Rampersad, Arnold. *The Art and Imagination of W. E. B. Du Bois*. Cambridge, Mass.: Harvard University Press, 1976.

Rasmussen, Wayne. *Readings in the History of American Agriculture*. Urbana: University of Illinois Press, 1960.

Reed, Adolph. *W. E. B. Du Bois and American Political Thought*. New York: Oxford University Press, 1997.

Rhodes, Colin. *Primitivism and Modern Art*. London: Thames and Hudson, 1994.

Ripley, C. Peter, ed. *Black Abolitionist Papers*. 5 vols. Chapel Hill: University of North Carolina Press, 1991.

Roosevelt, Theodore. *Citizenship, Politics, and the Elemental Virtues*. New York: Charles Scribner's Sons, 1925.

——. *Theodore Roosevelt: An American Mind.* Edited by Mario DiNunzio. New York: Penguin Books, 1994.

Rossiter, Margaret. *The Emergence of Agricultural Science.* New Haven, Conn.: Yale University Press, 1975.

Rousseau, Jean Jacques. *A Discourse on Inequality* [1755]. London: Penguin Classics, 1984.

Royce, Josiah. *The Basic Writings of Josiah Royce.* Edited by John McDermott. Chicago: University of Chicago Press, 1969.

Ruskin, John. *The Crown of Wild Olive.* New York: John Wiley and Sons, 1874.

——. *The Genius of John Ruskin.* New York: George Braziller, 1963.

Sale, Kirkpatrick. *Dwellers in the Land.* San Francisco: Sierra Club Books, 1985.

Saloutos, Theodore. *Farmer Movements in the South.* Berkeley: University of California Press, 1960.

Sanders, Elizabeth. *Roots of Reform.* Chicago: University of Chicago Press, 1999.

Schama, Simon. *Landscape and Memory.* New York: Vintage Books, 1995.

Schenck, H. G. *The Mind of the European Romantics.* London: Constable, 1966.

Scruggs, Charles. "Crab Antics and Jacob's Ladder: Aaron Douglas's Two Views of Nigger Heaven." In *Harlem Renaissance Re-Examined: A Revised and Expanded Edition,* edited by Victor Kramer and Robert Russ. Troy, N.J.: Whitston, 1997.

——. *Sweet Home.* Baltimore: Johns Hopkins University Press, 1993.

Sernett, Milton. *Bound for the Promised Land.* Durham, N.C.: Duke University Press, 1997.

Shaler, Nathaniel. "Nature and Man in America." *Scribner's Magazine* 8 (1890): 360.

——. *The Neighbor.* Boston: Houghton Mifflin, 1904.

Smith, Adam. *An Inquiry into the Nature and Causes of the Wealth of Nations.* 2 vols. Indianapolis: Liberty Fund, 1981.

Smith, Henry Nash. *Virgin Land.* Cambridge, Mass.: Harvard University Press, 1950.

Smith, Kimberly. *The Dominion of Voice.* Lawrence: University Press of Kansas, 1999.

——. "Mere Taste: Democracy and the Politics of Beauty." *Wisconsin Environmental Law Review* 7 (Summer 2000): 151–195.

——. *Wendell Berry and the Agrarian Tradition.* Lawrence: University Press of Kansas, 2003.

Smith, Rogers. *Civic Ideals.* New Haven, Conn.: Yale University Press, 1997.

Smith, T. Lynn. "The Redistribution of the Negro Population of the United States, 1910–1960." *Journal of Negro History* 51 (July 1966): 155–173.

Sobel, Mechal. *Trabelin' On.* Westport, Conn.: Greenwood Press, 1979.

South Carolina Narratives, from *An American Slave,* Supp. Series, ed. George Rawick. Westport, Conn.: Greenwood Press, 1977.

Spencer, Herbert. "Social Statics" [1851]. In *On Social Evolution,* edited by J. D. Y. Peel. Chicago: University of Chicago Press, 1972.

Spiller, G., ed. *Papers on Inter-Racial Problems Communicated to the First Universal Races Congress.* London: P. S. King and Sons, 1911.

Stanton, William. *The Leopard's Spots.* Chicago: University of Chicago Press, 1960.

Statistical Abstract of the United States, 1930, No. 52. Washington, D.C.: Government Printing Office, 1930.

Statistical Abstract of the United States, 1940, No. 62. Washington, D.C.: Government Printing Office, 1941.

Stephens, Lester. "Farish Furman's Formula: Scientific Farming and the 'New South.'" *Agricultural History* 50 (April 1976): 377–390.

Stewart, Mart. "'Let Us Begin with the Weather?': Climate, Race, and Cultural Distinctiveness in the American South." In *Nature and Society in Historical Context,* ed. Mikulás Teich, Roy Porter, and Bo Gustafsson. Cambridge: Cambridge University Press, 1997.

———. *"What Nature Suffers to Groe."* Athens: University of Georgia Press, 1996.

Stoddard, Lothrop. *The Rising Tide of Color against White World-Supremacy.* New York: Charles Scribner's Sons, 1920.

Stoll, Steven. *Larding the Lean Earth.* New York: Hill and Wang, 2002.

Szasz, Andrew. *Ecopopulism.* Minneapolis: University of Minnesota Press, 1994.

Taylor, Dorceta. "Blacks and the Environment: Toward an Explanation of the Concern and Action Gap between Blacks and Whites." *Environment and Behavior* 21 (March 1989): 175–205.

———. *Race, Class, Gender, and American Environmentalism.* Washington, D.C.: U.S. Department of Agriculture, Forest Service, 2002.

Taylor, Yuval, ed. *I Was Born a Slave.* 2 vols. Chicago: Lawrence Hill Books, 1999.

Thornton, John. *Africa and Africans in the Making of the Atlantic World, 1400–1680.* Cambridge: Cambridge University Press, 1992.

Tillinghast, Joseph. *The Negro in Africa and America.* New York: Macmillan, 1902.

Tompkins, Jane. *Sensational Designs.* Oxford: Oxford University Press, 1985.

Toomer, Jean. *Cane.* Edited by Darwin Turner. New York: W. W. Norton, 1988.

Treitschke, Heinrich von. *Politics* [1892]. 2 vols. Translated by Blanche Dugdale and Torben de Bille. New York: Macmillan, 1916.

Turner, Darwin. "Another Passing." In *Jean Toomer: A Critical Evaluation,* edited by Therman O'Daniel. Washington, D.C.: Howard University Press, 1988.

Tylor, E. B. *Primitive Culture* [1871]. 2 vols. New York: Harper and Brothers, 1958.

Upton, Dell. "White and Black Landscapes in Eighteenth-Century Virginia," in *Material Life,* ed. Robert St. George. Boston: Northeastern University Press, 1988.

U.S. Commission on Civil Rights. *The Federal Civil Rights Enforcement Effort,* vol. 6, 1975.

Van Vechten, Carl. *Nigger Heaven* [1926]. Urbana: University of Illinois Press, 2000.

Vlach, John. *Back of the Big House.* Chapel Hill: University of North Carolina Press, 1993.

Waldron, Jeremy. *God, Locke, and Equality.* Cambridge: Cambridge University Press, 2002.

Walker, Alice. *Meridian.* New York: Pocket Books, 1976.

Washington, Booker T. *The Story of My Life and Work* [1900]. New York: Negro Universities Press, 1969.

———. *Working with the Hands.* New York: Doubleday, Page, 1904.

Westmacott, Richard. *African-American Gardens and Yards in the Rural South.* Knoxville: University of Tennessee Press, 1992.

Weston, Anthony. "Beyond Intrinsic Value: Pragmatism in Environmental Ethics." In *Environmental Pragmatism,* edited by Andrew Light and Eric Katz. London: Routledge, 1996.

Wheeler, Michael, ed. *Ruskin and the Environment.* Manchester, UK: Manchester University Press, 1995.

White, Deborah. *Ar'n't I a Woman,* rev. ed. New York: W. W. Norton, 1999.

Wildavsky, Aaron. "Aesthetic Power or the Triumph of the Sensitive Minority over the Vulgar Mass." *Daedalus* 96 (Fall 1967): 1115–1128.

Williams, Vernon. *Rethinking Race.* Lexington: University Press of Kentucky, 1996.

Williamson, Joel. *The Crucible of Race.* Oxford: Oxford University Press, 1984.

Wintz, Cary. *Black Culture and the Harlem Renaissance.* Houston: Rice University Press, 1988.

Wood, Gordon. *The Creation of the American Republic, 1776–1787.* New York: W. W. Norton, 1969.

Woodward, C. Vann. "*Strange Career* Critics." *Journal of American History* 75 (December 1988): 858–860.

Worster, Donald. *Nature's Economy,* 2nd ed. Cambridge: Cambridge University Press, 1994.

Wright, Richard. *Native Son and How "Bigger" Was Born.* Cutchogee, N.Y.: Buccaneer Books, 1940.

Yarbrough, Jean. *American Virtues.* Lawrence: University Press of Kansas, 1998.

Young, Arthur. *A Six Months Tour through the North of England* [1771]. 4 vols. New York: Augustus M. Kelley, 1967.

Zamir, Shamoon. *Dark Voices: W. E. B. Du Bois and American Thought, 1888–1903.* Chicago: University of Chicago Press, 1995.

INDEX